One-Minute Wellness

Other Body by God Books

Body by God
The Owner's Manual for Maximized Living

by **Dr. Ben Lerner**

and

Bouncing Back from Pregnancy
*The Body by God Plan for Getting
Your Body and Life Back after Baby Arrives*

by **Dr. Sheri Lerner**

One-Minute Wellness

The Health and Happiness System That Never Fails

Dr. Ben Lerner
with Dr. Greg Loman

NELSON BOOKS
A Division of Thomas Nelson Publishers
Since 1798

www.thomasnelson.com

Published in Nashville, Tennessee, by Thomas Nelson, Inc.

Scripture marked NKJV is taken from the NEW KING JAMES VERSION. Copyright © 1979, 1980, 1982 by Thomas Nelson, Inc. Used by permission. All rights reserved.

Scripture marked NIV is taken from the HOLY BIBLE, NEW INTERNATIONAL VERSION®. Copyright © 1973, 1978, 1984 by International Bible Society. Used by permission of Zondervan Publishing House. All rights reserved.

Scripture marked NCV is taken from *The Everyday Bible, New Century Version,* copyright © 1987 by Worthy Publishing, Fort Worth, TX 76137. Used by permission.

Only your medical doctor can prescribe drugs, tell you to get off of drugs, or provide medical advice. *That's the practice of medicine.* The opinions in this book are not designed to replace the advice of your medical doctor. The role of this book is to make you aware of the hazards of poor lifestyle decisions and alert you to the inherent dangers of medications, while helping you to create optimum function and healing for your body.

With the guidance of your prescribing physician, you need to make your own best decisions on drug use and whether or not you can avoid, reduce, or eliminate medications.

Library of Congress Cataloging-in-Publication Data

Lerner, Ben.
    One-minute wellness : the health and happiness system that never fails / Ben Lerner.
      p. cm.
    Includes bibliographical references.
    ISBN 0-7852-0964-6 (hardcover)
    1. Health—Religious aspects—Christianity. 2. Happiness—Religious aspects—Christianity.
I. Title.
BT732.L47 2005
261.8'321—dc22   2005008735

Printed in the United States of America

05 06 07 08 09 QW 5 4 3 2 1

Special thanks to these doctors,
who are trusted providers of the science and principles
found in *One Minute Wellness.*

Alabama

Dr. Patty Long
Meridianville

Dr. Kyle Lopez
Fairhope

California

Dr. Jeff Gancas
Citrus Heights

Dr. Ken Moger
Citrus Heights

Arrow Chiropractic
Rancho Cucamonga

Colorado

Dr. Brent Berlener
Highlands Ranch

Dr. Jess Baldwin
Centennial

Dr. Kristen Kells
Colorado Springs

Dr. Paul Price
Centennial

Dr. Ty Johnson
Colorado Springs

Dr. Chris Pellow
Greenwood Village

Dr. Dustin Ferrell
Broomfield

Dr. Kevin Noffsinger
Denver

Dr. Joseph Singh
Lakewood

Dr. Susie Rivard
Colorado Springs

Florida

Dr. Daniel Yachter
Lake Mary

Dr. Erik Lerner
Orlando

Dr. Scott Stoltz
Seffner

Dr. Tony Nalda
St. Cloud

Dr. Gary Bolen
Venice

Dr. Roger Romano
Sarasota

Dr. Scott Ewing
Niceville

Dr. Dean Jacks
Niceville

Dr. Sheri Lerner
Celebration

Dr. Maryella Loman
Naples

Georgia

Dr. Chad Hyatt
Suwannee

Dr. Chris Lockerman
Hiram

Dr. Fred Roberto
Powder Springs

Dr. Mark Domanski
Savannah

Hawaii

Dr. Mark Hoffman
Honolulu

Illinois

Dr. Ashly Ochsner
Palos Park

Dr. Charlie Majors
Romeoville

Dr. Nathan Thompson
Yorkville

Dr. Paul Stoetzel
Lemont

Iowa

Dr. David Diehl
Pella

Dr. Tim Stackis
Dubuque

Kentucky

Dr. Lewis Misinay
Burnside

Michigan

Dr. Mark McCullough
Battle Creek

Dr. Guy Lasich
Marquette

Minnesota

Dr. Brian Arvold
Oakdale

Dr. Pete Wurdemann
North Branch

Dr. Brenda Kress
St. Paul

Dr. Emmett A Blahnik
Bloomington

Dr. Cory Couillard
Eagan

Dr. Jeffrey D. McComb
Bloomington

Dr. Sean M. Primus
St. Paul

Dr. Ryan J. Mayeda
Maplewood

New Mexico

Dr. Ben Bowles
Albuquerque

New York

Dr. Eric Ashburn
Fishkill

Dr. Tom Kovacs
New York

Dr. Craig Fishel
New York

North Carolina

Dr. Megan Powell
Shallotte

Dr. Marc Surprenant
Charlotte

Dr. Terri Wells
Shallotte

Dr. Sonya Young
Wrightsville Beach

Ohio

Dr. Louis Valentine
Cincinnati

Dr. Jonathan Snyder
Circleville

Oklahoma

Dr. David Dick
Broken Arrow

Dr. Lance Bailey
Tulsa

Pennsylvania

Dr. Lawrence Bellows
Mansfield

Dr. Laura Bellows
Mansfield

Tennessee

Dr. Alan Arstikaitis
Memphis

Dr. Reed Johnson
Memphis

Texas

Dr. Jim Labrecque
North Richland Hills

Dr. Randy Johns
Texarkana

Dr. Jimmie Lee
Brantley, Jr.
McKinney

Washington

Dr. Troy Dreiling
Vancouver

Canada

Dr. Joel Bohemier
Winnipeg, MB

Dr. Rolly Bohemier
Winnipeg, MB

Dr. Colin Elkin
Brantford, ON

Peru

Dr. Thomas Myers
Lima

Contributing Writers

Dr. Nick Athens, San Francisco, CA
Drs. Lise Cloutier and Mike Reid, Ontario, Canada
Dr. Gerard Clum, Hayward, CA
Dr. Patrick Gentempo, Mahwah, NJ
Dr. Bob Hoffman, Jericho, NY
Dr. Chris Kent, Maywood, NJ
Dr. Erik Lerner, Orlando, FL
Dr. Sheri Lerner, Celebration, FL
Dr. Maryella Loman, Naples, FL
Dr. Fabrizio Mancini, Dallas, TX
Dr. Matthew McCoy, Woodstock, GA
Dr. Joseph Mercola, Schaumburg, IL
Dr. Daniel Murphy, Auburn, CA
Drs. Marty and Tony Nalda, Saint Cloud, FL
Drs. Jennifer and Palmer Peet, Shelburn, VT
Dr. Guy Riekeman, Marietta, GA
Dr. Terry Rondberg, Rancho Santa Fe, CA
Drs. Stuart and Terry Warner, Point Pleasant, NJ
Dr. Dan Yachter, Lake Mary, FL

Additional Resources

Dr. Bruce Lipton, www.brucelipton.com
Dr. Joseph Mercola, www.mercola.com

Testimonial Contributors

Dr. Deborah Adams, Kirkland, WA
Dr. Brad Butler, Oakland, NJ
Dr. Gavin Grant, Newport Beach, CA
Dr. Terry Harmon, Morganfield, KY
Dr. Rick Hellmann, Louisville, KY
Dr. Keith Helmendach, Charlotte, NC
Dr. Keppen Laszlo, Arvada, CO
Dr. Mark McCullough, Battle Creek, MI
Dr. Lewis Misinay, Burnside, KY
Dr. Makenzie Pamer, Powell, OH
Dr. Matt Pamer, Mansfield, OH
Dr. Roger Romano, Sarasota, FL
Dr. Holly Ruocco, Salem, NH
Dr. Patrick St. Germain, Apopka, FL
Dr. David Stender, Tucson, AZ
Dr. Terri Wells, Shallotte, NC
Dr. Dan Yachter, Lake Mary, FL

Contents

Introduction

Out of the Country of the Blind

In H. G. Wells's story "The Country of the Blind," Nuñez the explorer comes across a mythical world, lost deep in the mountains, inhabited by only blind people. Immediately Nuñez recalled an old proverb: In the Country of the Blind, the one-eyed man is king. "What an opportunity to serve," Nuñez said to himself.

These people knew nothing of sight. They believed in a life and philosophy and religion that thought the "world" was their city, that there was no such thing as a sky, as Nuñez went on about, but that a big rock hung over their heads to protect them. Many important things they lacked for health and a pleasant survival surrounded them, but they could not see.

Nuñez tried on several occasions to tell them of sight. "Look here, you people," he said. "There are things you do not understand." He spoke of the beauties of sight, of watching the mountains, of the sky and the sunrise, and the resources all around. However, they were nothing but condemnatory, and they labeled him insane.

In the end, when he explained that the noise they heard was the mountain tumbling down upon them, it didn't work. No one would "see." No one would listen. Eventually, the Country of the Blind was destroyed and gone forever.

The mythical Country of the Blind, so vividly illustrated in H. G. Wells's story, still exists today—and not just in the ancient lore of the Andes. Its counterpart is alive and thriving in postmillennial America, in every city, every suburb, every small town and rural community. The mountain above is falling, but the country's inhabitants—the vast majority of Americans—are unable to see the threat or refuse to listen. A threat that's beginning to affect an entire world.

So what is the threat? It's a *health-care system* that has blinded people to the truth about themselves, their bodies, and a quality of life that is well within their reach; *and a culture* that has lost its vision and is heading in the wrong direction. In America's "country of the blind," people have been led to believe that an array of physical, emotional, and mental illnesses and disorders are an inevitable fact of life or poor genetics, and that their only hope for coping with their health problems is some combination of medical visits, hospital stays, and over-the-counter drugs and prescriptions. Or they simply ignore them, writing off their health problems as the normal course of living.

Nothing could be further from the truth. But in a country of the blind, truth is obscured.

Step out of the country for a minute; let your mind wander and your eyes open. Imagine a society in which health and happiness are common—flowing freely and abundantly, creating a life without walls and success without boundaries. Where you are not predestined to fail by bad luck or preprogrammed for failure by poor genetics—but have something to say about your future. Imagine that kind of life being made available to you in just one minute—one life-changing "Aha!" moment of revelation and insight into the truth. Imagine, too, a series of one-minute treatments, thoughts, and lifestyle decisions that also take only a minute, or a few minutes, but can begin to change the way your body heals, functions, and responds to potentially harmful influences.

That's what *One-Minute Wellness* is all about: going beyond traditions, societal norms, fads, and drug ads that aren't creating the life you want, in order to open your eyes to the truth and lead you out of the country of the blind forever. Restoring your sight, and showing you life as it was meant to be experienced. Lifting off the veil so that you may have a clear view of the beautiful life you've been missing out on but were born to live.

You would be hard-pressed to find someone in this world right now who would tell you that things are as they should be. I, Dr. Ben, consider life and health to be our greatest gifts. Yet, with depression, childhood obesity, and lifestyle-induced diseases being more prevalent than ever before, it's evident that we've lost all respect for those gifts. Moreover, with divorce, adult obesity, and many diseases reaching all-time highs, it's also clear that our methods for dealing with life are incongruent with what it takes to create health or peace.

As a husband and a father, when I look around at the current state of affairs, I have obvious concerns for my family's welfare as well as their future.

I've worked with Olympic and professional teams as well as tens of thousands of patients the world over, so I have seen a whole lot of suffering and witnessed en masse how hard it is for people to care for themselves in a way that brings the pleasing outcomes we all desire. With the help of my good friend and performance expert Dr. Greg Loman and some of the most knowledgeable and healthiest people on planet Earth, we tell a story and share facts that we hope will help you find your way out of this failing system the way our families have. This book is written by people whose families have a level of physical, mental, and emotional health that is rarely or never seen in the general population today. It's all about Maximized Living! What we've written about here is a new system, a natural system, the Health and Happiness System That Never Fails.

The contributors and resources come from a variety of fields: leaders in the chiropractic profession, top health experts, consumer advocates, and research coming from the fields of science, medicine, nutrition, mathematics, economics, and the world's leading medical and alternative medical journals.

The original ideas, thoughts, action steps, and procedures here, while taking only a minute to realize, conceive, or receive, bring results for a whole new world of abundant health and happiness. They are One-Minute Wellness.

A Book with the Power to Save Lives

This is an incredibly unique book. ON THE LEFT-HAND PAGES, you have a dramatic, inspiring, Rocky-like story of two people who discover that the life, the emotions, and the bodies they once believed they were stuck with can change and that their dreams were not lost, but just deferred out of a need for new direction, new thoughts, and new actions.

ON THE RIGHT-HAND PAGES, you have the explanation and documentation of how and why their lives so radically improve. These factual, "how-to" pages will show you how the new principles, methods, and scientific discoveries of the natural Health and Happiness System That Never Fails can transform and even save your life, along with saving a sick, suffering, sighing, dying world.

In the following pages you'll meet two people, Elijah and Hope, whose lives have been forever changed by a new way of living and thinking. Through building health rather than treating disease, embracing the lifestyle their bodies were intended to follow, and receiving treatment that cooperates with the way the body was designed to heal, they become the great American story— two people who overcome the odds and discover their dreams. Though they're both fictional characters, their stories are representative of those true experiences we have seen again and again in our offices around the world. Accounts of people who emerged from darkness and blindness to all that God had in store for them and gained an entirely new perspective on life.

Your eyes can be opened as well . . . it takes only *one minute*.

| 1 |

A System in Crisis

America is the technological superpower, the wealthiest nation in the world, and spends significantly more of its gross national product, and spends more per person, than any other nation in the world on health care.[1] So where, then, does America stand on health? We should be at the top, right?

Startling Statistics

First of all, let's look at the statistics. Depending on the source, current data show that as many as five out of six Americans will die from heart disease and cancer, with the numbers of those being affected by other degenerative and neurological illnesses—such as diabetes, Alzheimer's, Parkinson's, and multiple sclerosis—growing every day. What's worse, the U.S. has the highest rate of mental illness (anxiety disorders and depression), with more than a quarter of the population suffering versus as little as 4.7 percent in other countries.[2]

In our children, we're watching learning disorders, asthma, allergies, infections, and mental illness reach unparalleled levels. With childhood obesity reaching epidemic proportions, the numbers for degenerative disease, neurological conditions, hypertension, and high cholesterol can be expected to skyrocket in the future and become prevalent at younger and younger ages. As a result, we'll be watching the first generation of American children experience life expectancies that are shorter than their parents'. With diabetes and high blood pressure setting in at younger and younger ages, parents may also begin outliving their children.

Where Does the Technological Superpower Rank in Terms of Health?

Saying that the level of health and wellness in America is poor is not an overstatement, an emotional reaction, or a "grass is always greener" in some other country commentary. It's the truth.

Of thirteen countries studied in a recent comparison, the United States ranked an average of twelfth (second from the bottom) in sixteen available health indicators. More specifically, the rankings of the U.S. on several indicators were

Elijah's Story

Gasping for what might very well be his last breath, Elijah thrashed about on the gurney, straining to find the one face he most needed to see. Wild with fear, surrounded by strangers in white, Elijah could form only one thought: *Mommy!* Where was she? As an orderly tried to calm him down, a doctor placed an oxygen mask over his mouth and nose. Still, his breath would not come.

Rushing through the corridors of the emergency room, the staff surrounding the gurney did their best to help Elijah, who continued struggling to breathe. Hooking him up to a ventilator and giving him an injection of a sedative, they managed to stabilize him and restore a semblance of rhythmic breathing. Barely conscious, Elijah heard a nurse asking questions about his medical history.

"Well, I know he's had these episodes before. They say he has allergies," said a voice Elijah knew all too well. Opening his eyes and struggling to focus, he saw her face, confirming his assumption. The voice and face belonged not to his mother but to his well-intentioned but hardly equal-to-the-task babysitter.

Lying in his hospital bed, this newly admitted patient—Elijah Knight, male Caucasian, age seven, medical history unknown, parent notified but not present—gave in to the fatigue of this latest ordeal and drifted off to sleep, his last thoughts for the night centering on defeat. His lungs had failed him once again. Just as his family had.

- #13 (last) for low birth-weight percentages
- #13 for neonatal mortality and infant mortality overall
- #11 for postneonatal mortality
- #11 for life expectancy at one year for females, #12 for males
- #10 for life expectancy at fifteen years for females, #12 for males
- #10 for life expectancy at forty years for females, #9 for males
- #7 for life expectancy at sixty-five years for females and males
- #3 for life expectancy at eighty years for females and males
- #10 for age-adjusted mortality
- #13 for years of potential life lost (excluding external causes)[3]

Look carefully at some of these problems in detail.

The U.S. is the worst place in the world to be pregnant or have a baby. The first three items on the list above indicate that our babies are born with the poorest health (last for low birth weight) and have the least chance of making it to or through birth. Why?

With the emphasis we place on pediatrics, the construction of the megapediatric hospitals, and the trillions we spend on pediatric research in the U.S., how is it possible for us to rank eleventh for one-year-old females and twelfth for one-year-old males—not in health but in life expectancy?

We're ranked high—third—in life expectancy for those who actually make it to age eighty. But have we kept them living, or simply breathing? Are they experiencing Maximized Living?

The most dramatic stat, however, is that America is dead last for "years of potential life lost," excluding external causes (such as getting hit by a bus). In other words, if God created you to live to eighty, you have the least chance of reaching that age if you live in the U.S. Ultimately, this stat shows that our system has managed to stop God's intentions for our lives better than any other system in the world.

These stats are backed up by recent World Health Organization (WHO) studies that ranked America at #23 for life expectancy, #15 for overall achievement, and #72 for "performance on the level of health," which is how well the health-care system actually improves a citizen's overall health.

Why Is the U.S. in Such Bad Shape?

At first thought, most people might suspect that the American lifestyle is to blame. We are people who are behaving badly—drinking, smoking, eating too much fast food, and so forth—so therefore, sickness is what we deserve. While this may be

Seven miles north of Arlington County Medical Center, Miriam Knight took another drag on her cigarette as she sat on the stoop behind the convenience store. Despite the October chill, she preferred the stoop to the confinement of what was laughingly called the employee break room. *Better pneumonia than claustrophobia any day*, she figured. Besides, back here she could take a swig from the flask of vodka she kept hidden in her jacket pocket, and no one would be the wiser. And at least out here she could inhale some fresh air along with her Winstons.

Elijah—poor kid. He deserves better. The thought of Elijah jarred her, and she struggled to think of something less stressful, like the wickedly handsome guy who came in every evening just after her shift started for a cup of coffee (light, no sugar) and a *USA Today*. It was useless. Instead of his image, all she could see was Elijah fighting for his next breath. And all she could think of was her disturbing conversation fifteen minutes earlier with Joanna, who could make her feel like an unfit mother faster than Dr. Phil or Judge Judy.

"Miriam, you've got to get to the hospital right now!" Joanna had said after convincing the store manager that this was a genuine emergency. "Elijah's on his way now in an ambulance—he had another breathing fit."

"I can't leave work. You go."

"What? Are you crazy? He needs his mother, not a babysitter!"

"I can't leave," Miriam whispered hoarsely as she cupped the mouthpiece with her free hand. "I'll get fired, and you know it."

true on one level, this study showed that we actually rank fairly high in the different lifestyle categories that were measured.

- The proportion of females who smoke in the U.S. was 24 percent (fifth best). For males, it was 28 percent (third best).

- The U.S. ranks fifth best for alcoholic beverage consumption.

- The U.S. has relatively low consumption of animal fats (fifth lowest in men ages fifty-five to sixty-four years in twenty industrialized countries) and the third-lowest mean cholesterol concentrations among men ages fifty to seventy years among thirteen industrialized countries.[4]

So if our lifestyle is bad, but about the same as or better than other countries in the study, and if technology, science, and the miracles of modern medicine produce health, which country should be the healthiest? America, of course.

So, then, what is it? Why are we so sick?

The author of the *JAMA* report is Dr. Barbara Starfield of the Johns Hopkins School of Hygiene and Public Health. As she so shockingly describes, the answer is that *the U.S. health-care system itself, and not lifestyle or a lack of technology, is actually the major contributor to our low rankings and our poor health.*

Iatrogenic Death—Our Deadly Health-Care System

The word *iatrogenic* means death induced in a patient by a physician's activity, manner, or therapy. This term is used especially if there is a complication following a treatment or during the course of stay at a hospital. The people who die due to what are classified as iatrogenic causes are people who would not have died if doctors had properly diagnosed and treated them.

While some studies, using limited numbers, have the iatrogenic deaths listed as the third leading cause of death in America,[5] new research shows that the estimated total number of deaths induced inadvertently by a physician or surgeon or by medical treatment or diagnostic procedures—in the U.S. annually—is between 783,936 and 999,936.[6] From these updated numbers it becomes evident that our conventional, modern medical system is itself the leading cause of death and injury in the U.S., as approximately 699,697 Americans died of heart disease in 2001 and 553,251 died of cancer.[7]

These numbers are derived from the total deaths directly caused by adverse drug reactions,[8] medical error,[9] bedsores,[10] infections,[11] malnutrition in hospitals,[12] outpatient practices,[13] unnecessary procedures,[14] and procedures related to surgery.[15]

For fear of being sued and other negative repercussions, as few as 5 percent and no

"Look, all I know is, this kid could die, and you need to be with him. I don't even know what to tell them."

"Tell them to call me—wait, better not—Matt is already ticked off at me. One more long phone call and I'm probably out the door for good. Look, I've got to get back on the register. Matt's shooting me his 'I'm the manager and not a cashier' look. Let me know what happens, okay?"

"You can't hang—" Miriam finished Joanna's sentence in her head. No point in continuing the tirade. She most certainly could hang up, and she did, heading back to the register and sighing with relief that her scheduled break was just a few minutes away.

Now, sitting on the stoop, Miriam glanced at her Timex wristwatch, the one she had found at Goodwill just last week. *Seven more minutes*, she thought as she looked up at the night sky and silently cursed the full moon. *Seven more minutes before I have to go back inside and put up with the loonies that will be coming in tonight.*

"Miriam!" Matt's voice interrupted her moment of ironic bliss. "You've got another call!"

Crushing her half-finished cigarette with her shoe—*what a waste of a good smoke! These things are expensive*—Miriam trudged back in and took the phone from Matt.

"What is it?" she asked Joanna as she glanced over at Matt, whose raised eyebrows signaled that he wanted to know if Elijah was all right. *As if he cares*, Miriam thought. "Yeah. Okay. Tell them his doctor is . . . well, he doesn't really have one. I mean, we go to the clinic. What do you mean, which one? I don't know the name—it's the one the county runs out on Grant near the bus stop by Medi-Mart. I told you—he doesn't have a doctor. We just see

more than 20 percent of iatrogenic acts are ever reported by doctors or hospitals.[16] This implies that if medical errors were completely and accurately reported, we would have an annual iatrogenic death toll much, much higher than 783,936 to 999,936.

The Cost of an "Inadequate" Medical System

By now it should come as no surprise that the U.S. health-care system is the most expensive in the world. The World Health Organization estimates that we spend $4,887 per person on health care each year, far exceeding the annual amount spent by other countries (Canadians, at number two, spend $2,792, while people living in the Bahamas come in at a distant third—$1,220). That's largely due to the higher cost of medical technology, the salaries of medical professionals, and ever-increasing hospital costs. As the prestigious *New England Journal of Medicine* put it, "The American healthcare system is at once the most expensive and the most inadequate system in the developed world."[17] Half of all personal bankruptcies are caused by medical expenses.

The number of prescriptions written per year in the United States, and the costs associated with them, is staggering. A recent report by the Kaiser Family Foundation indicates that in 2003, 3.1 billion retail prescriptions were filled in the United States at a cost of $163 billion. This translates to eleven prescriptions filled for every man, woman, and child in the country in 2003.

"What do we get for the most expensive health care in the world?" Dr. Mercola asks. "The best system for treating acute surgical emergencies—and a system that has failed at treating chronic illness. The high cost of the health-care system is considered to be a necessary burden. This, however, could be more easily tolerated under the assumption that better health results from more expensive care and more advanced technology."

Medicine Has Clear Benefits, but Carefully Weigh the Costs

While medicine has many lifesaving benefits, recent findings are revealing more and more that the cures may in fact be more dangerous than the diseases they were created to heal.

Again, if these statistics seem alarmist, consider the sources: they are the top schools and the most widely circulated and best-known medical journals in the world, such as the *Journal of the American Medical Association* (*JAMA*). The evidence concerning our health-care-system crisis is so compelling, the medical profession's own publications could no longer ignore it.

Dr. Gerry Clum, president of Life-West Chiropractic College, has some serious cautions and concerns when it comes to the concepts of drug therapy. While no

whoever is available. No, I don't have time to come down there. You sign the forms—this is exactly why I gave you the authority to do that. Tell them Elijah has a truckload of medical records, and half of them are in their own records department. Look, I have to get back to work."

She glared at Matt, who was covering for her on the register. "He's fine, all right? He made it. That's all you need to know." Brushing by him, she avoided making eye contact with anyone. "Next!" she called out to any customer in line who was brave enough to risk setting her off.

So he made it after all, she thought. *Is this ever going to end?*

———

From the moment he took his first breath, Elijah had been in deep trouble—trouble so deep that the doctors weren't even aware of its extent. The way Miriam saw it, his tiny lungs had failed to receive the message that the time was coming for him to be born, and they just sat inside his body, taking their sweet time and refusing to grow as they should. When Elijah was ready to make his entrance into the world, they still weren't strong enough to function the way a healthy set of lungs should.

When the doctors told Miriam that his lungs were underdeveloped, she wasn't concerned. After all, hadn't they emphasized that in similar situations the infants' lungs eventually caught up to the rest of their bodies? "Don't worry, Mrs. Knight," their pediatrician reassured her. "Children like Elijah grow up to live normal lives."

Maybe so, Miriam thought throughout the years, but Elijah

one would seek to return to the days before the availability of insulin or antibiotics, the unbridled and often illogical use of many medications is now causing, in the opinion of some health-care professionals, as many problems as they help.

People consume drugs in the United States for health-care and recreational purposes in a nearly mindless manner. Prescriptions are written, filled, and consumed on a robotic basis. Few questions are asked, few concerns are noted, and the cycle of use and reaction continues.

Every drug is to some degree a poison. Virtually any medication taken by the wrong patient, in the wrong dose, or at the wrong time has the ability to be harmful, if not fatal. The risk/benefit analysis of drug consumption—prescribed or otherwise—needs to be brought into focus for health and economic reasons.

Before you think that this view is alarmist in nature, consider the following facts about the use of one of the world's most common pain-related drugs, acetaminophen (available under the product name Tylenol, for example). Acetaminophen use is the number one reason for acute liver failure in the United States. It is also responsible for 8 to 10 percent of the end-stage renal disease in the U.S.[18] These statistics are associated with *one* extremely common, widely used drug that is considered so safe it is available without prescription to anyone with the money to pay for it. If the "nondangerous" drugs yield consequences of this nature, what is happening with products that require the restrictions of a prescription to obtain them? Think Vioxx and hormone replacement therapy!

Aside from adverse reactions from drug consumption, there are other reasons to be very cautious about drug usage, particularly antibiotics. Alexander Fleming discovered penicillin in 1928, and in the 1940s its use in humans was under way. Within months the developers of penicillin began to warn their colleagues about the consequences of overutilization of this newly discovered "wonder drug." Responsible physicians and researchers continue to echo these concerns by warning us about the consequences of widespread overutilization of antibiotics: the development of very strong, very powerful, very fatal microorganisms called "superbugs." Today every hospital in the world fears an MSRA (methicillin-resistant taphylococcus aureus) superbug outbreak, which could wipe out a nursing home or hospital ward in no time. This isn't science fiction—it is the reality of infectious disease today. The CDC warns that 90 percent of upper respiratory infections, including children's ear infections, are viral and that antibiotics do not treat viral infection.[19] More than 40 percent of about 50 million prescriptions for antibiotics written each year in physicians' offices are inappropriate.[20]

"Care, not treatment, is the answer," says Dr. Joseph Mercola, a Chicago-area osteopathic physician, in response to the health-care crisis. "Drugs, surgery, and hospitals are rarely the answer to chronic health problems. Facilitating the God-given healing capacity that all of us have is the key. Improving the diet, exercise,

hadn't. And the people around him hardly lived normal lives either.

Blissfully ignorant of what the future would hold for her, Miriam doted on her newborn son, convinced he wasn't just normal but perfect in every way. Not at all like her marriage had been. "Joseph and his wild ideas! Always talking about going out West and living the cowboy life!" her mother pointed out as often as she could. Miriam had stopped objecting; her mother was right, but she wasn't about to let her know that Joseph's many "wild ideas" were threatening their marriage.

To Joseph's way of thinking, Miriam was taking this whole marriage thing way too seriously. So what if he wanted to hang out with the guys after work? He always did that when they were dating. Nothing had changed except that they had said some vows and now lived under the same roof. Big deal. He'd keep going out with the guys. It's not as if he ever stayed out all night or did anything really bad—not that he hadn't had the opportunity a time or two.

No matter how much Joseph complained, though, Miriam knew she was the one who had gotten the raw end of the deal. What happened to that romantic, charming man she used to know? Where was the man who pledged his undying love in more ways and on more occasions than she could count? For that matter, whatever happened to the promises he made? The honeymoon in Rome (who knew there was one in New York State?), the Lexus LS430 that would replace her ten-year-old Toyota Corolla (which she was still driving), the brand-new, custom-designed house (their "temporary" apartment had been their home for two years)? His charm disappeared with his promises a long time before.

"Joseph's a different man—you'll see," Miriam told her mother

and lifestyle are basic." Dr. Mercola's views have motivated him to create a health-care Web site, www.mercola.com—which provides the most current wellness information and cutting-edge, natural solutions to the present crisis of our health system.

Drug Effects Abroad

As the U.S. health-care model spreads abroad, we're finding that no matter the race, creed, color, or continent, the "side" effects of the overuse of medication are hazardous.

Down Under

- Official Australian government reports reveal that preventable medical error in hospitals is responsible for 11 percent of all deaths in Australia. This is about one of every nine deaths.

- If we add deaths from properly researched, properly registered, properly prescribed, and properly used drugs to the number of preventable deaths due to private practice, it comes to a staggering 19 percent, which is almost one of every five deaths.[21]

In Canada

A February 2004 report from the Canadian Broadcasting Company (CBC) indicated that in the last five years, the adverse incidences among Canadian children due to medications increased approximately 300 percent.

Quick Facts About Drugs

- Studies suggest that there is a link between neurodevelopmental disorders, such as autism, and mercury exposure from thimerosal-containing childhood vaccines.[22]

- The flu shot has little effect against amorphous (different) strains.[23] Each year thousands of people who receive a flu shot still get the flu.[24]

- Ritalin is as potent as cocaine, yet prescriptions soar. (See page 13 for more information.)

- Forty to 60 percent of all prescriptions written in a given year were prescribed for conditions for which the prescription drugs did not have approval.[25]

- Hormone replacement medications are the second-most-prescribed drugs in the U.S., with 42 percent of postmenopausal women taking the medications, which may increase the risk of cancer, heart disease, and strokes.[26]

several months after learning she was pregnant. "He's really settled down. All he talks about are the things he'll be able to do with our children. He's going to be a great father."

At first he was, Miriam recalled. Those first few weeks after bringing Elijah home from the hospital were among the best of her life, as crazy as they were. The whirlwind "routine"—*now there's an unlikely word to describe this chaos!* Miriam thought early on—of scheduled bottle feedings and unscheduled diaper changes, scheduled pediatric visits and unscheduled family visits, replaced the implied accusations, belittling comments, and outright name-calling that had crept into their marriage.

In Elijah, Joseph found a same-gender ally, a child who would grow up to be just like his old man. Joseph could see it all now: teaching little Eli to catch, shooting hoops with him when he was older, watching Eli quarterback the varsity football team in his junior year. ("The jocks will eventually start calling him Eli, so we might as well start now," he once told Miriam.) He couldn't wait for Eli to grow up.

In Eli, Miriam also found what she had always longed for: a guy to love. Miriam could see it all now: Eli would be a model child. Eli would be her rock, her support, her shelter. Eli would take care of her when they both got older. Eli wouldn't break his promises to her. Eli would never disappoint her.

Miriam could hardly believe it. The Knights' fantasy world began to crumble before Elijah was even two months old. Awakened in the middle of the night to the sound of their baby gasping for air, Miriam and Joseph rushed to the emergency room, terrified they would lose Elijah. Shaking with fear, Miriam sat next

Overmedicating Children

Ritalin is prescribed for ADHD and hyperactivity even though there are no valid, established tests to prove those conditions are present. This medication has severe side effects, including but not limited to rapid heartbeat (palpitations, tachycardia), high blood pressure (hypertension), unusual heart rhythm, heart attack, psychosis, depression or excitement, convulsions, seizures, drowsiness, confusion, lack of sleep, agitation, hostility, impaired mental abilities, nausea, vomiting, eating disorders, growth problems, weight loss, hair loss, blood disorders, headaches, joint pain, blurred vision, and severe withdrawal symptoms.

This drug is under serious investigation, and in fact, the whole ADHD/hyperactivity diagnosis is facing serious scrutiny. The mass majority of this dangerous controlled substance is consumed in the U.S. and is actually not used at all in many major countries. In 1970, two hundred thousand children were on Ritalin and like substances, and now the numbers have exceeded six million.[27]

Similar medications such as Aderol, Concerta, Dexedrine, Dextrostat, and Metadate have similar concerns and side effects. Most important, in most cases, these drugs cover up and don't resolve or heal the more meaningful, complex underlying issues.

Painkillers—Killer Statistics

The 2004 recall of the popular drug Vioxx, one of the most widely advertised and prescribed medications at the time, was due to the finding that somewhere between thirty thousand and one hundred thousand Vioxx users reportedly suffered heart attacks and strokes while taking the painkiller. In a December 2004 *New York Times* article: "Federal drug officials said that the entire class of painkillers known as nonsteroidal anti-inflammatories—drugs that include Celebrex, Advil (naproxen), and Mobic—could cause worrisome effects on the heart."[28] "This illustrates the fundamental dynamic that all drugs have risks," said Dr. Steven Galson, acting director of the FDA's center for drug evaluation and research.[29]

There is a way that seems right to a man, but its end is the way of death.
—PROVERBS 14:12, NKJV

to her husband but felt miles away from him as they waited for the attending physician to return.

"Your son is breathing on his own now. He'll be fine," the doctor said. "He was experiencing bronchial distress caused by the croup. Just get this filled"—with that, he tore off the top page on his prescription pad and handed the page to them—"and follow up with his pediatrician. Any questions?"

Any questions? Was he serious? After the obvious ones—"What just happened? Didn't our son almost die? What if this happens again? This medication is supposed to cure him—how? What's the croup, anyway?"—Miriam could have added a dozen more. But she and Joseph stood mute, so confused and traumatized that neither could form a complete sentence. All they wanted was Elijah back in their arms.

Faithfully following the doctor's instructions, Miriam gave Eli the medication, and he seemed to be getting better. *Maybe it was just a fluke, some kind of bug that's going around,* she thought. A month later, though, the scene repeated itself, with another anguished, middle-of-the-night trip to the emergency room. Once again, they sat together in the waiting room, this time with a seat left vacant between them. "At least we know what to expect," Miriam said to Joseph, trying to convince herself more than him that everything would turn out just fine.

Knowing what to expect provided little comfort, especially when the attending physician prescribed an entirely different form of treatment after he had stabilized Elijah and had him breathing normally again. "Just run the water in the shower until it gets hot, and then hold the baby when you get in. The steam from the warm

Medicalization: "Disease Mongering"

The pharmaceutical industry is raking in unheard-of profits—more than three times the average of the other *Forbes* Fortune 500 industries—even after counting in all of the research and development costs. Much of this is done under the guise that it's for the greater good. However, the facts show that the system has become replete with research bias and conflicts of interest.

In an article titled "Selling Sickness: The Pharmaceutical Industry and Disease Mongering," the *British Medical Journal* traveled to the depths of the health-care-system crisis created by what they called the "medicalization" of society.

Medicalization is the medical industry's practice of turning commonly found symptoms into a "disease" so its members can prescribe a medication for it. In addition, the medical industry works to increase the awareness of its drugs and treatment to get more customers (i.e., lots of TV commercials, ads, bowl sponsorships, etc.).

There is what's been described as an "unholy alliance" between pharmaceutical manufacturers and doctors, who are informing the population that they are in fact ill. Medical doctors are intelligent, good people. They go through an extended educational process to learn how to help. Nonetheless, due to the speed at which information is coming across a doctor's desk and given how busy doctors are with their medical practices, they can't possibly keep up. As a result, for prescribing advice, they're forced to rely on the very skewed opinions of drug reps and the biased research paid for by their companies. I've heard it said that so much new information on medical treatment comes out each year that within four years, a medical doctor's training is obsolete. If you've ever seen a dozen police try to prevent a stadium full of college kids from rushing the football field after their school just won the big game, you'll get a slight idea of what medical doctors are being asked to handle during the course of their careers. So they've been taught, since the time they were medical school students, to rely on the pharmaceutical and medical-device manufacturers and their reps for reinforcements (help, support, education, and advice on practicing medicine).

In 2003, the *British Medical Journal* said, "Twisted together like the snake and the staff, doctors and drug companies have become entangled in a web of interactions as controversial as they are ubiquitous [everywhere]."

In 2001, all of the biggies—the *New England Journal of Medicine* (*NEJM*), the *Journal of the American Medical Association* (*JAMA*), the *Annals of Internal Medicine,* and the *Lancet*—put out an all-points bulletin throwing up a red flag warning that clinical research had really become little more than commercial activity (a way of making money).

John Abramson, MD, points out in his book *Overdosed America* that a 2002

air will cause his bronchial passages to relax, and he'll start breathing normally again," the doctor assured them. "Any questions?"

"What are we supposed to do, Joseph?" Miriam pleaded once
they got back in the car and headed home. "You know how long it
takes for that old water heater to pump out any hot water, and Eli
could die by that time. Plus, I'm totally confused now: do we keep
giving him medication, or do we just give him the steam baths?
None of this makes any sense, but they're the experts."

Half-expecting a snide remark from Joseph, whose Boy Scout
behavior had started to wear off, Miriam was startled when he
agreed with her. First thing the following morning, she called Eli's
pediatrician and described what had happened the night before.
"The doctor you saw last night was right—all Eli needed was a
steam bath. The medication is only to be given when he has the
croup," the pediatrician told her. *So how come you never mentioned
steam baths?* Miriam wanted to shout but opted instead for a less-
accusing approach. "But what's wrong with him? Why does this
keep happening?" she asked.

"Yours is not an abnormal situation," the doctor replied.
"Respiratory distress is a fairly typical childhood problem. The worst
thing you can do is worry about it. He'll grow out of it."

The worst thing I can do is keep listening to you, Miriam thought
but held her tongue. There weren't a lot of pediatricians in town,
and they couldn't afford to get on this doctor's bad side. Besides,
everybody knew this doctor was the best in the county.

Miriam's own health took a plunge as the Knights' "not abnormal" situation worsened over the next eighteen months. Tension
headaches, insomnia, chronic fatigue, low blood sugar, hormonal

article in the *Journal of the American Medical Association* showed that "59 percent of the experts who write the clinical guidelines that define good medical care [the standards to which doctors are often held in malpractice] have direct financial ties to the companies whose products are being evaluated." If doctors choose to ignore guidelines, they risk their reputations, their standing in the medical community, and being charged with malpractice.

"The exaggeration and distortion of the 2001 cholesterol guidelines that are responsible for the millions of Americans being treated with cholesterol lowering statin drugs [lipitor, zocor, prevachol, lescol, mevacor, crestor]—despite lack of scientific evidence of benefit of such widespread use—is presented as a case in point." Dr. Abramson further explains that if these new guidelines are followed, the number of people taking statin drugs will go from thirteen million to thirty-six million, with the only likely upside being drug-company stockholder profits, and not healthier people.

A key strategy of the alliances is to target the news media with stories designed to create fears about the condition or disease and draw attention to the latest treatment. This has led to problems on several key levels:

- People with benign, normal symptoms taking dangerous drugs. As we are convinced that natural signs of aging and common conditions are diseases or treatable symptoms, we take drugs for such things as balding, anxiety, mild bone loss, and indigestion, which put us at risk for issues that are not true illnesses or risks.

- People being tested regularly and undergoing unnecessary treatments with drugs and invasive surgery. Very few people after middle age can pass tests without being told that they have some sort of "risk." This risk is turned into a pseudodisease leading to such things as dangerous breast and colon surgery and "preventive" medications. For example, a male patient over forty goes to the doctor for a sore throat and finds the doctor's finger up his rectum. The doctor informs him that he has a prostate issue and removes it, causing the man to be impotent for the rest of his now-miserable life.

- Fear and a loss of clarity in the important practice of medicine. As a result of "disease mongering," the more the medical industry influences a nation, the sicker that nation "considers itself to be." It eats away at our self-confidence and teaches us that we're weak and incapable of staying well—that all signs and symptoms are potentially dangerous conditions and diseases. Truly, this sort of marketing has blurred the lines of when we need drugs and surgery and when we don't.

imbalance—Miriam had it all, but she had no time to deal with any of it. With Eli experiencing severe shortness of breath every few weeks, it was all she could do to keep up with his needs, let alone her own. What's more, the unrelenting stress of constant worry, frequent doctor and emergency room visits, unanswered—or perhaps, unanswerable—questions about his chances for a normal life, endless waiting for the hot water to make it to the shower head, petty arguments over whose turn it was to hold Eli in the shower—all that began to expose the Knights' marriage for the sham it was.

Shortly before Eli's first birthday, Miriam sensed that their lives—and her own emotions—were beginning to unravel. Another night, another episode—only this time, Elijah had turned blue by the time she woke up. No time to wait for the hot water; this was an undisputed 911 situation.

As several paramedics worked to resuscitate Eli, another worked to calm down a frantic and panic-stricken Miriam. They brought Eli around quickly enough, but Miriam was another matter altogether. "Mrs. Knight, you need to take a deep breath," one paramedic advised. "Make sure you talk to the doctor about her," he added, turning to Joseph, who was barely paying attention. "She needs something to calm her down. Are you going to be all right, Mrs. Knight?"

Sure, sure, Miriam thought, unable to answer. *I'll be just fine, just as soon as I slit my wrists.* That horrifying possibility shook Miriam back to reality. "I'll be fine, fine," she stammered. *I've got to keep it together for Eli. I've got to,* she thought as she climbed into the back of the ambulance for yet another ride to the emergency room. Once again, Miriam found herself worlds apart from Joseph as they

Worst of all, rather than people focusing more time and attention on their health as they age or as they see degeneration setting in, they settle for a diagnosis and the latest medications. The only winners are the ones who profit.

Suggestions from the *British Medical Journal* on disease mongering:

- Move away from using corporate-funded information on medical conditions and disease.

- Widen notions of informed consent to include information about controversy surrounding the definitions of conditions and disease.

- Lead people to participate in their health and not just in their disease (inside-out versus outside-in).[30]

What stands in the way of change: powerful pharmaceutical and medical technology companies, along with other powerful corporations with incredibly large vested interests in the medical business. This kind of money and influence can tip the scales of opinion from professional caution to uncritical acceptance. If you look at the people who make up governmental, FDA, hospital, and medical health advisory boards and their financial ties to pharmaceutical companies, you clearly see conflicts of interest. Sadly, the public is mostly unaware of these interlocking interests and continues to believe in the sanctity of medicine. An industry that's forgotten that its sole purpose was to serve the people and not itself. It's reality. We can live with it—just beware.

I truly don't believe that the people in the medical industry are bad people. I know that, for the most part, their chief aim in life has been to help. The problem lies in the fact that in the eyes of their patients, they have become like gods. Without caution or investigation, they've been given total authority in the health-care world. With seemingly nowhere else to turn, we have completely handed over to them the public trust—so much so that out of fear, no one dares doubt them—even in the face of a broken, desolate, and ever-failing health-care system.

Caring doctors enter this system, but the system simply has scientific, philosophical, and ethical flaws. It just doesn't work.

As people and other health delivery systems begin to challenge and shake the foundation of the medical industry, the industry is fighting fiercely to deny alternatives or control them—a practice that certainly is more for self-preservation and not for the preservation of the public.

I really believe in what were originally the true principles of medicine. Many friends, patients, and family members of mine have been saved by the power of emergency medical intervention. Unfortunately for all, what was once designed to save us from disaster or death in the case of extreme circumstances has now crept

rode to the hospital. The one weak link that held them together had almost died.

———

"Hey, man, what do you expect?" Gary asked. "Your kid almost dies just about every month, and you're thinking about leaving. Man, I'd be out of there."

That's not exactly what Joseph wanted to hear. Draining his bottle of Coors, Joseph looked away from his buddy and struggled to find a reason to go home. "Yeah, but Eli needs me. Miriam, I could do without, always whining about her headaches and stuff. But Eli's my son."

"You sure about that?" Gary tilted his own bottle and sneaked a sideways glance at Joseph.

"What's that supposed to mean?"

"Come on! You mean you haven't thought about that, not even once? Look at you—you're a rock! Man, every guy in your family, every one that I know anyway, is a bruiser. And Miriam's brother— what was his name? Oh yeah, Hal—he's got as many trophies for football as all the Knights put together. So how come Eli's so weak? Think about it, man."

He did, and he had. Too often. Sure, Miriam had been a real goody-two-shoes when they were dating, and with him around, she hardly had any reason to look elsewhere. But this thing with Eli— it had to be genetic. Lousy gene pool, that's what everyone joked about these days whenever something went wrong. Well, maybe that was the problem with Eli—somebody else's stinking gene pool.

into our everyday lifestyle. Symptoms of all kinds have been labeled "disease" or "deadly," causing us to now fear every sniffle, cough, ache, or pain. What's worse, we now seek passive medical retribution for both our physical and mental well-being rather than actively participating in it. When symptoms arrive as a result of how poorly we've neglected our bodies and minds, rather than taking personal responsibility for our own wellness (restoring wholeness) and trusting in the God-given recuperative powers of our bodies, we seek those who are now only too willing to take on this role for us. There's a 24-hour pharmacy on almost every busy corner now!

As a result of handing the full authority of our lives over to the industry of medicine, the pharmaceutical and medical establishments have become so bloated, profitable, and powerful that we're now witnessing their becoming completely out of control.

While on one hand I personally owe much to the practice of medicine, experts are finding that the harm the present health-care delivery system is causing now outweighs the good. It's time that balance is restored—taking the good of medicine and replacing the bad with new ways of thinking and more appropriate ways of taking care of our bodies. You must choose doctors and advice very carefully and recognize that you can take back the authority over your life!

He would *not* put up with this for the rest of his life. He would *not* spend twenty years raising a weakling, a boy who would likely turn out to be a sissy. And he would *not* take a chance on being around if his son died. He could take the money he'd been secretly squirreling away ever since he got married—tips from generous do-gooders who didn't think twice about handing him a twenty after he set up their cable service, cash from odd jobs, even occasional poker game winnings, all money that Miriam knew nothing about. That was plenty for him to strike out on his own. Yep, that's what he'd do. He'd walk out and leave it all behind. Every bit of it. Come Friday.

"Where you going? It's early yet!" Gary called as Joseph headed for the tavern door.

"I'm out of here," Joseph said.

———

By Saturday, Miriam figured out Joseph was gone for good. He seldom came home before midnight anymore, but last night was different. He never came home at all. By the time Miriam discovered that some of his clothes were missing and began putting it all together, Ohio was four states away in his rearview mirror.

At first, she frantically tried to find him, enlisting the help of a single mother in the neighborhood who gave her advice on which agencies would actually help her find him and which would not. "I'd give up and go on welfare if I were you," her neighbor Kelly told her. "Guys like Joseph know how to get lost and stay lost. They'll never find him."

| 2 |

A Saner Approach to Life and Health

The governor of California is perhaps best known for his reinforced rubberized skin, mechanical endoskeleton, humanlike features, and robotic emotions. As the Terminator, Arnold Schwarzenegger was the image of a man in the body of a machine. In the movie of the same name, using objects that could be found in a garage or tool kit, the Terminator could fix or replace any damaged, broken, or blown-up parts, and the mechanical human was "repaired."

That's not so different from the philosophy of current traditional health care. Modern medical wisdom takes a *mechanical* approach to health-care solutions. This approach relies on technology, chemistry, and, yes, machinery for the solutions to our problems and treats people as if they were machines rather than complex, vital, biological beings capable of self-healing.

The tendency for medicine to follow a mechanistic model comes from the limiting point that we don't know how to make a body or create life, so we can't know everything about how to fix a body or a life. Therefore, since we do know how to make machinery and high-tech equipment, we apply our mechanical solutions to the care and treatment of people. Unfortunately, that means our understanding is based on our ignorance, which always creates an obstacle to success and is a large part of the reason behind the horrific health-care statistics we are now seeing in the U.S. and abroad.

While technology has always been associated with the future, ironically, when it comes to our well-being, the future relies on the power of people, not machines. Humans have a vital, miraculous power that machines don't. People are a whole lot more than the sum of their parts. To ignore this is not only to be ignorant of healing, but to interfere with healing. Thus, we have all the side effects people experience from modern medications and treatments.

Our health-care future relies on embracing this vital, human power and not using mechanistic thinking alone. We need to utilize not only high-tech treatments but also care that cooperates with the God-given life force that exists in living, breathing human beings—with the understanding that anything that doesn't cooperate interferes. Then instead of having understanding that is based on ignorance, we'll have ignorance that is based on understanding.

She was right. Convinced that Joseph had headed for Denver, a place he had never visited but always romanticized, Miriam pointed investigators in that direction. "He always wanted to be the next Marlboro man," she told them. "Said he was a mountain man inside and wanted to someday prove it by living in the wilderness." She left out the part about sitting around a campfire, drinking with tough-as-nails mountain men and even tougher mountain women.

But if Joseph ever made it to Denver, he left no evidence of his presence there. He simply disappeared. Miriam decided that when he was old enough, she would tell Eli that his daddy had died in a car crash on his way to Colorado to find a better job and make a new life for the three of them. As much as Miriam hated to make Joseph sound like a saint, she figured Eli had enough strikes against him. Learning one day that his father had abandoned him was one strike too many.

Miriam had much more to worry about than finding Eli's elusive, deadbeat father. Without the health insurance plan offered by the cable company Joseph had worked for—and without any hope of ever seeing a child-support check—Miriam became accustomed to waiting what seemed like forever to see a doctor at the free clinic run by the county. That seriously cut into her job-search time, which in turn eliminated any hope of finding job-training time.

"How do you do this?" she asked Kelly, who lived in the apartment upstairs and had been on welfare as long as she could remember. Wrong person to ask, but the only one available. "How can you get a good job when you need money to live? I mean, how can I go get training for a better job when I have to spend all my time making money and taking care of Eli?"

When we completely humanize life's divinity, we eliminate common sense, morality, humble respect, and the value of life. Resultantly, we get the kind of disastrous statistics we are seeing today. Humans need *healing*; they can't just be "repaired." If we continue to ignore our vitality and seek only to manipulate it with technology, all the while disregarding the side effects, we can expect not only a lack of wellness, but a future that is so cataclysmic, it would look like a movie in which Governor Schwarzenegger could actually star.

Fortunately, science is finally beginning to understand the powerful, intelligent design of human biology and what you can do and how you can live to create healing and transformation in your body.

Today's Biology: New Discoveries Reveal Your Vital Power

Despite the fact that science knows you're not just a bunch of mass or matter and has begun to recognize an intelligent, immeasurable, spiritual component to your life, medical students still are taught that the body is merely a physical machine. This leads to the belief that you're just simple equipment—programmed, predestined, or "fated" by age, genetics, geography, or gender for either good or bad physical or emotional health.

As a result of this way of thinking, all research and traditional medicine ever tries to accomplish is to attempt to come up with the next drug treatment that can manipulate destined-to-fail systems that are present as a result of gene defects, bad luck, or because "hey—you're just old." So, while there are new diagnostic tools coming out all of the time telling you you're sick based on some hypothetical norm and newer, stronger drugs that can alter function to greater and greater degrees, none will ever make you, in fact, healthy. And these new tests and stronger drugs are apparently very hazardous to your health.

Doctor Bruce Lipton, a former medical school professor and research scientist, points out in his book *The Biology of Belief* that this Darwinian viewpoint of genetic determinism or fatalism make up part and parcel of the current medical model and are the "Central Dogma" of science today. According to this theory, if you're born with defective genes, hello unhappy life—sooner or later you'll become a victim of depression, obesity, illness, and the express lane to an early grave. This dogma supports that in the "survival of the fittest," you're weak. It looks at your cellular systems as some sort of simple, incomplete, unidirectional machinery. In this scenario, all that's left for you is a lifetime of dependency on medications.

Fortunately for all of us, today's scientific community is revealing that you're much, much more than a machine fated for peace and health or misery or disease. As Dr. Lipton states, "Genes can't turn themselves on and off. Something that effects your [internal] environment has to trigger them."

"Beats me," Kelly said, applying a top coat of polish to her pinkie. "You need to get in the system, girlfriend. It's the only way you're going to get through this."

"Forget I said anything," Miriam said, frustrated by the idea that welfare was the only answer. She'd just have to take whatever job she could get, even if it paid little more than minimum wage, and even if it meant working more than one job.

The little money she got for her good-for-nothing, rusty Corolla, now almost fifteen years old, netted her a security deposit on a dingy, one-bedroom apartment in what she liked to call a "safety-challenged" neighborhood. She did manage to get a fairly good deal on the high-tech stereo system Joseph left behind in his haste to get her out of his life. He'd bought it during his "country superstar" phase, when he'd convinced himself that they should move to Nashville so he could have a better shot at a recording contract. That was one flight of fancy that paid off; another starry-eyed future celebrity—just a kid, but an extravagant one—met her asking price, no questions asked. Miriam figured he'd eventually learn the fine art of haggling, but she was delighted with his current level of enthusiasm—and ignorance.

Meanwhile, Elijah's episodes continued, now exacerbated by chronic bronchitis, increased susceptibility to pneumonia, and the latest diagnosis, allergies. The last one particularly rankled Miriam. "What do you mean he's allergic to cigarette smoke? Isn't everybody?" she asked the clinic nurse during an especially frustrating visit.

Despite all this—the poverty, abandonment (Elijah was old enough now to doubt the car-crash story), frightening health problems, a mother who seemed to be growing numb to the truth about what their lives had become—Elijah displayed all the

The truth we're beginning to understand proves Darwin's evolution and Newton's mechanistic physics are heavily flawed. Most scientists now realize that there's an intelligent design to life as well as acknowledge that there's a "Designer." This "new biology" doesn't seek to humanize our divinity or the incalculable miracle of cell life. Life is not fully explainable through measurable physics and chemistry alone. We're incredibly complex and non-linear. There are so many connections, interconnections, and communication pathways going on in the body that we can't ever possibly understand how they work. And that's just how God probably wants it.

Essentially, medicine does not look only at the spiritual part of our makeup— it denies it's even there. Fortunately, the belief that you're a frail biochemical robot controlled by genes and predestined to either fail or succeed has given way to an understanding that you are vital and powerful beyond what you could ever fully fathom. You are more than just the sum of a bunch of parts that can be studied in a laboratory. As it turns out, you are a remarkable, dynamic being capable of programming or reprogramming yourself to be a healthy, creative, purpose-filled, and joyful person. God's magical, creative, healing power exists within your cells, and with any cooperation on your part, balance can be sustained or restored and you can begin experiencing all that He has designed you to be.

The fact is, genetics are a tendency, not a death sentence. Genes for heart disease, breast cancer, mental, emotional disorders, etc., are like the trigger on a gun—they're only dangerous if you pull them. Inside of just one nucleus in one of your fifty trillion cells is six feet of DNA material. This is similar to cramming thirty miles of wire into a cherry pit. This DNA comes in forty-six different sections called chromosomes, which is subdivided into your genes. These genes encode information for molecules that perform a bewildering number of functions. We barely have a glimpse of the monstrous complexity of genes and how they specifically affect our behaviors and respective biology. To say that a "gene" causes obesity, depression, alcoholism, or chocolate addiction is insane. We truly don't understand 5 percent of what's going on, and that percentage never improves because with each new discovery, we also discover that there's even more mystery.

When it comes to cellular success, it's nurture and not nature that makes the biggest difference. The vast majority of diseases we face aren't due to our poor DNA. Dr. Lipton shares that "single gene disorders affect less than 2 percent of the population"! That means 98 percent of us are born with the ability to live with outrageous health and incredible happiness. These new discoveries show us that there is an ongoing creative power in our lives, and we are not "fated" at birth to feel a certain way, act a certain way, behave a certain way, and die a certain way at a certain time. *No.* At this point we know that we have something to say about that. The diseases, depression, aches, and pains we face today are not the results of

resiliency of a typical boy. Sure, he knew he was different. All the other kids could play longer, run faster, climb higher, and throw farther, but Eli seemed to have adjusted to his limitations. He'd rather be playing than sitting on the sidelines, but he also enjoyed watching his friends chase each other after he had reached his limit. Besides, he hated what happened when he overdid it. He was content being a spectator once in a while.

That is, until he entered middle school.

Things were different then. Back in elementary school, the worst that happened was that Eli wouldn't be able to play dodge ball or climb the monkey bars or run races during recess. But now, just about every athletic activity, both during school and after, was centered on one concept: the Team, with a capital *T*. Baseball, basketball, football, soccer—all were team sports, and the competition among middle-school boys was notoriously fierce and cruel.

No one wanted a sickly kid like Elijah on his team. Not once was he actually chosen, even when the phys-ed coach forced the team captain of the day to "choose" him. No, the team that got stuck with Eli had gotten him by default, and along with him they got a special team name for that day: *losers*. When one particularly malicious group of boys created a chant ("E-li's / Gonna cry! E-li's / Gonna cry!"), Elijah begged his mother to homeschool him. No chance that would ever happen; with two, and sometimes three, jobs, she had no time for teaching her son.

"Mom, I can't breathe!" Eli called out to Miriam at least one morning a week, always on a school day. He had to be careful not to overplay his hand, but he knew full well his mother couldn't and wouldn't ignore his cries for help. Getting out of school one day a

dysfunctional grandparents, but because we've lived and thought in such a way that created disharmony in our bodies.

"It's the environment, not the DNA," says Dr. Lipton. "When I provide a healthy environment for my cells (under the microscope), they thrived; when the environment was less than optimal, the cells faltered. (Most importantly,) when I adjusted the environment, these 'sick' cells revitalized."

You can no longer shift the blame for your present or future problems away from you and simply rely on the medical establishment anymore. You must take responsibility for your well-being. Any negative, unloving, stressful attitude, any manipulation of the body, any removal of parts, any interference to normal function, or any artificial invader (such as medications and refined, artificial, chemical-laden, or genetically modified foods in your diet) entering the body will alter this natural, safe internal environment, throw it out of balance, and cause chaos in the cellular community. This will create an incredible disadvantage to cellular survival and reduce quality of life. It will show up as pain, depression, disease, and a general failure to thrive. The quick-fix solution of choice may be medication, but as they say in TV game shows—*Beep, wrong answer!* Chemicals don't create harmony, order, or balance; they disrupt it. The real solution is to embrace what is necessary to create a healthy cellular environment once again so the body can restore, rejuvenate, and heal. The problem is that there's not trillions of dollars in allowing the body to get back in balance and heal itself. Therefore, it may be a while before "modern" medicine accepts this new understanding, and it's unlikely to be supported by research dollars from drug companies anytime soon.

It is, however, the future.

> Where science once sought the replacement of God, today's cutting-edge scientists, when asked if they believed in God, would say, "Of course I do. I'm a scientist."

The Mechanical Model: An Outside-In Approach

The mechanistic model of health care focuses on the diagnosis and treatment of disease and the symptoms of disease. "Modern" medicine uses mechanistic thinking when it takes an outside-in approach to discovering where disease and symptoms come from and what to do to treat them (i.e., the body has a tendency to break down like a machine, and when it does, we tinker with the mechanisms or remove or replace the parts altogether).

week was better than nothing; he just had to make sure he varied his symptoms—sometimes pain in his lungs, sometimes shortness of breath, sometimes deep coughing he'd learned to fake. But one morning, he failed to notice his bedroom door was open just slightly—just enough for Miriam to see in.

"Mom! Hurry! The pain—it's awful!" Joseph, calmly sitting up in bed, began his hacking cough routine. Little did he know that Miriam had been watching him all along.

That put an end to the fake episodes. Besides, the real ones were frequent enough, and Eli was getting tired of having to remember which symptom he had used the last time. Doing his best to hide his shame and humiliation from his classmates during school hours, Eli spent his time just trying to get by. Life pretty much settled into the routine of a crummy drama played out on three sets: big school, tiny apartment, and a crowded clinic that pushed the limits on the definition of "sterile environment."

By the time he was twelve, Eli felt as if he lived at the clinic. The treatment he received had become so routine that he started mouthing the nurse's words behind her back: "Elijah Knight's here again. Put him in three, give him oxygen—you know, the usual." But on one occasion, Elijah was surprised to see a new doctor at the clinic. He could see the immediate change in his mother's entire demeanor when the young doctor greeted them with what actually appeared to be a genuine smile.

Buoyed by a sense of hope that even she knew was unrealistic, Miriam pleaded with the doctor to listen to her concerns and realize that she had been through it all for nearly twelve years—she had heard it all, seen it all, experienced it all. She wanted to know exactly

Mechanical Outside-In Disease Model

1. The cause of health issues. Current medical thinking looks at the cause of disease as something we're stuck with, something that's "sudden," or something that jumps out (or in) and attacks us from the outside. Heart problems are an example of something we're told is in our families. Cancer "suddenly" strikes, or a cold and flu bug somehow bores its way in from the outside and gets us.

2. The cure for health issues. The responsibility for healing is placed on something outside the body. Diseases are treated or symptoms are masked from the outside in, using either medication (such as antibiotics, muscle relaxants, and anti-inflammatory drugs) or an outside-in resource, such as surgery (repair, replacement, or removal of the organ, muscle, or tissue).

If this has been your understanding of the treatment of disease, it's time you learn about new research that is proving this concept to be limited, potentially dangerous, and necessary far less frequently than doctors prescribe it. It's not that this approach never has any warrant, but on the whole it makes no sense and has failed to keep us well. Doctors learn this model, which does not train or prepare them to create health, only to treat disease, and medical science continues to support it despite its failure to create a more healthy and happy world.

A traditional doctor looks at disease as a single entity or event and at the human body as a sum of its parts. This type of doctor may "specialize" in a part or system. He doesn't see the body as a powerful, vital, complex, healing, living, breathing organism. But the body is not a bunch of parts; it's a symphony of parts working together in harmony. After all, what's an eye or an intestine without the rest of the body?

The new vital, nonmechanical model of health utilizes today's new biology by looking not from the outside in, but from the inside out.

Vital Inside-Out Dis-ease Model

1. The cause of health issues. The cause of health problems comes from the inside out due to the existence of "dis-ease." This is a lack of normal function, balance, harmony, or "ease" in the body. It's the presence of dis-ease on the inside that creates an unhealthy environment for your cells to thrive and causes a disruption in vital health. *You are no longer working according to intelligent design.* This allows bugs, cancers, heart disease, and other illnesses to overcome you—on the inside.

Dis-ease (a lack of cooperation among cells) results in breakdown, disrepair, imbalance, and lowered resistance. Effectively, over time, symptoms of illness can arise, along with a full-blown, diagnosed disease.

2. The cure for health issues. Don't treat the symptom or disease; treat the cause. By following this new way of thinking about disease, you don't look on sickness and disease as something you're stuck with, that attacks you, or that's getting you from the outside in, but rather as resulting from dis-ease, or a lack of proper function and

what was wrong with her son, and she wanted to know if he could be cured. And most of all, she wanted to know *now.*

Fresh out of medical school, the young doctor listened carefully and announced confidently, "I think I know exactly what will take care of this problem," he said. "We'll do some more blood work, but I think this battery of tests will give you the answers you're looking for." Weary, beaten down, both her senses and her common sense dulled by repeated disappointments, Miriam relented.

The test results came in the following week. The verdict was in: Elijah was suffering from asthma. *Great,* Elijah thought, *another ailment. Oh goody! And another doctor—this just keeps getting better.* The doctor of the day at the clinic reminded Eli of the Tin Man—stiff and rusty, with a frozen expression on his face.

"So, Elijah, when you begin to feel short of breath, just place the inhaler in your mouth"—the doctor demonstrated, using a non-working inhaler—"and press down on the top of the little bottle attached to it. A puff of medication will enter your lungs and clear them so you'll be able to breathe normally."

"But will this cure him?" Miriam asked.

"No, no. This will relieve the symptoms," he said, tearing off a page from the top of his prescription pad and handing it to Miriam. "Any questions?"

Furious, but too worn out to act on her anger, Miriam left the clinic with Eli and headed for the bus stop. A torrential downpour drove them instead to a Medi-Mart, where they'd have to ride out the storm until their bus arrived in a half hour or so.

Already in a foul mood, Miriam scowled as she entered the store—the store whose manager had fired her when she was late

balance inside the body. You do what you can to restore normal function and "ease" and so that you can build resistance to germs and prevent illness. In this way, the responsibility for healing does not lie on something outside you, but within you.

God has made the body to be a self-healing, self-regulating, self-perpetuating organism and has placed the answers to disease within the body. So the key to health is to treat the cause, not the effect: to detect, identify, correct, and remove that which interferes with proper function and balance. Only when you eliminate the interference can you establish "ease" in the body. With balance restored and "dis-ease" eliminated, then and only then can you create an internal environment that supports not only getting rid of your symptoms and disease but also actually restoring health—from the inside out. Just as it was *designed* to do.

> Find out the cause of this effect,
> Or rather say, the cause of this defect,
> For this effect defective comes by cause.
> —SHAKESPEARE

Don't Blame the Germs

In 1865, French chemist and biologist Louis Pasteur developed the germ theory, which presumes that bacteria and viruses attack the body from the *outside in*, causing diseases to develop in the organs. His theory, however, was immediately challenged. Another belief existed that disease was a side effect and had nothing to do with attacking germs. It did, however, have everything to do with the body's lack of resistance, thus showing that the cause of disease was dis-ease.

This latter theory proved and has continued to prove Pasteur wrong through evidence showing that: many healthy people carry pathogens (germs) but do not exhibit the symptoms of disease, not all people are susceptible to all pathogens, certain diseases develop only when an opportunistic pathogen invades a susceptible host, and not all diseases are caused by microorganisms (many are caused by dietary deficiencies [scurvy, rickets], abnormality in chromosomes, or environmental factors).

Pasteur's way of thinking has always been accepted and firmly adhered to by medicine and a population who, when sick or suffering, want so badly to believe that there's a cure lurking out there somewhere. In their time, not too long ago, leeches, bloodletting, and drilling holes in the head to let out evil spirits were the premier treatments of the day. Those practices seem barbaric to us now, but as more and more of our health-care practices prove to be harmful and even deadly, how much of what we do today in this cultural generation will also be considered barbarism tomorrow?

one too many times after dealing with Elijah. Avoiding her former coworkers and anything that might entice her or Eli into buying something, Miriam wandered over to an area where a woman was giving some kind of demonstration. (*It's always something here,* she thought. *One week a miracle arthritis preparation, the next a miracle cure for wrinkles. Wonder what they're up to today?*)

"Free Spine Screening," the sign read. *What on earth is that?* Miriam wondered. She watched as the woman ran an instrument up and down a customer's back. The readings on the instrument uncovered a misalignment of the man's spine. "You'd benefit greatly from having your spine adjusted by a good chiropractor," the woman said, handing the customer a packet of literature.

Still scowling, Miriam considered the demonstration to be one step above a traveling snake-oil exhibition. *I swear, what are people thinking? It's just another scam, and a health scam at that! I've about had it with charlatans, and I'm not about to fall for anything like this.*

"What about you, ma'am?" the woman asked Miriam, interrupting her critical thoughts.

"No, um, no," said Miriam, who hated being put on the spot.

"How about your son?"

My son? Is she nuts? "Uh, no," Miriam said. "Look at the time, Elijah," she said, pointing to her miraculously faithful Timex. "It's almost time for our bus." She tried to make a getaway by steering Elijah toward the door, but the woman nevertheless managed to place an information packet in Miriam's hand.

"I do hope you'll consider seeing a chiropractor," the woman called after her.

Fat chance, Miriam thought.

The facts behind this anti-Pasteur theory reveal that while bugs may have a role in disease, improving the body's ability to maintain itself from the inside out is the most important answer to winning the war against sickness.

> If the germ theory of medicine was completely true,
> there'd be no one living to believe it.
> —DR. FRED BARGE

The Culture Principle

As we look at societies that experience a high degree of wellness—societies that lack the sophisticated tools we have in the United States—it becomes evident that health is not created by "things." It is created—or, in reality, destroyed—by our culture. This becomes particularly evident when people from other, healthier nations, such as the Japanese or the Scandinavians, are Westernized—either by moving to the U.S. or by American culture influencing their civilization. Once people from other nations are exposed to the Western lifestyle and its health-care system, they begin to suffer steadily from conditions and diseases once common only to the Western world.

In our culture, most adults and even many children use cell phones for chitchatting and doing business 24/7. McDonald's, Pizza Hut, and other fast-food vendors have franchises in the public schools. Few people can imagine a stress-free week or an unrushed moment. Consumers demand fast service and instant relief. People get their exercise by competing in intense sports competitions—on their Nintendo machines. And we have a blood supply that, in many areas of Seattle, California, and New York, is approximately 75 percent Starbucks.

To solve the incredible health, family, and emotional crises that exist in the U.S. and now, more and more, in the rest of the world, it's going to take more than a pill or the latest diet program. Clearly, dropping the latest blockbuster drug or fad diet into the same culture has failed again and again to make us fit, happy, or well.

There's a need for a new way of thinking—a shift in the way our culture lives, thinks, and looks at its bodies and each member. This change will not just save us but also the world, because when we change, the world changes.

What you thought before has led to every choice you have made, and this
adds up to you at this moment. If you want to change who you are
physically, mentally, and spiritually, you will have to change what you think.

— DR. PATRICK GENTEMPO, CEO,
Chiropractic Leadership Alliance

That night at work, Miriam reached into her pocket for her flask but came up instead with the pamphlets on the benefits of chiropractic care. One pamphlet in particular, titled *Kids and Chiropractic*, caught her eye. *Kids? There it is again. Why on earth would a child need to see a chiropractor? What these doctors won't do for a buck. Oh well. It's probably just for kids who get hurt playing football or something like that,* she thought.

Something compelled her to keep reading, however, and by the time her break was over, Miriam was surprisingly intrigued by the possibility that chiropractic care could be beneficial in a lot of ways she never considered. But her thoughts were interrupted by Matt reminding her that her break was over. Absentmindedly, Miriam threw the pamphlets into the trash can on her way back into the store, and the little bit she had learned was soon lost in the swirl of frenzied activity that her life had become.

Sixth grade proved to be among the worst so far in Eli's life. The taunts from the other kids became nastier and reached an all-time low when he returned to school after being taken off the football field on a stretcher—not because he was injured, but because he couldn't breathe.

"Why? Why, God—or whoever You are?" Miriam screamed as she pounded the pavement with her fists. This time, the call had come in just as she arrived at work for her four-to-midnight shift. Eli had been horsing around with some of the guys after school, trying to fit in with them as they played a spontaneous game of

Shifting the Culture:
The Evolution of a Paradigm

by Dr. Guy F. Riekeman, president of Life University in Atlanta, Georgia

The world we've created is a result of the level of thinking we've done thus far and it produces problems, the solution to which does not exist at the same level of thinking.

—ALBERT EINSTEIN

In 1956 Thomas Kuhn introduced the word *paradigm* into the culture, defining it as a model of reality so deeply held that its truth or validity is no longer questioned. Paradigms generally evolve through the following stages:

1. A new idea appears to provide solutions to old problems. The new idea is perceived to be a perfect or "total" solution, which later proves to be unrealistic.
2. The new model evolves and gains widespread acceptance.
3. Questions evolve that the initial model can no longer address.
4. The population is ready for a new paradigm, or "paradigm shift."

While this process generally evolves slowly, every now and then an atypical shift occurs that alters the thought process of a culture—a point at which the culture challenges the basic functions of science, religion, politics, and so forth.

So what about health? For thousands of years we have asked, *How do we eliminate suffering and disease?* The unstated assumption is that the elimination of disease is the path to health. So deeply held is this thought process that few people have ever questioned the notion. Therefore, shifts in health-care delivery (paradigm shifts) occur not as shifts in thinking, but as shifts in technology. We substitute leeches for casting out evil spirits. Then we replace leeches with drugs, radiation, and surgery, each time believing we are only a few dollars and some research away from the ultimate cure for disease (stage 1 of the paradigm).

Stage 2 of the paradigm is acceptance. Think about how much of our cultural effort and economy is caught up in the diagnosis, research, and treatment of disease. It's a staggering thought. Who, like Copernicus, would dare challenge the very theory that this worldview is built upon?

football. Once again, Eli had to be taken off the field on a stretcher. Once again, Eli was taken to the hospital. Once again, Miriam was called at work. For the first time, Miriam cracked—publicly. Very publicly.

"Why me? Why my son? What do You have against us?" she screamed at the sky again, bloodying her hands on the broken glass in the parking lot.

Matt tried to restrain her from hurting herself any more than she already had. "I've called for help for you," he said, warding off the blows from her amazingly strong arms. The sizable crowd that had gathered around them managed to part just enough for the ambulance to pull into the parking lot.

For once, Miriam would ride to the hospital as a seriously agitated patient rather than a seriously anxious parent.

It was the following day before Miriam was lucid enough to talk or listen to the doctors. Now she had a double dose of turmoil to deal with: her own and her son's. Elijah was fine for now, they told her; her new neighbor Joanna, whom Miriam had listed as an emergency contact on every medical form she had filled out since moving to the smaller apartment, was caring for him at her home, and he was responding well to the temporary treatment they had prescribed.

"What do you mean, 'temporary'?" asked Miriam, antsy to get out of the hospital and see her son.

"Well, Mrs. Knight"—how she hated that name!—"there's been a bit of a complication. Elijah's problems this time were more than respiratory. We were afraid he'd injured his body, so we took some X-rays when he came in. We discovered he has a congenital problem known as scoliosis. Most people call it 'curvature of the

But questions have begun to arise (stage 3). Why do we still have so much disease? Why is such a high percentage of disease produced by the treatments of other problems (iatrogenic disease)? Isn't public health, not specific drug treatment, really the key factor in increased life expectancy and elimination of major plagues? Why are the treatments often worse than the disorders for which they are prescribed (such as drugs put on and pulled off the market like thalidomide, Phen-Phen, and Vioxx)? And frighteningly, why is our health-care system now a leading cause of death, just behind cardiovascular disease and cancer?

Based on these and other questions, I believe the population is ready for a shift (stage 4). Studies by David Eisenberg at Harvard Medical School determined that alternative health care increased throughout the 1990s to the point where it exceeded the number of visits to medical doctors. In 1999 there were 629 million visits to alternative practitioners and only 380 million visits to those in mainstream medicine. The question for our generation is whether we are simply going to shift the technology, such as gene therapy, while still holding the treatment of disease as a path to health, or if we are going to shift our level of thinking.

Can we end war by building a bigger war machine? Can we eradicate hate by attacking those who hate? Can we eliminate disease by treating disease? Perhaps we need new paradigms of peace, love, and health.

Is it time for a new paradigm? Will it happen? The choice is yours.

Cowardice asks the question, "Is it safe?" Consensus asks the question, "Is it popular?" Conscience asks the question, "Is it right?"

— MARTIN LUTHER KING JR.

When Convention Doesn't Work Anymore

With America ranking at or near the bottom in nearly all of the indicators that are used to determine the health of a nation, perhaps it's time to change the way our culture views health care. *Innovative thinkers have always been maligned and rejected at first.*

What Dr. Riekeman shared about Kuhn's evolution of the paradigm and how it becomes entrenched in society also shows why the challenge in launching a different paradigm is so immense. The change from the traditional, mechanical, medical paradigm that treats symptoms and diseases to a nontraditional, vital, disease-care paradigm that looks for the cause has met with violent opposition

spine.' It's generally hereditary. Do you know if there is a history of scoliosis in your family? Or maybe Elijah's father's family?"

Her brain still foggy from the myriad drugs she'd been given to calm her down the night before, Miriam did her best to answer the doctor's long list of questions. By the time he left her room, though, about all she could remember was that Elijah needed to see a pediatrician. And that her good-for-nothing husband was probably the genetic culprit this time around. And that she was angry, very, very angry at the dozens of medical "professionals" who had failed to detect this 'curving spine' or whatever it was called over the ten-plus years she'd been running from this doctor to that specialist, from this hospital to that clinic, from one bogus diagnosis to another even more bogus diagnosis.

Physicians familiar with the Knights, who by now had become regulars at the hospital as well as the clinic, determined that it was in Elijah's best interest to allow Miriam to go home, provided she continue taking the Xanax they prescribed for her and make an appointment to see a counselor on staff at the clinic. Assuring her that she was not "crazy"—her word choice, not theirs—but simply stressed out, they released her from the hospital.

But now, Miriam and Elijah faced another round of medical procedures. Years later, Miriam would look back and wonder how they ever got through Eli's middle school years. At the time, however, it was simply more of the same routine they had become accustomed to, only this time with new faces to look at and new titles attached to the new faces. The clinic was not equipped to handle this new problem.

First there was the new doctor who had recently joined their

from conventional wisdom. That makes sense when you look at German philosopher Arthur Schopenhauer's insights into the three steps all truth goes through before it is accepted:

1. It is ridiculed.
2. It is violently opposed.
3. Finally, it is accepted as self-evident.

Too often, patients make health-care and life decisions based on the opinions of coworkers, friends, family members, and the established paradigm or conventional wisdom. But often that wisdom, along with those opinions and paradigms, is based on both prejudice and faulty information. Still, people often oppose and write off as a scam or quackery anything that criticizes the existing system and offers newer or different ideas—even if these ideas show evidence of being lifesaving.

Hopefully by now it's becoming obvious to you that conventional paradigms of health and well-being are not working out and that it's time to accept a new paradigm.

Alternatives to medicine are becoming popular. Sadly, there is so much conflicting health and wellness information that it's challenging to decide which steps and direction we should take. What will be the new paradigm? What will work?

We send a message around the world in a second and a half, but it takes twenty-five years to get an idea through a quarter-inch of skull.

—CHARLES KETTERING

pediatrician's practice. After examining Eli's X-rays, he concurred with the hospital's diagnosis: scoliosis. He ran some more tests—no surprise there—and began a treatment program that involved a series of bending exercises designed to help Eli's body adapt to the misalignment. That didn't work.

Next came the physical therapist, who fitted Eli with a wedge-shaped board and strapped him down, demonstrating the exercises he was to do at home: "Lift your legs, one at a time, to a forty-five-degree angle, and rotate them X number of times, increasing the frequency as you begin to feel stronger. Oh, and sleep on the wedge every night," he said. Eli felt stronger, that's for sure—strong enough to kick off the straps and rid himself of the torturous contraption forever. So that didn't work either.

On to an orthopedic specialist, who designed a molded plastic body brace for Eli that extended from his hips to his underarms. A brace that Eli was expected to wear every day of his life. A brace that would undoubtedly eliminate every last shred of human dignity and self-esteem he possessed. That treatment didn't last long—and it didn't work either.

In the midst of all this, Eli's pediatrician determined that he was suffering from depression ("Good grief! Who wouldn't be?" Miriam asked.) and placed him on a low dosage of Valium. When that didn't seem to help much, he increased the dosage.

Cost so far: tens of thousands of dollars, just on the scoliosis treatments alone. "Even with what Medicaid covers, I can't imagine what our bills are going to be," Miriam whimpered to herself.

Next stop: the office of one of the finest orthopedic surgeons in the Mid-Atlantic, if not the entire country. By this time, Matt had

| 3 |

What Wellness Really Is

As the American public continues to be disappointed with its current level of health, and more and more of the drugs people are taking are being removed from the market, these people are beginning to doubt the wisdom of traditional medicine and turn toward alternatives. A growing number are beginning to embrace a not-so-well-defined concept called "wellness." While the notion of wellness is a shift in the right direction, has our current definition of wellness been working? Where has the present wellness paradigm taken us?

A History of the Wellness "Industry"

1961: Weight Watchers holds its first meeting.
1970: Cigarette ads are banned from TV and radio.
1978: The Soloflex is introduced.
1980: Going to the gym becomes popular.
1986: Suzanne Somers begins doing ThighMaster infomercials.
1986: Bowflex is introduced.
1987: Sheena Easton popularizes washboard abs.
1988: Healthy Choice releases its frozen-dinner line.
1990: Spandex becomes popular.
1995: ESPN launches the *Body by Jake* television workout show.
1997: Nordic Track unveils the Ellipse exercise machine.
1998: Tae-Bo is popularized.
1999–2004: Body for Life, Atkins, South Beach Diet, Dr. Phil, and various fitness and weight-loss programs take America by storm, and "alternative medicine," such as vitamins, herbs, foreign juices, and natural doctors, finds ever-increasing popularity.

Today: The idea of wellness is to get more fit and lose weight. On the contrary, obesity numbers have soared in the last three decades, tripling and even quadrupling for adults as well as children in the U.S. and abroad.

rallied community support for the Knights and managed to collect enough money to cover many of their excessive medical costs, including the cost of the thousand-mile round-trip. Encouraged by his efforts and the doctor's reputation, Miriam once again experienced a renewed optimism.

Much to her relief, this acclaimed surgeon said the words she so desperately wanted to hear: "We've analyzed your son's X-rays, and we're confident we can help him."

Twelve years spent in one long medical nightmare about to come to an end—eighteen months of that time devoted to scoliosis alone. For the first time in years, Miriam allowed herself to feel genuinely happy—in fact, genuinely hopeful.

"Here's the procedure we recommend," the surgeon continued. "We'll place a rod in his spine. What that involves surgically is an incision that will extend from his shoulder blades to his tailbone. Once we open up the incision, we'll be placing two-inch screws in his spinal vertebrae."

The flush of excitement completely drained out of Miriam's face. Pale and ashen, she couldn't stop trembling.

"At that point, we'll insert the rod and fuse it to his spine. We want to make sure you understand that this will not 'heal' Eli's scoliosis; his spine will never be straight. But it will stop the curvature from worsening.

"You also need to understand that once the rod has been inserted and fused, it cannot be removed."

With that, the surgeon began to recite the dangers inherent in this kind of procedure, along with an abundance of statistics covering every possible outcome. But Miriam had long since quit listening.

While record amounts of diet, exercise, and positive-attitude books, infomercials, products, tapes, vitamins, and videos are being sold, we're more overweight, out of shape, sick, tired, and unhappy than when the "wellness revolution" began. This is because we're still in the "Country of the Blind". We've applied alternative treatments, but we're still using the same outside-in paradigms. Our cell-phone, fast-food, fast-relief, double mocha latte–driven culture and cultural mentality still don't support health.

Today's concept of wellness has made very few strides toward creating healthier people. What we need is "*real* wellness."

Real wellness is going to take more than "alternatives"; it's going to take

- a *real* change in thinking,

- a *real* cultural paradigm shift,

- more than another pill or fad program.

Real wellness is going to require actions that maximize life inside your body by creating the kind of function and environment that allow health and peace of mind to flourish. It's the newer discoveries that embrace our vital power and teach us to cooperate with the intelligent Designer by no longer breaking the laws of life.

Wise is the one who sees with his own eyes and listens with his own heart.

—ALBERT EINSTEIN

The Definition of Health

Almost no one knows what the definition of health really is. Therefore that which they believe about health cannot be true.

—DR. IAN GRASSAM

To have a true wellness revolution, first you must answer the question: *What is wellness?* The term has been badly abused. Clinics offering abortion often call themselves Women's Wellness Centers, and doctors and hospitals offer "wellness visits" through which they provide expensive exams and tests in an effort to create "early detection" of disease. Unfortunately, "early" is still after the fact, and the treatments involve more prescriptions and surgery. Injectable drugs and prescriptions are given even to children and the elderly in the name of "wellness."

To know what *real* wellness is, you first have to define what health *really* is. Most people would say they're healthy when they have no pain, no runny nose, no

She would *not* subject Eli to such a dangerous operation. She would *not* allow any surgeon—not even the best in the world—to implant such a dubious, permanent fixture in her son's body. She would *not* be intimidated by this man's credentials, or his degrees, or his stellar standing in the medical community.

She and Eli returned to Ohio, overwhelmed by the circumstances and feeling more alone than ever.

Within a week, though, doubt began to cloud Miriam's thinking. Had she decided too quickly? Had she made the right decision? Had she declined this opportunity only because the procedure sounded so—so *gruesome*? Who was she to doubt the opinion of such an esteemed doctor?

And then there was Matt. God bless that man! Not only had he collected money on behalf of the family to help out with their medical bills, he also had graciously promoted his hardest worker—Miriam—to assistant manager, making her eligible for the company's health insurance plan. ("I had an autistic son," he told her shortly after her breakdown in the parking lot. "I know what you're going through. A whole lot more goes into determining an employee's value than a spotless attendance record," he had added, with a twinkle in his eye.) It wouldn't take effect for another sixty days, but after twelve years, sixty days seemed like no time at all.

After second-guessing her decision for more hours than she cared to remember, Miriam decided to schedule the surgery. "You've made the right decision, Mrs. Knight," the surgeon intoned when she called to tell him she had changed her mind. The next three weeks were nearly lost in a flurry of paperwork, both legal and medical.

headache. In other words: *I'm healthy when I feel good.* In today's fad-diet-and-home-exercise-infomercial world, health has also come to mean losing weight or looking good.

There are three problems with this. First, when you think health is feeling good, what do you usually do when you feel bad? You take a drug to feel good and then assume you're healthy. Yet, as you now know, you do not automatically become healthy when a drug eliminates your symptoms, and in fact, you may be even sicker.

Second, when my father died of a heart attack at the age of fifty-two, he died without prior symptoms of heart disease and had passed previous medical evaluations. His doctor told us that in more than two-thirds of people who have a heart problem, the first sign is a heart attack. Then, in two-thirds of those, the people die. Or, for the majority of people, the first sign that there is a heart problem is a person's death. As my family discovered, that's a little late to begin looking into it.

I could go on with story after story of people I've seen in my clinics who chose to not follow through with care based on the fact that they felt fine—only later to discover disease that was so far along by the time they discovered it, it was too late. By the time you actually know you have cancer, Alzheimer's, diabetes, and other physical problems, these conditions have typically been ravaging your body for years. The same is true even for spine and extremity pain. By the time it hurts, MRIs and X-rays often show massive arthritic degeneration and/or disk damage that's been developing for years.

Third, there's the "if it ain't broke, don't fix it" myth. Thinking, *If I have no symptoms of a disease, then I don't have to worry about disease,* is one of the most colossal errors in judgment you could ever make concerning your health. You might not have a diagnosed disease, but dis-ease can go on for years without warning before being discovered as disease. This type of thinking will, without argument, eventually shorten your life.

The following is a list from the *Merck Manual of Medical Diagnosis.* These are some of the most common diseases we face today and are all present in the body without any signs or symptoms noticeable to the victim:

Heart arrhythmia	Glomerulonephritis (kidney disease)
Atherosclerosis (plaque in arteries)	Hypertension (high blood pressure)
Osteoarthritis	Ovarian cancer
Benign prostatic hypertrophy	Ovarian cyst
Breast cancer	Paget's (bone) disease
Cardiomyopathy	Spinal degeneration
Polyps of large bowel	Cervical cancer
Prostate cancer	Cholelithiasis (gallstones)

Word spread through the community that Eli, the child whose face was pictured on countless donation jars at stores throughout the area, had a date for the operation. Among those who got the word was Sharon Peters, the mother of a boy around Elijah's age who had also been diagnosed with scoliosis. New to the community, Sharon had never met Miriam, though their sons would be attending the same school the following year.

"Do you think we could get together?" Sharon asked Miriam after reaching her at home. "My son was diagnosed with scoliosis, and I find it helps to talk to someone who shares the same problem."

Elated, Miriam readily agreed. The chaos of her life had left little or no time for friends, and here was a woman who knew what she was going through. It was just like an answer to prayer, only Miriam seldom prayed, and when she did, she had no clue who or what she was praying to. Maybe meeting Sharon was a result of all that New Age psychic energy stuff the girl with the purple hair at work had told her about. She didn't care who or what was responsible; all she knew was that this was too good to be true.

Over lunch the following day—Sharon insisted on treating her to a *real* lunch at the Olive Garden—the two women shared war stories about the various therapies and procedures doctors had put their sons through. Throughout their conversation, one thing puzzled Miriam: her newfound friend positively oozed serenity. She could not fathom how this woman could be so calm, so pleasant, so positive in the midst of what Miriam could only assume was a nightmare similar to her own. *Once I get to know her better,* Miriam thought, *I'll ask her what medication she's on. It might help me, too.*

"You know, my son is scheduled to have a rod put in his spine

Pulmonary valve stenosis	Renal calculi (kidney stones)
Coronary artery disease	Renal (kidney) failure (chronic)
Diabetes mellitus	Retinoblastoma (cancer of the eye)
Diverticular (colon) disease	Scoliosis (curvature of the spine)
Emphysema (lung disease)	Tooth decay
Fibroid tumors of the uterus	Valvular heart disease

Seeking freedom from symptoms is easy to do and may even guarantee those results. The only thing it can never bring you, however, is health. In fact, as the *Merck Manual* shows us, being free from symptoms may just cover up signs of disease and keep you ignorant of your perilous predicament.

Real Wellness Is Maximized Living

Realistically speaking, symptoms are the worst measuring stick to use to determine your health. Sure, healthy people feel good. Actually, truly healthy people feel great. But people who believe they are healthy simply because they have no current severe ache or pain often find they have disease—and drop dead without warning.

Assuming that the absence of disease equals health is like assuming that people who do not divorce have perfect relationships. But if health is not the absence of disease, then what is the goal?

The *real* definition of *health*, according to *Dorland's Medical Dictionary*: "Health is a state of optimum physical, mental, and social well-being and not merely the absence of disease or infirmity."

With a true understanding about health, you can then define *real wellness*. Real wellness has the goal of achieving true health and not just obtaining absence or early detection of sickness.

Despite the immense challenges it has faced, the wellness industry has recognized a real need in the lives of the American people: the need to take ownership of their own health and well-being. How people do that will determine whether the wellness industry has truly met that need or only offered a smoke screen as an alternative to what economist Paul Zane Pilzer calls the "sickness business" of traditional medicine.

When wellness is just the next trendy program in the History of Wellness, it will have the same failed results as medicine—the same failed results it's been getting.

"People become customers [of the sickness business] only when they are stricken by and react to a specific condition or complaint," Pilzer writes in *The Wellness Revolution*. "The [real] wellness business is *proactive*. People *voluntarily* become customers—to feel healthier, to reduce the effects of aging, and to avoid becoming customers of the sickness business."

in a few weeks. They say it won't completely correct the problem, but it will improve it and keep it from getting worse," she told Sharon. "I guess that's about all we can hope for."

"Well, not me," Sharon said quietly, aware she was venturing into a sensitive topic for discussion. "I'm hoping for a lot more than that."

"What do you mean? How can you say that, after all you've been through with Jeremy?"

"Well, I haven't told you 'all' I've been through. We've been seeing another doctor, the first one who has ever actually helped him."

"Who is he? I've been to every doctor in a fifty-mile radius and even beyond, and not one has helped Eli."

"His name is Mark Johnson, but he won't be of much help to you. He was our doctor back in Atlanta before my job was transferred here. But he did refer us to a local doctor he knows through an association they both belong to. We've only had our initial consultation with him, but we like him a lot. His name is Timothy Abraham."

Timothy Abraham . . . Timothy Abraham. Where do I know that name from? Maybe some directory of local physicians? It sounds so familiar, Miriam thought as she sipped her iced tea.

"He's a chiropractor," Sharon said, sensing Miriam's bewilderment.

"A chiro—Hold it! He's the Medi-Mart doctor!"

Now Sharon was the bewildered one. "The Medi-Mart doctor?"

"He was there. Well, not him, but his assistant, doing 'spine screenings' or something like that. His name was at the bottom of all the pamphlets they were handing out that day. I don't know

Since health is not the absence of anything but the presence of well-being, *real wellness* doesn't work merely to eliminate but to build: *to build the body's inherent vitality and to restore balance and ease from the inside out.* It's called *Maximized Living*—something for which there is no alternative.

Alternative Medicine Isn't Real Wellness/Maximized Living

Alternative medicine and weight-loss programs fail here as well. Most of what are called "alternative therapies" treat symptoms and illnesses with natural remedies. The good news is that it's unlikely you'll die from a bad side effect, but it's still an outside-in, mechanical, disease-treating model. It doesn't work, no matter what the treatment.

Similarly, weight-loss and many bodybuilding and fitness programs focus on outside appearance rather than also focusing on health.

To experience *real* wellness, complementary or alternative medicine isn't the answer if the approach is the same as with regular medicine. For building health, it's best to not use anything with the word *medicine* in it.

Healing in a *Real* Wellness World: Medications, or Maximized Living?

Do desperate circumstances call for desperate measures and a need for whatever chemicals and methods are available? Sure, sometimes. The question is, is it really a desperate circumstance? Doctors usually say yes.

You have more power than you realize. Real wellness can only be attained through Maximized Living. Maximized Living through nurturing your body toward good health and trusting in that power is the only real medicine. It's healing, the only real cure. It's science, the only real future for *real* wellness.

God made your body with the power to overcome. *Real* wellness is anything that removes interference with your body's ongoing, natural balancing process. By restoring balance, you can reach your maximum level of health (optimum physical, mental, and social well-being), allowing you to get well if you are sick and helping you to stay well if you are not.

So when you are sick, if it's an emergency, you may need medical technology, much of which can save lives. But you have probably needed Maximized Living for some time. Wellness is even more necessary in times of emergencies so that in addition to just getting past the crisis medically, you can actually get well.

With health being "optimum mental and social well-being" in addition to

what ever became of those pamphlets, but I'm sure that was his name at the bottom."

Amused at the image of Timothy Abraham as a convenience-store doctor, Sharon continued, again treading carefully as she recalled her own knee-jerk reaction to the word *chiropractor*. "You know, nobody was more shocked than I was to find myself in a chiropractor's office. Me! My whole life I'd been told they were quacks. Get this—my ex-husband is chief oncologist at a major teaching hospital, and he threw a fit when he found out I had taken Jeremy to Dr. Johnson. He threatened to send Protective Services after me on a child-endangerment charge, and he even got his own radiologist to take new X-rays of Jeremy's spine. But he shut up after the radiologist compared his X-rays to Johnson's—turns out the guy refused to testify against Johnson, since Jeremy's spine—and overall health, I might add—had clearly improved under his care. End of threats."

"You've got to be kidding me. He couldn't get anyone to testify for him?"

"Well, I'm sure he could have eventually. But his colleagues, the ones who reviewed Jeremy's history, that is, all said they'd have a hard time disputing what was right there in the files. Bottom line, Jeremy's dad loves him. He saw a depressed, miserable, practically handicapped child transformed into this bright, happy boy who can finally shoot hoops. Big improvement in his grades, too—really big."

Brother! Miriam thought. *That would be a miracle.* With everything else going on, she'd had no time to deal with Elijah's grades. If his grades kept sliding the way they had been, he'd be in middle school till he was twenty-something.

"But Sharon, how can this guy—Dr. Abraham, was it?—and the

"physical well-being," you need to seek doctors and methods that take into consideration not only the body but also the life and the whole person.

Some have applied the term *holistic* to New Age ideas. Holistic healing, however, really should be called whole-istic healing. Maximizing Living includes optimizing the function of the whole person: body, mind, and spirit. Only doctors who keep this in mind are able to help make and keep you healthy and *whole*.

The Times, They Are a-Changin'

In a 2004 survey, the U.S. Centers for Disease Control and Prevention found that nearly two-thirds of Americans regularly use alternative forms of health care, with chiropractors being the leading alternative health-care providers and prayer for healing and natural products being the most common alternative practices.

If traditional health care were effective, there would be no need for alternatives. The reality is that while nonmedical, nonsurgical wellness treatments such as prayer, supplements, and chiropractic care are considered "alternative health care," there is no alternative to doing the things that genuinely bring health and happiness. True health and *real* wellness rise beyond mere symptom relief and doing what it takes to look good. What is often called "alternative health care" really should be called "no-alternative health care," if health and happiness are the goals.

"No alternative" forms of health care make up the Maximized Living revolution and form the Natural Health and Happiness System That Never Fails.

guy in Atlanta be better than a real doctor? I mean, look at us—before Joseph left and ever since Matt raised support for us, we've had the best care possible: the best pediatrician, the best hospital, the best physical therapist, the best orthopedic specialist, and now the best orthopedic surgeon, possibly in the whole country. How could they be wrong?"

"Well, first of all, chiropractors *are* real doctors. Second, having the best doctor in the world perform the wrong procedure doesn't transform it into the right procedure. You already told me how scared you are about having the rod fused to Elijah's spine. You said you knew, without a doubt, as you sat in that doctor's office and he explained the operation to you—you knew it was all wrong. But as you said, it was your only hope, so you started second-guessing your decision. I'm here to tell you, though, that it's not your only hope. You have another hope, one that's nowhere near as invasive and risky as a rod fusion is.

"If you're still confused, go home tonight after work, sit quietly, and think through the answer to this one question: is Elijah any better off today than he was *before* he got all this excellent medical care? I can tell you this, Miriam, when I applied that same question to Jeremy, the answer I came up with changed our lives."

With that, Sharon dropped the subject and picked up the check. If Miriam wanted to continue with the conversation, fine. But Miriam needed a breather, a chance to take in all that Sharon had said to her and let it settle deep down inside her. The surgery was still several weeks away; as they walked out to the parking lot, Sharon silently prayed that would give her enough time to earn Miriam's trust and convince her to call it off.

| 4 |

Maximized Living

The Natural Health and Happiness System That Never Fails—One Minute at a Time

First, let's define *Maximized Living*.

What does Maximized Living really include? At this point you know that it doesn't include the next blockbuster drug or plastic surgery. What it does include is exercise, a thoughtful diet, discovering a compelling purpose for your life, building strong relationships, and the use of nontoxic, noninvasive forms of health intervention, such as prayer, chiropractic care, supplementing missing nutrients, and rehabilitative techniques.

Maximized living is "*real* wellness." You now should realize that you must change your paradigm from an outside-in, mechanical, medical, or wellness model in which you fight or treat disease and symptoms to an inside-out, vital, real-wellness model.

In the new model, you

- build health as the best prevention and defense of disease,
- nurture a nontoxic internal environment for your cells,
- cooperate with the intelligent design of your body, and
- embrace care that corrects the cause of issues by removing interference or eliminating dis-ease—

all of which is the inherent consequence of a natural lifestyle that respects your body and falls into alignment with the ultimate intent God has for your life. Remember: health and happiness is your choice 98 percent of the time and an ever-present reality through the tools of Maximized Living.

As Dr. Gerry Clum puts it,

Rather than looking at every symptom as another problem that has been visited upon you by your genes or bad luck, look at the message your body is sending you. We couldn't live for very long without a functioning pain response system in our bodies, we couldn't live for very long without efficient temperature control

Later that night when Miriam got home from work, she first went in to the apartment's one tiny bedroom and checked on Elijah—*two o'clock, breathing normally, maybe we'll make it through the whole night this time*—and then dropped her tired, aching body onto the recliner by what passed as the front window, a filmy pane of glass protected on the outside from intruders and window-washers alike by burglar bars. Her thin jacket hardly kept the chill in the apartment at bay, but she left it on all the same. *Beats wasting energy taking it off,* she figured. Suddenly aware of the intrusive weight of her shoulder bag, Miriam let it drop off her shoulder and onto the floor.

I have never been so completely drained in all my life, she thought. *I can't do this anymore. I'm living on this roller coaster that never stops long enough to give me a chance to decide if I want to take another ride. Maybe Sharon's right. Or maybe the surgeon's right. Where the heck is Joseph, anyway? He should be here helping me decide what to do. Shoot, he should have been here all these years helping me decide what to do.*

Sharon . . . she really seemed to know what she was talking about. Miriam chuckled at how she almost spit out her coffee when Sharon told her that her ex-husband was an oncologist. *That does say something for her trust in chiropractic, though. She's been through this as a "real" doctor's wife and as a mother. And if Dr. Johnson had really been a quack, Dr. Peters would have continued going after him, with a vengeance.*

Oh, God, I just don't know. Miriam was addressing no one in particular, but she was especially doubtful that the God she learned about in the Bible would be listening in on her thoughts tonight.

systems within our bodies, and we couldn't live very long without active and effective cough and gag responses. So we need to support these helpful signs and warnings as a way of building good health rather than continually suppressing them, which actually causes damage to our health.

The reason we have such an aggressive and active drug supply system in the developed world is because people don't look at the true nature of the symptoms they are demonstrating and because there are huge sums of money to be made from giving people a quick fix, as opposed to asking them to take more responsibility for their health and well-being. Building health is complex and can never come by a quick fix.

That's also the point Dr. Patrick Gentempo made in his 2001 testimony before a White House commission on alternative medicine. Traditional medicine, he said, is "sick care"—the diagnosis and treatment of disease and crisis intervention. Genuine health care focuses on "quality of life, performance, and potential. This means that a person doesn't look at health care as fighting disease, but for the purposes of improving overall health and well-being and quality of life."

Hidden away in the inner nature of the real man is the law of his life, and someday he will discover it and consciously make use of it. He will heal himself, make himself happy and prosperous, and live in an entirely different world. For he will have discovered that life is from within and not from without.

—RALPH WALDO EMERSON

No, He had much better things to do than to waste His time on a confused doubter like her.

Sitting in the dark, paralyzed by indecision, fatigue, and the cold, Miriam drifted off before she even had a chance to get into bed—or what passed for her bed, the lumpy sofa she had gotten from Goodwill. She could easily have slept on the recliner all night had a stabbing pain in her right shoulder not abruptly awakened her. Rubbing it to try to relieve the stiffness, Miriam remembered that her shoulder bag had felt unusually heavy tonight. *Oh no! I totally forgot! Sharon handed me a package as we left the restaurant. I should have opened it hours ago.*

Gingerly reaching down to pick up her bag, her aching shoulder being most uncooperative as she did, Miriam managed to lift the oversized purse high enough to rummage around inside for the box. After realizing it would help to switch on the lamp by the recliner, she pulled out a mug-sized box with a card attached. "Open this last" was written on the outside of the envelope. "Okay, whatever you say," Miriam said out loud, realizing she was bordering on giddy at the very idea of receiving an actual gift from a friend.

Inside the box was a jasmine-scented jar candle, the kind they sell at Cracker Barrel. Tucked inside the box was a pack of matches and a handwritten note: "The matches are a bonus"—Sharon had drawn a little smiley face here—"just in case you don't have any. The candle is to remind you of the hope you have. Whenever you light it, remember that hope."

Miriam reached for the card. What more could Sharon possibly have to say? Hadn't she said it all in that little smiley-faced note? As

| 5 |

The Essentials of Maximized Living

Many people today are living on an island of pain while surrounded by a sea of wellness. A *real*-wellness doctor committed to Maximized Living will walk you through these five components, not with the goal of symptom relief alone but of true health and wholeness:

1. Avoidance and Reduction of Medications
2. Maximum Nerve Supply
3. Quality Nutrients
4. Optimum Oxygen Levels and Lean Muscle
5. Peace of Mind and Strong Relationships

Where medicine once considered wellness "subacademic," science has now caught up to realize that wellness is on the cutting edge of health care. While many medical practitioners have embraced some part of wellness, many conventional physicians and medical companies have become increasingly frustrated as they see business move away from them and into the hands of the patients and wellness providers whose alternative approaches run counter to theirs.

Standard medical care today is like driving the pony express just when man invented trains. There is a superior way. Trying to create better drugs and surgeries now is like trying to find a faster horse—and a horse can never outrun a train.

Let's walk through what it takes to jump on the Maximized Living train so that rather than ending up at the Sick and Suffering Station, you arrive at Health and Happiness.

We'll look at the first two essentials here, the rest in the following chapters.

Essential #1: Avoidance and Reduction of Medications

Healthy lifestyles are the biggest threat to the growth and expansion of the drug industry and its consequences in our society. A recent *Forbes* magazine cover article, titled "Pharma's New Enemy: Clean Living," thoroughly addressed this subject from

she opened the envelope, a piece of paper fluttered to the floor. She'd get it in a minute. First, the card.

Miriam,

    I want you to know what kind of person Dr. Abraham is, not just the kind of doctor he is. And I want Elijah to have the best possible chance for a normal—no, make that an exceedingly wonderful—life. Enclosed is a gift certificate, which is what Dr. Abraham gives each of his regular patients to pass along to someone they know who needs chiropractic care. Please accept it as a gift from one who has been there, a mother just like you who only wants the best for her child.

Love, Sharon

Stunned, Miriam bent down to retrieve the paper that had fallen out of the envelope. It was indeed a gift certificate. For the Abraham Chiropractic Clinic. In the amount of two hundred dollars.

Miriam switched off the light. *Was Elijah any better today than he was before he received all this excellent medical care?* She knew the answer. Miriam Knight cried for the first time since that night in the convenience store parking lot. This time her tears reflected not despair, but gratitude.

But the battle was far from over. An increasingly despondent Elijah—so much for the Valium—had become stubborn and exceptionally strong-willed for such a weak child. "I'm not going to try any more new doctors!" he said before stomping off to his room when Miriam tried to talk to him about her decision to cancel the surgery and have him checked out by Dr. Abraham. His grumpy

the position of the consumer as well as from the position of the investor. Consider the following perspective from the article: "Do you really need all those prescription pills you are popping? Maybe not. There's a backlash building against the cost, risk and side effects of medication, and it's bad news for the pharmaceutical industry." As the article notes, "Every few years the ultimate medical catastrophe: a miracle cure that turns out to be toxic."

The One-Minute Wellness Drug Policy

By now you should be fully aware of the dangers of taking either prescription or over-the-counter medications, and you should know to think twice when someone tells you to "take two and call me in the morning." However, only your medical doctor can prescribe drugs or tell you to get off drugs. *That's the practice of medicine.*

Our role is to make you aware of the hazards of poor lifestyle decisions while helping you to create optimum function and healing in your body. *That's the practice of real wellness.*

In time, you must begin to judge for yourself whether your medications are keeping you alive, merely palliating symptoms of an unhealthy body, or actually causing some of the ailments you suffer from. The bottom line is that taking any drugs will cause some level of adverse side effects. With the guidance of your prescribing physician, you need to make your own best decisions on medication. As you heal, work with your medical doctors to help you reduce or eliminate the drugs you're on.

Essential #2: Maximum Nerve Supply

Food, vitamins, exercise, and sometimes even drugs have benefits to survival. Yet they do nothing to help a dead body. In order for the body to function, heal, and experience wellness, it must have life. Life is that mysterious something that animates cells and keeps them digesting, circulating, reproducing, moving, resisting illness, etc.

The study of embryological development shows that the brain is the first organ to develop. The brain then sends creative power through the spinal cord and nerves to create every cell and organ in your body. (The brain, spinal cord, and nerves make up the central nervous system, the main headquarters of the whole body.) From that neonatal moment on, the brainpower flowing down the spine and nervous system continues to control all function and healing in the body for the rest of your life. Consequently, the spine is your lifeline. Cut it, and life ends.

mood threatened to ruin a rare day off for his mother. She let him simmer down for a while before knocking on his bedroom door.

"Look, do you really want to go through with this operation? That's what it sounds like, but you didn't seem so hot on the idea when you first heard what it would involve," she said as she entered the room.

"No. I don't want to have the operation. I don't want to go to that new doctor. I don't want to go to school, I don't want to go anywhere, and I don't want to see anybody. Ever again. I've had it." He covered his mouth with his hand, hoping his mother hadn't seen his bottom lip start to quiver. He was too old for this, too old to cry. Unable to hold the tears back, he lashed out at his mother. "Just leave me alone!"

Just then, the phone rang, breaking the tension in the room. "Oh, hi," she said as she answered, her eyes glued to Elijah. She was not about to walk away from this fight. She stood her ground in his room, his sacred space, talking on the cordless phone. "Sure. We'd love to. Maybe we'll pick up a video from the library on the way over. See you then."

"We're going to Mrs. Peters's house for a pizza and movie night," Miriam said, her eyes riveted to Elijah's. "We can stop off at the library if there's a movie you'd like to borrow, but she says they have plenty. Get ready. We're leaving in a half hour."

Seldom had she spoken so clearly and directly to Elijah; most of the time, their lives were so rushed that they barely had any time to actually talk to each other at all.

Sharon Peters had anticipated Elijah's reluctance to try a new doctor—she'd been through the same thing with Jeremy—and she

All *real* wellness is ultimately dependent on the spine and nervous system's ability to provide *maximum nerve supply.*

The central nervous system—the life-power supply—is so powerful and complex that it is able to control your fifty trillion cells within dozens of operating systems all at once. This is done without you, the user, even consciously thinking or even knowing about it. While the body can go days without water, weeks without food, and minutes without oxygen, it cannot last even a second without nerve power.

The statement that "the body heals itself" is really only partially true. Bodies don't really heal. A deceased body (one without any remaining nerve supply) can no longer improve or help itself. Without God's mysterious power still present in the body, it cannot heal, function, or experience life. That is why we say, "Only God heals—because it's His life power alone that's keeping you alive."

While there are those who argue where this vital power comes from, there are few left in or out the scientific community who deny its existence or importance. This debate has existed for centuries. This is evident in a comment made by the founder of chiropractic, Dr. D. D. Palmer, in his book *Science, Art, and Philosophy of Chiropractic:* "In the early years of chiropractic, I used the term *Innate* (Spirit), *Innate Intelligence* (Spiritual Intellect), *Universal Intelligence* (God) because they were comprehensive, and the world was not prepared to receive the latter terms just mentioned in parentheses. It may be even now premature to use them."

Another partial truth, which means it's also a partial lie, is that drugs, food, minerals, vitamins, herbs, and such can heal. Look at this scenario to see if that's true: Let's say paramedics arrive at the scene of an accident and find two victims. One is dead, and one is barely hanging on. The surgical staff at the hospital surgically seal all of the wounds, give the patients vitamin C, and pour massive amounts of medication down each of their throats. Who's got the best chance of making it?

The obvious, laughable answer is the one who is just hanging on. He's the only one with nerve power still flowing through his body, so his body is the only one that stands a chance of utilizing the treatments to get better.

If your body lacks adequate nutrition and exercise, then certainly your body can use food, supplements, and a regular exercise program to function better and build health. But none of these things actually heal. It's a tough concept, but a true one.

The body cannot even use food, water, or vitamins unless life supply is fully flowing into and out from all pertinent operating systems that deal with assimilating and absorbing these nutrients. On the other hand, despite the fact that nothing some people eat contains any decent nutrition and everything they ingest is toxic, this inborn, God-given life supply is so incredible that when operating at its peak capacity, it can miraculously remove these toxins and use whatever is left to keep them alive for remarkably long periods of time.

was convinced Eli just needed to talk this whole thing out with someone his own age. But first, she convinced Miriam.

Getting the boys together away from school proved to be a godsend. It took another two weeks, but Eli eventually consented to see Dr. Abraham, thanks to a glowing report from Jeremy, who described the chiropractic adjustments as "pretty cool—it doesn't hurt. It feels kinda good." On that, Eli was now inclined to acquiesce to the notion of the "cool" doctor.

Opening the door to Dr. Abraham's office, Miriam looked around at what could almost have been someone's living room. *Oh no! I'm in the wrong place!* she thought, double-checking the name on the door. No, this was the right place, but it sure didn't look like a doctor's office. Eli raised his eyebrows, expressing the same opinion, but pleased to not be looking at the typical kinds of threatening machinery and sterile white walls he was used to seeing at other doctors' offices.

"You must be Mr. Knight," a receptionist said, making eye contact with Elijah and extending her hand to him. "Welcome!" No doctor's assistant had ever treated Eli like an adult before, and none had ever welcomed him before, either.

"Hello, Mrs. Knight! And welcome to you, too!" With that, the receptionist led them to a corner where they could sit and talk until it was time to go in to see the doctor.

What an odd place, Miriam thought, taking in the entire office area. *No little sliding window separating the staff from the patients, and it looks like everyone who works here wears regular clothes.*

"Thank you for having Elijah's records sent to us. We couldn't read through it all; that would take years, I'm sure"—with that, she

Maximum nerve supply should be your chief aim in life when it comes to establishing real health. If you were to interrupt the central nervous system (life) supply to any cell, it would begin dying. If you cut the nerve to any cell, it would cause immediate cell death (think black tooth). A healthy lifestyle is critical for supporting real wellness but is secondary to a powerful central nervous system—that transmitter of life.

> *The mission of God's inborn intelligence within the human body is to maintain the material of the body of a "living thing" in active organization.*
>
> —RALPH W. STEPHENSON

About the Spine and Nervous System

As you've seen, your spine is your lifeline. The spine and nervous system control all function and healing. Because health, by definition, is how well you are functioning and healing and not simply how well you look or even feel, the spine creates the foundation for health.

Due to the importance of the life supply coming through your brain and spinal cord, those body parts are encased in a bony armor. The skull protects the upper brain, and the bones of the spinal column protect the brain stem and spinal cord. A common and a very likely way to interfere with maximum nerve supply is for the spinal column to become damaged, to shift, or to rotate out of place. Slips, the thousands of childhood falls, poor posture, sleeping in contorted positions, auto accidents, sitting for long periods of time, sports trauma, stress, toxic emotions, and even the birth process itself can all cause spinal abuse.

> *Look well to the spine as the cause of disease.*
>
> —HIPPOCRATES,
> the father of modern medicine

A basic, fundamental, underlying predictor of all health or lack of health is how well your spine is functioning. Yet, next to your stomach and liver, it's the most regularly abused part of your body. Determining how well your spine is positioned and performing is a major factor in determining whether or not your body is producing a state of health (optimum physical, mental, and social well-being) or in a state of dis-ease (the precursor to disease).

Checking Out Your Spine

The two primary methods for evaluating proper alignment and position of the spine are posture and X-ray.

smiled at Elijah—"but we can tell you've been through quite an ordeal. One of the things I love most about working here is seeing lives like yours turned around. It's nothing short of a miracle."

After filling out the requisite forms (*At least he has real doctor paperwork,* Miriam thought, enjoying her attempt at comic relief to ease the nervousness she felt), Miriam and Eli were taken to Dr. Abraham's exam office for an initial consultation. Once again, they were both concerned that they were in the wrong place. Standing in front of them was an older man in regular clothes—no white jacket, nothing to indicate that he was anyone special.

"Hello, Elijah, Mrs. Knight. I'm Dr. Abraham. It's good to see you."

Both Knights managed to mutter a response of some kind. Sensing their discomfort, the doctor explained that he had reviewed Elijah's history but wanted to hear them describe the problems in their own words.

Miriam had been through this so many times that she could recite this speech in her sleep. But this time, she had the uncanny sense that Dr. Abraham was really listening to her. What started as a monotonous recitation of myriad symptoms and treatments soon became an impassioned plea for the help they so desperately needed.

"What we do here is different from what you've experienced before," he said when she finished. Taking care to make eye contact with Elijah as often as he did with Miriam, he continued, "The symptoms and the treatments you described are important in that they are a part of a very painful history for the two of you. But that's exactly what it is—history. We're starting fresh here,

The old adage of the mother nagging her child to sit up at the breakfast table has turned out to contain much wisdom. As science continues to reveal, posture is a major key to good health.

Posture

When you look at a person from the front, his spine should be straight. The head, shoulders, hips, and feet should be lined up. When you look at a person from the side, the ears should be back over the shoulders and the shoulders should be back over the pelvis.

His posture and spine are abnormal if

- his head is visibly tilted, shifted, or rotated in one direction.

- his head is jutted out in front of his chest and shoulders (forward-head syndrome).

- one hip is higher than the other, turned in one direction, or shifted to one side.

- one shoulder is higher than the other, turned in one direction, or his whole upper body is shifted to one side.

In any case of abnormal posture, a person's central nervous system is experiencing interference or being damaged.

X-Ray

The most accurate method for measuring the condition of the spine is the use of X-rays.

When looking at the front-view X-ray, the spinal bones (vertebrae) should also be straight. The bones must not be rotated or tilted, and no curvatures to the side (scoliosis) should be present.

The side-view X-ray must reveal three well-placed arcs. The most important arc is in the neck (cervical spine) between C1 and C7 (the first and last cervical vertebrae). This cervical arc is known as the *arc of life* because mental life impulses travel directly from the brain down this part of the spinal cord to bring life to the rest of the body. Losing your arc of life causes the most severe obstruction to the central nervous system. The other arcs occur in the thoracic (middle) spine and the lumbar (lower) spine.

If your central nervous system is unhealthy, you cannot become truly healthy simply by exercising or eating right. You can be healthier, but you cannot live at a "normal" or optimal condition of wellness. Any abnormal position of the spine, misalignment of the bones, changes in these curves, or damage to

and I can assure you that it won't take years to begin to see improvement."

In all their years of medical care, neither Miriam nor Elijah had ever heard a doctor explain the way the body works, what happens when things go right and what happens when things go wrong. One by one, pieces of the puzzle that formed Eli's medical condition began to fall into place as Dr. Abraham continued to talk, occasionally pointing to charts and diagrams to illustrate the point he was making.

"Elijah and Miriam, we don't treat disease, we restore health. You can't fight the darkness; you can only turn on the light. The problem here is that all the doctors you've seen in the past were simply treating symptoms, and not just with medication but also with other forms of therapy. But Elijah's health continued to go downhill. That's because true health does not and cannot come from a pill, a potion, or an operation. Health can come only from within, from the capacity for healing that has been inside your body from the day you were born—actually, even before that.

"What we do here in this office is educate you on how the body functions and provide correction for those areas of the body that have been allowed to malfunction for too long. What we do will not only help correct Eli's problems but also change the path of his life."

Dr. Abraham turned and pointed to a diagram of the brain. "God put the most amazing power in that brain and spinal cord— power to heal, power to control everything from your heart beating to your stomach digesting. Do you understand what that means? It means that all healing comes from within."

the bones and disks indicates a serious problem. It's simply the way health is defined.

Posture is the window to the spine. Poor posture is a result of poor X-rays. As a result, just trying to "sit [or stand up] straight" as your mother or teachers may have told you would be impossible. If the spine is misaligned on X-ray, forcing yourself to sit or stand up straight would be impossible to do for very long—which unfortunately leads to more nagging.

Posture affects and moderates every physical and mental function in the body. Spinal pain, blood pressure, headaches, pulse, lung capacity, and mood are only a small portion of the body's functions that are most easily influenced by posture.

—DR. C. NORMAN SHEALY,
Shealy Institute

Vertebral Subluxation: The Key Cause of Interference

In popular wellness, it is well understood that poor nutrition, stress, or a lack of exercise can interfere with health (normal function). But spinal interference would certainly create a more damaging effect on overall health, since it would strike right at the core of what causes the body to function.

Take, for example, the unfortunate case of Christopher Reeve. A fall off a horse jarred his head and caused a vertebra in his upper neck to become fractured and misplaced. As a result, all function in the body was compromised or stopped altogether. In accidents of this nature, it's clear: without spinal column integrity, there's nothing that can be done to create wellness.

This is a telling example of the horrifying effects of something called *vertebral subluxation*. Vertebral subluxation is any minor or major misalignment of an individual spinal vertebra or several vertebrae (*global subluxation*). These misalignments, which can be so small that they have to be measured with an instrument, invade the spinal cord space, put pressure on the spinal cord, compress nerves, and/or push soft tissue out of the way and into delicate neurological tissue.[31] Subluxations at the top of the spine, like the one Christopher Reeve suffered, also cause pressure or damage to the brain stem[32]—the area of the nervous system responsible for breathing, heart rate, and many vital automatic functions. The upper cervical spine and brain stem area is so sensitive that Reeve's doctors said you could cover up the damage to his cord and brain stem with the width of the tip of your pinky (approximately one centimeter).

God? I've never heard a doctor mention God before. Miriam leaned forward in the upholstered armchair and tried to concentrate on what he was saying.

"If I were to cut Elijah's arm right now"—he reached over as if he really was about to follow through—"several things would happen. The skin would split, and bleeding would follow. A sensation of pain would immediately surround the cut. But then, right at that very moment, the power that created the body—the power that God put in the brain and the spinal cord—would begin to heal Elijah's arm. In a few weeks, the healing would envelop the cut completely.

"There isn't a doctor on the face of the earth who can make that healing take place. If the cut is deep enough, Elijah might need a suture to hold the cut together, a Band-Aid—or two strong and tireless hands willing to hold the cut together for the next two weeks. But the suture, Band-Aid, and hands wouldn't heal; they would just allow the power in the body to heal.

"It doesn't matter what kind of disease is afflicting Elijah's body. If his body is functioning on an optimal level, his body will know how to heal that cut. All we need to do is find out what has been causing Elijah's body to perform at a less-than-optimal level for all these years, to discover what we call the 'interference' that has existed in his body since birth. When we find that interference and remove it, then Elijah's body will have its best chance to come back to life.

"Eli, I know you've had more X-rays than you can count, and I'm sure you're tired of all this. But what we're going to do is take a very specific X-ray that will show any misalignments of the spine that are interfering with your own ability to heal and function. If we find these misalignments and begin to correct them, the pressure on

Vital information travels from the brain and spinal cord to all of the parts of the body. Not only does information travel down the nerve, but also information from the peripheral parts of the body is sent back to the brain and spinal cord at the same time. When this information is interfered with [by vertebral subluxation], a problem arises in the body.

—DR. DANIEL J. MURPHY

Vertebral subluxation and the accompanying poor posture and positive x-ray findings are caused by a number of very common sources:

- a challenging birth process (particularly with medical intervention)
- falls and collisions as a child
- sports injuries
- auto accidents and other traumas
- poor posture (computer work, long-distance driving, position at work, etc.)
- improper sitting and sleeping positions (includes pillow and mattress problems)
- the viscero-somatic reflex: organ problems (viscero) triggering skeletal problems (soma)
- any physical, mental, or chemical stress (chemical stress is caused primarily by processed foods, medications, and environmental toxins)
- lack of exercise: weak or tight muscles

When interfering with the central nervous system, these subluxations can be a severe deterrent to health and wellness. When you interrupt the brain-body connection, you throw the entire body out of balance. As a result, chaos and disorder erupt and your internal environment is no longer conducive to cellular harmony and well-being, resulting in a state of dis-ease.

With the level of inactivity and mental, physical, and chemical stress that exists in the world today, the presence of spinal misalignment is epidemic.

Subluxation Degeneration

According to the laws of physics (Wolf's law), the longer vertebral subluxation exists, the more damage it creates. Wolf's law shows us that degenerative arthritis begins to kick in when there is any unequal pressure for any amount of time on a bone. Therefore, the longer subluxation exists, the more degeneration and damage to the spine and sensitive central nervous system.[33]

your nervous system will be relieved, and the power will be restored to your body. Do you want that to happen?"

Dr. Abraham was speaking Eli's language now—power! "Yes!" Eli nearly shouted.

Dr. Abraham proceeded to give Elijah a complete physical examination and then took the X-rays that would help him find the cause of his health problems. At the end of the session, the receptionist scheduled two additional appointments for them: a follow-up visit in which the doctor would review Elijah's X-rays and outline a course of treatment customized for his particular needs, and an orientation session called the Doctor's Report, in which a group of new patients would receive instruction on exactly how chiropractic works and how it can truly help.

As Miriam left the office that day, the light at the end of the very long tunnel that characterized their lives became more than a faint, illusory glow, which in the past had always turned out to be a hallucination. No, this light was bright and clear, even if it was an unknown distance away. The possibility that there were answers to Elijah's health problems was becoming a reality to her.

Still, her hopes had been dashed too many times in the past for her to completely embrace the idea that chiropractic was *the* answer. *How can it possibly be this easy? There's no way it's as simple as Dr. Abraham says—that all you need to do is find the light switch that's shut off, turn it back on again, and his body will function just fine. There's no way that could happen.*

What Dr. Abraham told her in that room contradicted most of what she had been led to believe for years, that there was something so drastically wrong with Elijah's body that no doctor could ever

Organs are "organ-ized" cell systems. The longer these systems have to deal with a chaotic disorganization, toxic environments, and a lack of balance, the more damage is done. A dis-organ-ized state is a dis-ease state.

Important note: As I mentioned earlier, a lack of pain does not mean you're well. This is particularly true of vertebral subluxation, as it is not normally accompanied by back pain. By the time there is pain, there is damage. (Most people are shocked to find that although the pain just began, their MRIs or X-rays reveal significant long-term damage due to the effects of subluxation degeneration.) It would be a very dangerous assumption to think that because your back doesn't hurt, spinal problems don't exist.

Who knows what might have been the outcome for Christopher Reeve and the thousands like him if there had been normal spinal alignment prior to their accidents and the maximum ability to absorb forces existed? Potentially, these incidents could have gone from deadly events to just another fall as they do tens, hundreds, and thousands of time a day. Correction prior to pain gives you your best chance for wellness, prevention, and safety.

Today's Scientific Chiropractic

Among scientists, it's commonly understood that one can't prove, disprove, or improve that which one can't measure. Today, nutritionists, exercise physiologists, and chiropractors have the means to measure their results. Chiropractors in particular have taken the best of what neurological and chiropractic research has to offer and combined it to discover even more about what a healthy spine should look like and what can be done to treat the unhealthy spine than has ever been known before.

Chiropractic was founded on the accurate and specific measurement of the spine, particularly the upper cervical spine, which houses the lower brain and most of the vital parts of the spinal cord. Newer research on the brain and nervous system, as well as ever-advancing methods for measuring the normal alignment of the healthy spine, has built upon that foundation to bring the science of chiropractic to an unmatched cutting-edge level in today's wellness world.

Based on neurological research, the laws of physics, engineering, mathematics, and endless studies of the spine, doctors, scientists, and researchers of all kinds have developed an optimum model of the upright spine. These models have been published in the world's most prestigious medical journals. We can now distinguish a normal, healthy spine and nervous system from an abnormal, unhealthy one, using measurable factors. Just as we know normal, healthy blood pressure or cholesterol ranges, we now know normal, healthy spinal ranges as well as abnormal, unhealthy ones.

correct it. That "something," which no doctor had adequately identified, had weakened his immune system, and he was going to have to live with the resulting negative effects for the rest of his life.

In no time, she was practically back to square one, in denial that anything that sounded so easy could ever be truly effective. *Eli's other doctors had state-of-the-art machines and technology at their disposal, high-tech hospitals, and hundreds of millions, even billions of dollars' worth of research and diagnostic tests. There's no way all those doctors could be wrong and this one guy in khaki pants and a polo shirt could be right. It just can't be that easy.*

That night, she talked her concerns over with Sharon.

"Miriam, I know just how you feel. I grew up believing that if you looked up *chiropractor* in the dictionary, you'd see an illustration of a duck and a one-word definition: *quack*.

"My mother used to read me a story from the Bible that I've never forgotten. It's about this blind man who claimed that Jesus had healed him and restored his sight. The religious establishment—they were the ones who hated Jesus—started to give the man a hard time. They wanted him to admit that Jesus was a false prophet.

"I've always loved the man's answer. It went something like this: 'Look, whether He's a false prophet or not, I don't know. All I know is, up until this morning, I was blind my whole life. Now I can see.' That's the way I respond when people accuse me of going to a quack: 'Look, all I know is, my son's spine was curved, and now it's straight. My son couldn't run after the ice-cream truck no matter how much he wanted a Popsicle, and now he's on three sports teams. My son hated his life, and now he loves it. If you think a quack could transform him to that extent, well, I guess

A chiropractor can now attain precise measurements of your spine, make an accurate assessment of the damage to your spine and nervous system, make equally accurate recommendations for care, rehabilitation, and determine a clear-cut prognosis. Success rates are very high and very proven both clinically and in research, particularly in the case of techniques such as Chiropractic Biophysics (CBP), Pettibon, Upper Cervical Specific, and several others.

In addition to using the spinal X-rays and examination of the patient's posture to evaluate spine and nervous-system health, advances in technology have brought tests like EMG (electromyography, which records the electrical activity of muscles and reveals how the central nervous system is functioning) and computerized range-of-motion and muscle evaluations to give even more insight into the presence of neurological interference, abnormal spinal alignment, malposition of the spinal curves, joint degeneration, and other parts of the vertebral subluxation complex.

The Chiropractic Fight for Survival

Palmer and his son, B. J., began to develop the techniques of spinal analysis and adjustment that would eventually characterize chiropractic care. In 1897, D. D. Palmer opened a chiropractic school (which later became known as Palmer Chiropractic College) to train others to provide this vital type of care. Chiropractic made many steps forward scientifically and politically through an ever-growing body of knowledge and the support of satisfied patients.

Despite the high clinical success rate of the Palmer adjustments (or maybe because of it), the medical profession vehemently opposed chiropractic.[34] Consequently, and as their numbers grew, chiropractors experienced increasing hostility from physicians. Morris Fishbein, secretary of the American Medical Association (AMA) and editor of its journal from 1924 to 1949, was one of the most influential of the antichiropractic forces, grouping chiropractic along with osteopathy as "nonmedical cults" and referring to the profession as "chiroquactic."[35] These myths, prejudices, and stereotypes are still in existence and believed by the many uninformed today.

In 1963, the AMA formed a Committee on Quackery that worked aggressively, both overtly and covertly, to destroy the chiropractic profession.[36] One of the principal means the AMA used to achieve its goals was to make it unethical for physicians to associate professionally with chiropractors. This essentially resulted in a boycott, preventing chiropractors from obtaining hospital privileges or access to medical diagnostic services, and eliminating any cooperation between the two groups in the delivery of health-care services. Several lawsuits were filed by or on behalf of chiropractors, and in 1987, in a landmark U.S. District Court decision (*Wilk v. AMA*), the AMA was found guilty of violating the Sherman Act, which made illegal every combination or conspiracy in restraint of trade.[37]

that's something you have to give some serious thought to.' Usually, that ends the conversation."

After she got off the phone, Miriam decided to give this three more days—that's all. If the follow-up visit the next day and the orientation session on Thursday night did not convince her—and Elijah—that this was the direction they should take, then they would go ahead with the surgery. Otherwise, she would call the surgeon first thing Friday morning to cancel. (*That should be a fun phone call*, she thought, anticipating a not-so-gentle talking-to from the surgeon.)

After the follow-up session, Miriam's pessimism waned a bit, but she remained doubtful. That night, though, she came home from work to find Eli awake and waiting to talk to her. "What happened?" she asked, anticipating the worst. "Are you all right?"

"Mom, I'm fine. Calm down—I just want to tell you something." He waited for her to settle into the recliner. The more relaxed she was, the better this would go. "Look, I really like Dr. Abraham. He doesn't treat me like an idiot or a little kid." He hesitated again, gauging his mother's mood. It seemed safe to proceed. "And this afternoon I went to the library, and Jeremy was there, and he told me about this group of kids in Atlanta who all had scoliosis, and how they'd meet up sometimes at the chiropractor's office, and how Doc Abe does the same thing—"

"Doc Abe?"

"Yeah, that's what they call Dr. Abraham, and anyway, in Atlanta the kids would have their own Doctor's Report, and they'd all get to know each other and talk about how weird all this scoliosis and spinal cord stuff is and Jeremy said it was so cool and other

The courts are still in the process of disbanding the medical Committee on Quackery (which also opposes nutrition, homeopathy, acupuncture, chelation, etc.) even today. Unfortunately, much damage has been done by the myths and bias that remain.

> *Great pilots are made in rough waters and deep seas.*
> —DR. B. J. PALMER

How Not Having Your Head on Straight Can Affect Your Health

Current information on normal placement of the upright spine reveals the importance of head position in relationship to your body. It's important that the position of the cervical spine allow your head to sit back atop your shoulders. Unfortunately, the effects of gravity, poor posture, the weight of the head, or past trauma can cause neck and skull misplacement, leading to a condition called *forward-head syndrome*. The forward displacement of the head, which is accompanied by the loss of the normal cervical curve, is a situation in which the chin juts out in front of the shoulders and chest and causes pathological (disease-causing) tension on the spinal cord and brain stem.

In his book *Rejuvenation Strategy,* Dr. Rene Cailliet, director of the Department of Physical Medicine and Rehabilitation at the University of Southern California, wrote this description of the deadly forward-head syndrome as well as humpback syndrome:

1. Incorrect head position leads to improper spinal function. [It is a major and complex form of vertebral subluxation.]

2. The head in forward posture can add up to thirty pounds of abnormal leverage on the cervical spine.

3. Forward head posture results in loss of vital capacity. Lung capacity is depleted by as much as 30 percent. Loss of lung capacity leads to heart and blood vascular problems. [Jut your chin out and flex your head down and try to breathe. You can barely do it. Then tuck your chin in and extend your head backwards. Now you can really fill your lungs.]

4. The entire gastrointestinal system is affected, particularly the large intestine. Loss of good bowel peristaltic function and evacuation is common to forward head posture and loss of spinal curve.

5. Forward head posture causes an increase in discomfort and pain. Freedom of motion in the first four cervical vertebrae is a major source of stimuli that causes production of endorphins. As a result of this loss of endorphins

kids went through all the stuff I went through, and we're going to talk again tomorrow and—"

"Eli, slow down. I can't keep up with you."

After a disturbingly long pause, Eli stood up to go to bed. "Mom, just don't make me get that rod in my back," he said before turning to leave the room.

If that didn't settle the matter, the Doctor's Report orientation session certainly did. Doc Abe—getting used to that would take a bit more time for Miriam, but she was trying—spent the first part of the session explaining his foundational belief that at the time of their birth, God placed within all people's bodies all that they needed for their future health and well-being. When people become sick, it's because the "light"—the "power" designed to keep them healthy—is off, causing the body to get sick, and that he needed to turn the power back on.

As he went on, something occurred to Miriam that she had not given any thought to before that moment: here she was, sitting in a doctor's office, listening to him carefully detail his method of treatment so his patients clearly understood the procedures—at eight o'clock at night. This man, Doc Abe, had seen patients all day long, and yet he was devoting his evening to educating them. And according to the schedule posted on the wall, he did this twice a week, week after week, all year long. Amazing. She didn't know a single other doctor who would do that—and she knew *lots* of doctors.

He even had a care plan that included payments she might even be able to afford! If he wasn't a saint, she'd be willing to make a nomination.

Shortly before the session ended, Dr. Abraham pointed to a

(hormones that reduce pain and affect emotions), many otherwise non-painful sensations are experienced as pain.

6. Forward head posture causes loss of healthy spine-body motion. The entire body becomes rigid as the range of motion becomes diminished; the person's body becomes hunched.

7. Associated with humpback syndrome or "hyperkyphotic posture" was found in an October 2004 study published in the *Journal of the American Geriatrics Society* to significantly increase the likelihood of death. Studies at Cornell and John's Hopkins found kyphosis to both increase the chance of uterine prolapse and decrease physical function and mobility respectively.

The Spine-Brain Connection

With the ability to measure brain activity and health improving each year, studies and theories on the brain-body connection are finding ever-increasing popularity. The more we discover about the functions of the brain and the pathways through which it communicates with the cells and senses, the more likely we are to expand our mental, emotional, and functional capacities and overcome disease.

With so much emphasis on the brain-body connection and how the brain keeps the body going, a logical question arises: What keeps the brain going? Paradoxically, the answer to this question is simply *the body*. While the brain is keeping the body healing and vibrating along, nutrients from eating, drinking, breathing, and the products of cellular function keep the brain healing and vibrating.

Nutrients essential to the brain for survival—such as oxygen, glucose, and others—are transported from the body to the brain through the fluid that flows inside your spinal canal. This fluid is called the cerebrospinal (brain-spine) fluid, or CSF. This fluid gets from the spine to the brain with the use of a CSF pump. This CSF pump doesn't use electricity. The power for the pump is generated by movement of the sacrum (lowest portion of the spine) and the cervical spine (upper portion of the spine).

In order for the CSF pump to move effectively, you need a healthy spinal column. Irregular or reduced motion of the sacrum and/or cervical spine due to vertebral subluxation in either of those areas will lead to abnormal and reduced flow of oxygen, glucose, and other important nutrients to the brain. That is why the spine-brain connection is so important. A bad back or a bad neck will literally give you a bad brain.[38]

Correcting your spine not only gets you functioning better, it gets you thinking clearer.

resource table and mentioned one title in particular. "There's a story in that book called 'Country of the Blind' by H. G. Wells," he said. "I'm about to tell you a condensed version of that story, and if you like it, feel free to sign up to borrow the book so you can read the whole thing."

With that, he briefly told how Nuñez had discovered a hidden village tucked away in a valley, how all the villagers were afflicted with blindness, and how they refused to believe Nuñez's warnings of imminent danger because they could not *see* the danger coming.

"It's my mission to lead people out of the country of the blind, a place where the people have been led to put their faith and trust in an established belief that has blinded them to the truth," Dr. Abraham said. "I've made it my life's work to change the way Americans think about health care in order to lead them out of the country of the blind, one person at a time."

Miriam Knight's eyes finally began to open.

As she predicted, the phone call to the surgeon's office did not go well. Unaccustomed to asserting herself with medical professionals, Miriam found herself stuttering and stammering with each argument the surgeon posed in favor of proceeding with the operation.

"You realize that you could be doing unthinkable harm to your son's body by not having the rod inserted," he said. "This could set him back for years. I don't know who you've been talking to or where you're getting your information, but you need to consider the fact that we've been doing this type of surgery for years and have an extensive amount of experience as well as expertise in this particular procedure. I believe you're making a serious mistake in canceling the operation."

"As a man thinketh in his heart, so is he." How about "As a man is in his brain, so does he thinketh"?

— DR. B. J. PALMER

The Adjustment: Unlocking the Mystery and Overcoming the Myths and Fears

One of the great medical myths has to do with what people think a chiropractic adjustment is. Most think it is some sort of "popping" of the neck or "twisting and cracking" of the back—not unlike popping your own neck or twisting and cracking your spouse's back when he or she feels tight after work.

With this kind of ignorance about what an adjustment really is, is it any wonder so many people do not get chiropractic care or actually fear chiropractic adjustment?

The truth about a chiropractic adjustment is that there are dozens of ways to analyze vertebral subluxation and more than a hundred ways to adjust and correct spinal problems. There are light-touch adjustments, small- and large-instrument adjustments, adjustments using trigger points and reflexes, adjustments using specialized tables, multiple forms of hand-only adjustments, as well as techniques that focus on only certain areas of the spine. Vastly dissimilar to manipulations performed by osteopaths and physical therapists, specific scientific chiropractic adjustments are not generalized mobilizations of the spine. Rather, using various methods of evaluation, chiropractors actually use precise contact points designed to gently shift an individual segment or segments of the spine and extremities in a very specific direction.

AAA Safety Rating

Chiropractic adjustments are incredibly safe. Malpractice insurance carriers do not use myth or bias to determine their premiums. They use raw data based on the likelihood that a doctor would injure someone and be sued. While medical professionals can pay in excess of a hundred thousand dollars per year for their malpractice coverage, chiropractors pay barely a fraction of this, with premiums as low as only a few hundred dollars per year. Given the prevalence of the myths, prejudices, and fears, this is hard to believe, but absolutely true.

Remember, when a chiropractor works on your spine it's called an *adjustment*, not a *crack*. "Crack" is

- what you do to an egg in order to release its contents,
- found in old wood or thin ice,
- a dangerous addictive drug,
- the sound a well-hit ball makes when it strikes a bat,
- a different way of saying someone "told" a joke.

Maybe so, she thought, *but I think not.* Though the conversation was awkward, Miriam felt a certain amount of pride in the fact that, for once, she had trusted her maternal instincts and what little intelligence God had given her and whatever measure of intuition she possessed. For once, the decision she made *felt* right.

The following week, Eli developed a new interest in his own health. He began collecting books, journals, and newsletter articles to learn more about his body and to correct the misalignment in his thinking. Although he was only twelve, all he had been through had made him seem older and wise beyond his years. He decided it was time for him to take charge of his life and his health. Already, he realized how little he had understood about his own body for all those agonizing years; how much more was there to discover? For the first time in his life, Eli and books became inseparable—Doc Abe even let him borrow some of his textbooks from chiropractic college. Even though he didn't understand a lot of it, Eli soaked up as much information as he possibly could.

Eli's spine slowly began to move toward healthy alignment, much to the surprise of both him and his mother. Sure, they both had expected improvement, but this was turning out to be more effective than they thought. It took time, and it took patience, but when the moment came for Dr. Abraham to take another set of X-rays, they realized that it had been well worth it.

Standing in Doc Abe's office and seeing with his very own eyes what had taken place inside his body impacted Eli more than words ever could. His life had changed, and he knew it; the evidence was right in front of him. In the left X-ray view box was the image of his misshapen, misaligned spine that Doc Abe had taken that first day

Two Important Associates of the Chiropractic Adjustment

1. Therapeutic Reconstructive Care

With many spinal problems, including complications such as forward-head syndrome, disk degeneration, osteoarthritis, scoliosis, and loss of normal curves, certain additional spinal care techniques need to be applied in addition to the adjustment.

Therapeutic and reconstructive care includes

- stretching and weights used to correct the position of the skull (eliminate forward-head syndrome) and restore or increase the curves in the neck (arc of life) and upper and lower back;
- strengthening the musculature in the back of the neck and upper shoulders to hold the head, neck, and upper spine in normal positions;
- stretching, exercises, and blocking to correct imbalances in posture and lateral curvatures (scoliosis); and
- the use of specific chiropractic equipment for the rehydrating of disks and the regenerating of bone.

Note: Only highly trained chiropractors can offer these treatments. Standard manipulation, exercise, and physical therapy will not resolve forward-head posture, scoliosis, disk degeneration, or arthritis. Neither will taking medications or having surgery for the resulting effects of these conditions.

2. Spinal Hygiene[39]

There was a time when nearly everyone over forty had false teeth—or needed them. Fortunately, Timmy the Tooth and hundreds of other consumer-awareness campaigns led by the American Dental Association showed us that we need something called "dental hygiene."

While dental hygiene is important, it isn't as vital to your health as *spinal hygiene*. Poor posture, bad sleeping habits, sitting too much, and all forms of stress act as sugar does to your teeth. Just as with dental hygiene, you need to address these deleterious factors on a regular basis if you do not want decay and to lose the use of your spine before you hit fifty.[40]

Some forms of spinal hygiene include

- exercises to strengthen the paravertebral (back) musculature, abdomen, and quadriceps (front of legs), which all become weak or atrophied due to sitting too often;

in his office. On the right was an image of his spine taken the previous day—and his spine was now almost perfectly aligned.

Although Doc Abe had restored his spine, there was nothing Eli could do to restore his standing right away with the other kids at school. Once branded a weakling, always branded a weakling. Eli Knight's brand was so firmly entrenched in the minds of his peers that he may as well have had a gigantic *W* branded on his forehead, standing for Weakling. Or Wuss. Or Wimp.

In the past, each time Eli confidently took a swing at a fastball when it was his turn at bat, the other kids laughed, despite his growing strength. He knew they expected him to miss, and he did—nearly all the time. Each time he found himself face-to-face with Grace—the girl he had liked as long as he could remember— he started to ask her out but chickened out before the words had any real chance of leaving his mouth. What was wrong with him? Why couldn't he do a simple thing like connect the bat with the baseball or talk to a girl the way the other guys did?

Now, he remembered what Doc Abe had said about power. "The power inside of you is far greater than any problem outside of you." *My power's on,* Eli thought. *I don't have weakness in me, I've got greatness.* Soon, everything began to change.

Seeing those X-rays had a secondary effect in Eli's life. As it dawned on him that his body had actually—visibly—come back to life, something wonderful happened to his mind as well. Not only had the nerves that were crushed and damaged for most of his existence begun to come back to life, and not only had the breathing problems that had plagued him since birth—the croup, the pneumonia, the chronic bronchitis—vanished; Eli believed in himself

- proper stretching of anterior musculature—pectorals (chest) and anterior deltoids (front of shoulders) as well as the calves and hamstrings, all of which poor posture tightens.

While the exam, findings analysis, and rehabilitative procedures can take time, a highly trained, efficient chiropractor can perform the adjustment in as little as a minute. Nonetheless, that minute can mean abundant health that changes things forever. Thus, *One-Minute Wellness.*

Do Chiropractors Cure?

The biggest misunderstanding about chiropractic is that chiropractors claim to cure disease. Responsible chiropractors do not claim to "cure" anything. The medical profession tries to cure disease by using drugs and surgery. By contrast, chiropractic maximizes the natural, God-given strength of the human body and its capacity to heal without using dangerous drugs or surgery.

People go to chiropractors with heart disease, cancer, diabetes, infections, osteoporosis, high blood pressure, high cholesterol, hyperactivity, learning disorders, asthma, allergies, Parkinson's, Alzheimer's, multiple sclerosis, fibromyalgia, chronic fatigue, intestinal disease, aches and pains, and paralysis. In addition, chiropractors from the Carrick Institute, led by Dr. Ted Carrick, have gotten wonderful results working on patients with severe neurological disorders as well as reviving patients who are in a coma. While chiropractors do not heal these people, they use care of the central nervous system along with nutrition, diet, and healthy lifestyle programs to lead the suffering toward their greatest possible level of wellness.

Many do get well and call it a miracle. But it's really just a return to normal. The best miracles are the *silent* ones. These occur when people who were going to get one of these conditions or diseases go to a chiropractor for care before the disease or condition occurs. As a result of Maximized Living, people have their best chance to not get the condition or disease in the first place. That's the true goal and the ultimate miracle of *real* wellness.

The Cost of Chiropractic

In his testimony before the Senate Appropriations Committee, Dr. Christopher Kent explained the direct correlation between chiropractic care and reduced health-care costs. He cited an analysis of an insurance database that compared chiropractic patients with nonchiropractic patients over the age of seventy-five: The first group

for the first time in his life. He was more than healthy—he had been healed.

Over time, Eli became stronger. He became healthier. He started having more confidence. He began to realize that there was nothing wrong with him, that God had created him in His image, and that there was a source of strength deep inside him that could not be defeated.

Best of all, he became the star pitcher for his high school baseball team his senior year. And yes, he even got the girl. He took Grace to the senior prom.

reported better overall health, spent fewer days in hospitals and nursing homes, used fewer prescription drugs, and were more active than the nonchiropractic patients. Furthermore, the chiropractic patients spent 21 percent less time in hospitals over the previous three years.[41]

Hope's Story

"Daddy! Daddy! Look at me!" Little Hope Samuels looked down at her father as she stood poised at the edge of the diving board, her toes and legs and entire body in perfect alignment to perform the tricky one-and-a-half backflip she had learned just yesterday. But Thomas Samuels—one of the brightest stars in the King Advertising Agency—was lost in thought, poring over a sheaf of papers that could set him up for life, if only General Motors would agree to the terms in the contract he was holding.

"Da-a-ddy! Da-a-ddy!" Hope tried the singsongy, add-an-extra-syllable approach, but it was no use. She pushed off and nailed a perfect dive. It was a shame no one saw it.

From the time she was two years old, Hope and water had been nearly inseparable. When she wasn't at school, she was in the water. Actually, even when she was in school, she was in the water. When she grew to be a freshman, she was the only one to qualify for the girls' high school swim team. It helped that all the Samuelses' luxury homes had in-ground pools. Their seven-thousand-square-foot "vacation" home in the Colorado Rockies even had an indoor pool for those snowy and icy winter nights. And they almost always spent their family vacations near the water—Martha's Vineyard in the summer, the Caribbean and the Riviera at other times—though "family" vacations had become increasingly rare. More

| 6 |

Essential #3: Quality Nutrients

To efficiently run the numerous and intricate operating systems that make up your complicated body, each of your fifty trillion cells needs nontoxic fuel. This fuel is in the form of quality nutrition. A lack of quality food and an inadequate level of certain nutrients will interfere with normal body function and create a challenging environment for your cells to thrive in.

You are made out of what you ingest. The modern diet of convenient, processed, and chemical-laden meals poses a serious threat to the development of prosperous organs. Thus, most people's hearts are made out of McDonald's french fries and Krispy Kreme donuts.

These organs are then floating in body fluids that come from what you drink. For that reason, the quality of the liquids you consume is vital for supporting life. Bathing your organs (organ-ized cells) in coffee; cola; impure water; and red, green, and purple drinks also badly interferes with your state of wellness. If fish can't survive in a bowl filled with those beverages, what makes you think your cells will?

Essential #3 is a call to become considerate of your body and conscious of what you are putting into it in order to help create Maximized Living.

This rule is in close relationship to Essential #1. Your body is a divine mix of chemical reaction after chemical reaction. When you dump foreign chemicals into the body, like drugs or unnatural-synthetic-modified food, the side effects can be explosive.

The order for numbers two through four is determined by how essential those elements are to survival. You can go thirty to forty days without food, two to three days without water, two to three minutes without air, and a long time without exercise, but you cannot last a second without nerve supply.

Diet or Nutrition?

Most of today's nutrition guidance has been diluted down to the term *diet*. This is due largely to the fact that people have gotten so large. With obesity on the increase,

often than not, it was Hope and her mother, Abigail, who went away together. Peter was seldom home anymore.

On the surface—and who bothered to look any deeper anyway?—Hope appeared to be a fairly typical teenager. Other than her passion for swimming, her interests were pretty predictable: friends, boys, movies, music, and she was a solid student, earning more As than Bs. Her father never seemed to notice the As, only the Bs, and when he did, he ranted and raved and reminded her that she'd never get into an Ivy League school at the rate she was going. But she suspected deep down that even a perfect, straight-A report card wouldn't please him all that much, and she knew that if she could ride out his tirades, he'd forget about it eventually.

Abigail also got on her case about studying. But Hope sensed that it was more because she liked the prestige that came with having a daughter who got straight As—and because it validated her "good mother" status—than because she actually cared. Hope studied hard and wanted to get into a great school, especially a great swimming school, but some of the college-level courses were tough to get As in. What she really needed was help, not chastising. Fortunately, when Hope brought home a mediocre report card, Abigail forgot about it after a few days, and the whole issue blew over. Once or twice Abigail tried grounding her, but that proved to be a joke. When an opportunity eventually came up for Hope to go out, her mother had long since forgotten about the punishment.

In her senior year, Hope became an accomplished swimmer with a real opportunity to make the state championships. "Daddy,

it's no wonder that when you talk about healthy eating, people think South Beach Diet, Atkins, and Dr. Phil. The catch-22 is that the health-and-diet industry is in part responsible for the current outrageous level of obesity! Case in point: in past years the top-selling books were often novels. Nonfiction just could not compete against these categories. But in recent years, diet books have ruled the top of the charts and in many cases gone as high as number one overall and remained there for weeks. During that same time period, in which literally hundreds of millions of these diet books have been sold, obesity has skyrocketed, including going into hyperspace for kids.

While a dramatic shift from home-cooked, natural foods to fast, convenient foods is ultimately responsible for so many people being fat, diet programs have undoubtedly made us fatter. This is because we've gone to extremes; rather than simply returning to quality nutrition and clean water, we've been following funky, faddish weight-loss programs.

Besides, losing weight the wrong way may make you thinner, but not healthier. Atkins may allow you to have bacon at every meal, but is that good for you? You may lose weight, but all that means is you die lighter!

Maximized Living as it applies to eating is not a diet (*die* with a *t* at the end, for *torture*). It is leading people back toward making better choices about what they put in their mouths. When you consider only taste or filling yourself up when you eat, you are simply ignoring a major law of life.

A popular set of principles that many doctors of *real* wellness are using is called the Un-diet. It's a return to sanity by using a set of guidelines for normal eating. The Un-diet is *conscious* rather than *unconscious* eating or dieting. It's being considerate of our bodies' internal environment and letting health and weight loss take care of themselves.

Nine Million Obese Children—Under the Age of Six!

A story that ran in *USA Today* on October 1, 2004, opened many people's eyes to the epidemic of childhood obesity, revealing that a startling nine million kids are now considered obese.

Many health problems, such as diabetes, heart disease, cancer, and arthritis that are linked to obesity are becoming prevalent at younger and younger ages due to the childhood obesity epidemic. Providing children with nutritious meals and snacks, in addition to setting guidelines and educating them on good nutrition, will put them on the road to making healthy decisions as adults. Most important, parents serve as role models to their children. Exercising and eating right should be a natural occurrence in daily family life.

(**Tip from Dr. Ben: Can you say, "Pack your lunch!"?**)

I've got the district finals swim meet today! You said you'd get to at least one of my meets this year. Will you come?"

"I'll try—you know it's my—"

She finished the sentence for him. "I know: busiest time of the year."

That afternoon, she kept scanning the crowd. It was the biggest event for her team of the year, and every parent was there, bar two—Thomas and Abigail.

Somewhere along the line she'd stopped being disappointed. She wasn't sure what she felt. *They're busy; they don't like swimming; I don't know, who cares . . .*

Hope normally didn't pay attention to when her father arrived home, but that night she sat in the foyer on the bottom step of the winding staircase, practically breathless with anticipation. As soon as he walked in, Hope jumped up and squealed, "Daddy, you'll never believe how well I did!" She thought for sure that winning the district championship would impress him.

"What happened?" Thomas asked absentmindedly.

"Well, I . . . ," she began as she followed her father to his home office, where he began preparing for a night of even more work. Just as she got to the good part she heard the familiar shrill of her dad's cordless phone. No point in continuing; he was done for the night.

Clearly annoyed that Hope had not left the room to give him some privacy, Thomas placed his hand over the receiver and asked, "Well, what happened? Is it something that can wait until later?"

"Forget about it, Daddy."

Eating Is Not a Game of Perfect

It's pointless to look for the perfect diet. Rarely does anyone eat perfectly for even one day, never mind a whole week or a whole lifetime! That's what's so crazy about the new diets; no one can stick to nutritional programming very long. Forget dieting and begin Un-dieting.

The most important part of the Un-diet is to get started, get your bat off your shoulder, get off the bench, and just get in the game. You are never going to eat without error—and you don't have to. When you make mistakes, just get back in there. You can make several errors and still win. You lose only if you lose hope.

How can you do this forever? Let me introduce you to the Vacation Rule: Rather than calling it cheating, the Un-diet allows you to build two to three Vacation Meals right into your weekly eating schedule. These Vacation Meals can be chocolate on Wednesdays, pizza on Fridays, and ice cream after lunch on Sundays. Now eating what you love no longer means you've quit your diet; it's now part of your lifetime normal eating plan.

Eating for Three

In this world, committing to doing anything right is difficult. No matter what you do, challenges and natural temptations will always try to pull you away from it. What I have found is that fighting this is particularly tough when I am doing things purely for my own sake. On the other hand, if my commitment is to benefit the welfare of others, I have a whole other level of discipline.

Because a healthier eating program gives you more energy, greater strength, increased mental awareness, and significantly increased time here on the planet, what you put in your mouth affects others. When you consider what you are going to put in your mouth (which most people do not consider at all), remember that if you lead a longer, more vital life, you can do a tremendous amount more for God and the people you love. Pregnant women always say that they are eating for two. I always say that I am eating for three:

1. God
2. The people I love and serve
3. Me (I do like to look and feel my best.)

When I was growing up, my family definitely did not eat in order to live; we "lived to eat." I come from New York, and there's a reason why some of the most

"Hey, Mom! I got accepted at Georgia! I'm three for three!" Hope called out as she opened the front door, waving the brown envelope in her hand. "Mom! Mo-o-m!" She ought to know by now: extra syllables never worked on Dad, and now they didn't even work on Mom.

Hope poked her head into all the downstairs rooms before taking the steps two at a time to look for her mother upstairs. Where the heck was she? This was supposed to be her day off. "Mom? Mom?" Still nothing.

Picking up the phone in her parents' master suite, Hope pressed the code for voice mail. One message: "Hope, dear, I had to go to an early cocktail party—I had forgotten all about it, and it's practically in my honor! Well, not really, but the Reillys wanted to show off their new house. Not their 'new' house—oh, you know what I mean! See you later, darling!"

Ugh! Ever since her mom had taken a job with a hot new interior designer in town, she seemed to work all the time. And when she wasn't actually working, she was out "networking"—a code word for socializing and drinking like a lush. *I can't call her at the party—she'd kill me. Maybe I'll call Dad. Maybe not. When he's in Detroit, he does not want to be bothered, even with good news.*

Hope whispered, "It's like I'm invisible. It feels like I might just disappear altogether."

The phone rang, interrupting her thought. Startled, she picked it up a bit too quickly and lost her grip on it. "Hello?"

"Hey."

popular junk foods—such as cheesecake and pizza—have their own New York versions. It's because we love our food there—and it shows! While many people wake up and consider what they are going to do for the day, I still often wake up and think less about what I am going to do during the day than about what I am going to eat during the day.

My father lost close to a thousand pounds in his life yet died at fifty-two weighing his top weight. Any weight he lost dieting, he always regained. I remember when I was twelve, my father said to me as he was about to quit yet another fad diet, "If I have to eat well, I don't want to live."

In addition to wishing I knew about the Un-diet back then, I'd like to go back now and ask him to eat for my mom and my two brothers instead of for himself. I'll bet it would have helped. No one knows more about how hard it is to follow a consistent nutritious eating regimen than I do. But when I remind myself that I'm eating for three, I am far more likely to put the right things in my mouth.

Again, *real* wellness nutrition does not mean dieting or perfect eating. One thing all diets have in common is that they will eventually end. Maximized Living involves being considerate of your body, becoming more conscious of what you are actually eating, and making eating decisions that help create the future and body that please you.

The Food You Were Intended to Eat: Food by God

When God developed the body, He specifically created certain foods for its use. These are the foods that grow and exist in nature. They are Food by God. God has built into His food everything that is necessary to create a good environment for your cells. He put necessary materials inside, in just the right amounts and in the perfect balance, for the proper digestion, distribution, and elimination of nutrients.

The body's digestive system is an intricate network of food-processing organs whose purpose is to break down and utilize the food you eat. Each component of the digestive system is so divinely complex that no human could ever create or even completely describe it. Every single part is a universe unto itself. All the organs of this system have unique cells, glands, fluids, and functions that are divinely formulated to play a specific role in the amazing manner in which the very demanding human body processes food. When you take in Food by God in its natural state, the digestive system will easily break it down, dispense the nutrients to body cells, and quickly eliminate leftover toxins and by-products.

(Essential #2 Note: It's been said that you are what you eat. This, however, is not exactly true. The truth is, you are what you assimilate or digest. This is why nutrition is important. Still, nutrition plays a secondary role to maximum nerve

Whoa! She knew that voice. No doubt about it. Jacob Trask. *Oh, my.* "Hey back."

"What's up?"

If she was ever going to snag Jacob, she'd have to impress him. "Guess what? I just got accepted to Georgia!"

"Hey, that's great." His monotone voice betrayed his disinterest; her attempt at impressing him wasn't working.

"No, it really is. Georgia has the top division-one women's swim team in the country. In the *whole* country! I just know I could make the team!"

Even through the phone line, Hope could sense Jacob sitting up a bit straighter and paying a bit closer attention. She could just see his eyes—those unbelievably gorgeous eyes. *He may try to act blasé, but he's smart, and he knows this is big news,* she thought.

"Hey, Hope, that really is great. But didn't somebody tell me you were going to Auburn? Or was it Florida?"

"Well, it's my choice now! All three accepted me, and they have the top three women's swim teams. I'm three for three on acceptances!" This conversation was beginning to take effect.

"Hey, you know, we should go out and celebrate. Would a big division-one college swimmer like yourself be willing to get some pizza with a small hometown boy like me?"

Why not? Hope tried to act casual and stay in control to keep herself from screaming. She hadn't had a real date in months, and now Jacob! She'd had her eye on him since they first met at the Olympic-sized pool at Arlington Community College where she sometimes trained. He had the hottest bod in the whole pool!

Suddenly, Hope was beginning to feel visible. *Finally, someone*

supply. Without maximum nerve supply, even if you eat well—Food by God— your body can not fully break down and utilize the nutrients.)

Food by God is packed with living vitamins, minerals, water, fiber, and the enzymes needed to digest the food itself. These, along with dozens of other elements we know about—and countless numbers of elements only God knows about—are what make up Food by God.

Part of the inside-out, dis-ease, *real* wellness model for good health is understanding that when you do the things that are in alignment with nature, they produce optimal health.

Food by God and all of the vitamins, minerals, and other elements it contains have been put together by a natural, unlimited intelligence. Food by God is smart food. When you eat Food by God, such as an apple or an egg, it contains exactly what is needed for safe and effective use within your body. Your body knows exactly what to do with it. (For the Food by God list, see Appendix B.)

Food by Man

Food by Man is food human beings create or alter. It is also food that God did not intend for humans to use expressly on a regular basis. In reality, the problems with processed-food companies are very similar to the problems with drug companies. They add toxins in the forms of chemicals, colorings, and preservatives to foods. These toxins create an inopportune internal atmosphere for your cells, which in turn can only end up eliciting dangerous side effects in your body.

Many types of Food by Man are recommended by different diets that do not follow a *real* wellness model but rather a mechanistic model. These fad programs utilize unnatural, unintended foods such as processed animal products (pasteurized dairy, pork products, and the like), chemical-containing powders and meal replacements, and certain stimulant supplements in their recommendations, because they produce weight loss or energy.

The further you get from eating the foods specifically created for the body, or the further these foods are from their natural forms, the less efficiently the digestive system can break them down—if it can at all. This leads to interference with function or poor health.

Food by Man is barely even digestible. Because these foods cannot pass through the digestive system quickly and cannot be broken down efficiently, they will linger inside your body. This will block the processing of other nutrients, rob you of energy, contaminate your cells, create excess fat storage, affect your mood, and contribute to every type of symptom and disease known to humanity.

Food by Man lacks life or any truly *usable* vitamins, minerals, or other nutrients. Anything that is devoid of nutrition or life is unlikely to be able to *sustain* life.

who cares about my good news. I've got the right to celebrate! I'd much rather be doing it with Jacob than my parents anyway.

Jacob, a college sophomore, wasn't the best athlete on the swim team there—he spent too much time being interested in the girls' swim team to train hard enough to be good—but he was definitely the best-looking guy on the team.

Hope had long wanted to talk to him when she saw him at the student union, but he was always with a group, usually a group of girls. It wasn't until a week ago that she had finally mustered up the courage to introduce herself to him. She couldn't believe it when he asked her for her phone number.

Imagine her, a high school girl out with a college guy. She never thought she could do it. *I'm sure my parents wouldn't have thought so. My mom may not think it "looks proper," and Jacob's family may not be considered "socially acceptable."*

Before Jacob picked her up, Hope said to herself, "Slow down, girl. Slow down. It's just a date. That's all. No big deal."

But it was a big deal, the start of a very, very big deal. At least to Hope. Not that her mother or her father noticed. "Just don't let a boy interfere with the goals you have!" her mother said cheerily when she told her about her date with Jacob. "Is he related to the Trasks from Columbus?" she asked, concerned only with Jacob's pedigree.

Jacob might be the only person on earth who really understands and likes me for me. Fortunately, the parental units will never be home when Jacob picks me up.

Hope began to feel as if she was falling in love with Jacob. She had to admit that she couldn't be quite sure if he was serious about

The body has multiple protective mechanisms for cleaning out toxins and restoring harmony. This can keep you alive or at least breathing for a time. Unfortunately, Food by Man will not allow you to breathe too well or too long. (For a sample list of primary Foods by Man, see Appendix B.)

Important: Don't panic when you see the Food by Man list! We don't want crash dieting or rebound weight gain from the thought of giving up chocolate.

The Point of the Undiet:
Increase Food by God and Decrease Food by Man

Remember, wellness is more of what you should eat and less of what you shouldn't. A good start is 80 percent Food by God and 20 percent Food by Man. This is a particularly good ratio for kids. Plus, remember the Vacation Rule!

Vitamins, Minerals, and Herbs

Your health coach and wellness doctor may prescribe supplements for boosting immunity and giving you nutrients necessary for repair and recovery. These vitamins, minerals, and herbs can be of great assistance, particularly in the case of toxicity, weakness, damage, or breakdown from unknown long-term nutritional deficiencies or poor body function.

It's incredibly necessary to seek the counsel of a well-informed wellness provider (nutritionist, chiropractor, advanced personal trainer, or alternative doctor) who can assess your needs and lead you in the right direction. Otherwise, supplementation can cause problems and is likely to be a big, fat waste of time and money.

Remember, Essential #3 is "Consume quality nutrients." Using discount and drugstore supplements is like swallowing rocks, and they are going to come out of you looking almost exactly the way they looked on the way in. Wellness professionals typically have quality supplements available. They may cost slightly more than they do at the discount mall, but nutrients are not a good place to be frugal.

Supplements are just that: they are intended to be supplemental, in addition to taking in the right nutrients in the forms of nutritious food and clean water.

What's more, do you recall the two guys at the scene of the accident, one dead and one just hanging on? Keep in mind, vitamin C or any other letter of the alphabet can't heal the dead guy, only the one in which life-power remains. Supplements don't cure, but the right high-quality nutrients prescribed in the correct dosage can help facilitate a cure.

their relationship or only casually dating her. But then he'd call and tell her how beautiful she was and how much he missed her, and she'd talk herself back into believing that they were destined to be the perfect couple. He was attentive, encouraging, and most of all, affectionate—everything she wanted in a man.

One afternoon, his affection for her and her love for him took over. With no chance of getting caught, they made love right there in Hope's bedroom. Thomas was away on another one of his weekend business trips to Detroit, while Abigail would be at a Designers Showcase fund-raiser well into the night.

But they did get caught after all—three weeks later when the little stick turned blue.

Contrary to what she and her friends had heard for years, you most certainly can get pregnant the first time you have sex.

About all that Hope remembered from what was left of her senior year was that little blue stick and the sudden loss of the men in her life: the romance apparently died for Jacob after he found out she was pregnant. The last thing he said to her before he matriculated to a four-year university on the West Coast was, "Who says the baby's mine?"

Her dad also came clean, if you can call it that. It appeared that his "business trips" to Detroit had been business and pleasure. He moved to Detroit to start a new life with a lawyer for GM in June. He did keep one dirty little secret from Abigail and Hope until he was forced to confess during the divorce proceedings: he had squandered their wealth on lousy investments and lavish gifts for his lawyer friend. They weren't exactly broke, but Hope knew she couldn't count on her family to help her out financially once the baby came.

The Un-diet Food Guide

Step 1 to the Un-diet is to focus on eating Food by God. Step 2, in addition to eating the right foods, helps you to eat them in the right way when you are seeking to obtain a leaner, better-looking you.

By focusing on the right food categories (carbohydrates, proteins, and fats), in the right proportions and at the right times of day, you will see miraculous things begin to occur both inside and outside your body. Remarkably, you will see this happen even if you do not eat ideal Food by God. If you have any issues or conditions with your health, your weight, or your physical appearance, you will see improvements simply by eating according to the Un-diet Food Guide.

Step 1, eating Food by God, is incredibly helpful, but it's additionally beneficial when you consider what food is for. The Un-diet Food Guide is based on the different needs for carbohydrates, protein, and fats your body has throughout the day. These needs are as follows:

Serving Size Key: High = 2 + Servings
                                     Moderate = 1–2 Servings
                                     Low = 0.5–1 Serving

Serving sizes are approximate. In the Un-diet, what you eat and what type of food you eat are far more important than how much. *Serving size recommendation:* meat/proteins 4–6 oz., sweet potato—1 medium, 1 piece of fruit; follow guide on packaged foods—when in doubt, use the size of your fist as one serving.

Morning Food Guide
Carbohydrates
Today, a lot of people seem to be downright afraid of carbohydrates. Nevertheless, carbs are not really the enemy; unused carbs are. So if you eat a bowl of pasta and some bread at night, you've just eaten enough carbohydrates to run a marathon, but instead you go to bed. These unused carbs wreak havoc on your glands and systems, and the extra sugars they create are stored as fat. All this results in your getting up in the morning feeling more tired than you were when you went to bed.

In the morning, it has typically been six to twelve hours since you have fueled up, and you still have an entire day ahead of you. Therefore, you need a significant amount of energy- and nutrient-rich foods. Energy and the most significant amount of nutrients come from the foods in the carbohydrate category.

Eating the majority of your carbs in the morning gives you ample time to burn what you've taken in and leaves little left over for storage in the gut or butt.

The baby. He was due in October. Until now, Hope had hidden her pregnancy well; her slim, athletic build and well-toned swimmer's body working to her advantage. No one could tell she was four months pregnant when she walked across the stage to receive her diploma. But now it was late August, and it was obvious that she was very much with child. She said good-bye to her friends one by one as they left for college, her plans to enter Georgia—she never even applied to an Ivy League school, just to spite her father—on hold, if not dead in the water.

Feeling more alone than she ever had before, Hope threw herself into the task of preparing for the arrival of her child, a boy she would name Adam, for no particular reason except that she had never known an Adam and therefore had no bad feelings associated with the name. Her child would not be named Thomas or Jacob; that was a certainty.

Hope suspected she had shamed her mother beyond belief. (In later years, Hope would wonder if her decision to keep the baby, rather than go through abortion or adoption, was in fact a form of humiliating retaliation against her heavily distracted parents.) She and Abigail still lived under the same roof, but they may as well have lived on the other side of town from each other. And that roof wouldn't be over them for very long; under the terms of the divorce agreement, the homes had to be sold to pay off outstanding debts.

Between her job as a receptionist at a large real estate office and feeling queasy, Hope spent the last two months of her pregnancy more tired than she ever thought she could feel. More than once, she nearly lost her job; during her 3 PM break, she

Protein

Protein foods build and repair broken-down muscle and tissue. Because the body has been at rest, it doesn't have a significant need for proteins (building and repairing) in the morning.

Fats

Fats are not the enemy either, just bad fats. Bad fats include hydrogenated oils; nut, vegetable, and seed oils; and saturated fats from commercial meats. Good fats are those found in fish, avocados, walnuts, flax, olive oil, wild fish, and organic-grass-fed meats; these assist in the function of both the immune and cardiovascular systems. They're also important in protecting joint and brain tissue.

Fats support cell structure and healing. Large amounts of fats with large amounts of carbs make you fat. Because the body's been resting and because this is a carb meal, fats should be added to the morning meal but kept to a moderate-to-low level.

> **Morning Un-diet Summary:** Moderate-to-High Carbs/Low Proteins/Moderate-to-Low Fats

Afternoon Food Guide

Carbohydrates

There is now less day ahead of you, and unless you've been very active, you still have some unused carbohydrates in your system from the morning meal. Consequently, you have less need for energy, so less need for carbohydrates. Eat a moderate-to-low amount.

Protein

Because you have used your body to a moderate degree, it is now time to add a moderate amount of protein and vegetables. This is true unless you have made more rigorous movement. Then there is a greater need for more protein—the building and repair foods.

Fats

Accompany moderate proteins and carbohydrates with a moderate amount of good fats, which are also necessary for cell function and protection.

> **Afternoon Un-diet Summary:** Moderate-to-Low Carbs/Moderate Proteins/Moderate Fats

settled into the one comfortable chair in the employees' lounge and promptly fell asleep. Naomi, an assistant to one of the agents, saved her hide a couple of times when she noticed Hope's prolonged absence from the reception area and went to the lounge to wake her up.

Following the birth of her baby boy, Hope sank into a funk that threatened her own well-being along with Adam's. The stress of the last year had taken its toll on her; with her friends away at college, her mother back in her stay-away-from-home-as-much-as-possible routine, and her father and Jacob only God knew where, Hope found little reason to get up in the morning. With Adam still in a bassinet by her bed, she could pretty much go through an entire day without ever leaving her room—until her body started to shut down along with her emotions, and her breasts stopped producing milk. Only fear for Adam's survival got her up, showered, dressed, and down to the supermarket to buy formula for him. Fortunately for her, allowing for pregnancy leave was a corporate policy: her Donald Trump, *Apprentice*-watching boss had long wanted to say "You're fired" to her.

Good Lord, look at me, she thought, catching a glimpse of her reflection in a storefront window one day. Staring back at her was a misshapen, haggard wreck of a woman who looked twice her age. *Ha! I should be getting ready for the sorority Christmas party at Georgia right now, scouting out the oh-so-eligible frat boys to find that one future lawyer, future doctor—who am I kidding? I don't really care*

Evening Food Guide
Carbohydrates
During sleep, you have no need for energy foods, so you don't need to consume high-carbohydrate foods during this time. (Best is carbohydrates only from vegetable sources at night.)

Proteins
You have now used your body for an entire day, so you need a lot of rebuilding and repair protein foods. Additionally, sleep is the time when God created your body to accomplish most of its rebuilding and repair.

Fats
You can accompany a high-protein, low-carbohydrate meal with a larger amount of fats.

Evening Un-diet Summary: Low-to-Zero Carbs/Moderate-to-High Proteins/Moderate-to-High Fats

---

* This is basic nutritionl information for general well-being.

For more extensive information on supplementational nutrition and the Un-diet, see the book *Body by God: The Owner's Manual for Maximized Living* by Dr. Ben Lerner, or visit www.thebodybygod.com.

Another excellent source for diet and nutrition information and for those who have need for a more rigorous nutrition program is www.mercola.com.

what he does as long as he's a future millionaire!—that one guy who would fall completely in love with me and marry me, but not until I've graduated and I'm established in my own career.

Seven years later, Hope was living in a downsized dwelling with her mother and still plugging away at her job as a real estate assistant agent. She had taken the real estate exam, but with work and trying to spend time with Adam, she had yet to pass. Between the craziness of the real estate profession, the small income, and the craziness of Hope's home life, the postpartum depression of seven years before had developed into full-blown clinical depression. On top of that, her doctor had told her that the pain she was having was from something he termed "fibromyalgia" and that the weight she had put on and the fatigue were from what the doctor called a "sluggish" thyroid.

After another working Saturday, Hope drove to pick up Adam from the babysitter feeling guilty and distraught. *I'm twenty-five, and my body is shot. I've been living on coffee—lots of cream and sugar—food from vending machines, and McDonald's. I take more medications than my grandmother, and I can't even remember the last time I relaxed, or had fun, or swam, or did anything for* me. *Not to mention, I'm a lousy mom!*

Whack! A car came to a screeching halt in the trunk of Hope's VW, interrupting her thoughts, pushing her car into the path of oncoming traffic, and generally ruining her day. A string of four-letter words came to Hope's mind, but she was too jolted to say any of them. The next thing she knew, a paramedic was asking her questions: "Do you have any pain? Where? Does it hurt when I press here?" No broken bones, as far as they could tell;

| 7 |

Essential #4:
Optimum Oxygen Levels and Lean Muscle

If a cell's environment contains lowered levels of oxygen, it will accumulate toxins, develop disease, and eventually cause early cell death. The optimum way to have and develop the best intake and usage of oxygen is through regularly moving for sustained periods of time—also known as *exercise*.

More commonly known is that in addition to optimizing oxygen levels, exercise produces muscle. One way to measure health is by how much lean muscle tissue you have compared to fat tissue. Using this measurement, the more muscle you have and the less fat you have, the healthier you are. Many conditions, symptoms, and diseases are set in motion by a body with a low muscle-to-fat ratio.

You were born to move. God created you to hunt for food, build shelter, plant gardens, and fight for your life. But building a hut, killing a boar, and fighting off a bear are no longer parts of everyday life. As a result, movement today has become a rarity, sometimes occurring consistently only when a person walks from the computer to the refrigerator.

Every vital system in your body that keeps you alive—your heart, lungs, spinal cord, muscles, and arteries—requires that you move on a consistent basis. They need this to function properly or, in some cases, to even function at *all*.

Just as with the food you were created to eat, the *real* wellness model follows the idea that to be in alignment with God's will for our bodies and produce health from the inside out, we must be active. Otherwise we interfere with nature and fail to embrace those things that produce well-being. So, maximum nerve supply allows motion, and adequate nutrition gives you the fuel for motion, but it's up to you to go into motion if you want to receive this fourth necessity of health and happiness.

Everyone eats, but other than using the muscles of mastication (chewing), most people do not use their muscles on a regular basis. While many people believe you *swallow* health, nutrition—even though very important—has been shown to be less important than *exercising*. A study in 1999 of twenty-five thousand men showed that overweight men who are fit are half as likely to die as men who are thin and

no evidence of external bleeding. Placing her on a stretcher, the paramedics supported her neck with a collar and took her to the emergency room.

Once there, she insisted that she was fine—just a bit of tightness in her neck, but otherwise fine. They told her she might really begin hurting later so they wrote her a prescription for a painkiller, a muscle relaxer, and something to help her sleep. "Even if you feel okay," the nurse said, "it's good to take them as a preventive measure."

More drugs and more money on drugs, Hope thought to herself. *I guess if you need them, you need them.*

At the first possible moment, she dug her cell phone out of her purse and decided the only one she could probably reach would be Naomi, who also worked Saturdays and was still at the office. Naomi was a bit annoying, but she'd always been nice to her and had been willing to bail her out of a jam or two before. Besides, it was Saturday, so her mom was out on the town. Who else would come?

After hearing what had happened to Hope, Naomi came right away. The short walk to Naomi's SUV reminded Hope that she had just been in an accident. She was definitely stiff. But at least the X-rays proved there was no internal damage.

"Thanks for coming on such short notice," Hope said. "Would you mind swinging by Walgreen's first? I have three prescriptions to get filled."

"What for?"

"Well, for the pain."

"But just a minute ago, you told me you didn't have any pain."

"I don't."

unfit. "It's pretty clear that if you follow a healthy diet, don't smoke, but are unfit, you are still at high risk of disease and early death," said Steve Blair, author of the study and director at the Cooper Institute in Dallas. While other research shows that exercise does not completely negate all the dangers of obesity, Blair's study does reveal how important it really is to follow Essential #4: Optimum Oxygen Levels and Lean Muscle.

When you consider all of the preservatives, fats, colorings, sugars, and other contaminants in our modern, processed Food by Man diet, you start to see that you'd better get moving now more than ever. Exercise has even been found to be a viable, and at least equally effective, alternative to traditional medical treatment of depression.[42] All of this is why couches don't exist in nature. Hence, to experience Maximized Living, find quick, fun (or at least not so boring and painful) things you can do on a regular basis to keep yourself moving.

Optimum Oxygen Levels

One of the most important forms of movement is aerobic activity. *Aerobic* does not just mean leaping and dancing in tights. The word *aerobic* actually means "motion that requires the use of air/oxygen."

The aerobic cycle kicks in approximately fifteen minutes into a sustained movement that is increasing your heart rate. These movements include such activities as going for a brisk walk, running, bicycling, mowing the grass (with a push mower, not a tractor), raking, skating, or swimming.

Aerobic exercise is also called *cardiovascular* or *cardio exercise*, because it conditions two of the most important muscles in the body: the heart and the lungs. If you regularly perform aerobic (cardio) activities, every function needed for your body to acquire oxygen operates more efficiently.

When you are performing aerobic-level activities, all of the organs, vessels, and glands of the cardiovascular system adapt in a healthy way. They get stronger, more flexible, larger, smaller, or whatever is necessary to increase their efficiency.

The body's most important nutrient is oxygen. Remember, you can go weeks without food (or can at least *survive* for weeks) and days without water, but you can go only a few minutes without oxygen. Exercise "with air" causes the body to take in and handle oxygen more efficiently.

You stay alive by taking oxygen in through the lungs. *Real* wellness, as always, embraces the body's natural need for survival. Once the lungs have the oxygen, the heart and blood vessels pump it out to the rest of the organs. During aerobic activity, the body needs more oxygen than during inactivity, and it needs it faster than usual. That's why, when you do cardio-type movements, you cause your body to *adapt* by increasing the efficiency of the lungs, heart, and blood vessels to take in,

"So why take a painkiller?"

"I guess because they told me to. They told me I'd be in pain later on."

"Yeah, and maybe they're just treating you like a number and trying to clear out the packed waiting room with no regard for what happens to you once they've handed you your drugs and kicked you out the door. Adam's babysitter is over on Cedar, right? Backtracking to Walgreen's is out of our way, and you'll end up having to wait to get three prescriptions filled. Let's just go get Adam and get you home. You've had enough for one day."

This woman could really take charge of a person's life if they let her, couldn't she? I always did think she was a bit strange, especially when she started bringing me sermon tapes from her church and getting on my case about drinking so much coffee. Why does she think she knows more than trained medical professionals?

"But they said I need that medication. I think we should go back and get it, even if it makes me late picking up Adam."

"I always see you taking all those pills at the office; the last thing you need is more drugs. Tell you what—we'll go back and get them if you promise you'll let me put all six of your meds into a beaker and shake it up to see what happens. Bet you anything it'll explode. Just like they'll do when they hit your stomach and all those gastric juices get thrown into the mix. Did they check to see if the medications you are taking can mix with all of the new drugs they prescribed without some sort of dangerous reaction? Let me tell you something, girlfriend: you're a bad science experiment just waiting to happen."

"All right, all right. You win." Hope just wanted to get Adam

deliver, absorb, and store oxygen. In essence, you become a highly efficient oxygen-acquiring machine.

Health-care professionals working from a wellness perspective always seek to put people on a safe, personalized, regular cardiovascular exercise program for the vital benefits of fat reduction, improved oxygen levels, and enhanced cardiovascular performance. Regrettably, many well-meaning physicians will actually recommend avoiding exercise if people have cardiovascular challenges rather than create a beginning program that will work to create more *aliveness.*

Choking Yourself to Death?

When you fail to acquire optimum oxygen levels in the body, you interfere with the body's ability to meet basic oxygen demands. Instead of being a mean, lean, oxygen-efficient machine, your system begins to struggle with its ability to take in, store, carry, and absorb its most important nutrient. This means having higher levels of carbon monoxide waste in the body, fewer functional blood vessels, and a smaller, weaker heart that beats harder and faster because it is pumping less blood per beat.

As a result of less aerobic activity, the body, which needs oxygen to survive, is less oxygenated; in other words, it is literally *choking to death.*

Signs of Poor Oxygen Acquisition (Choking to Death)
Recognize any of these symptoms?

- Fatigue
- Injury
- Memory loss
- Joint and muscle pain
- Infection
- Sleep disorders

- Low blood sugar
- Depression
- Problems absorbing fat
- Decreased libido
- More difficult menstrual symptoms

Outside-in warning: as you can see, many of the common symptoms and diseases people suffer from are due to a lack of movement and insufficient oxygen.

The risk is that using an outside-in approach, people seek doctors to diagnose these symptoms as a "disease" and prescribe drugs. In reality, from an inside-out point of view, it's recognized that you don't have a disease, but dis-ease due to exercising below required levels for good health. You don't need drugs; you need to move . . . briskly and regularly.

When you are ill, ask yourself, *Do I really have an illness requiring drugs and*

and go to bed. She'd try to get someone else to take her for her medications in the morning.

"Good. That's right where I want you. Because what I'm going to say next is something you're not going to like."

Uh-oh. Here we go again.

"I know what you're thinking—*Here we go again. Naomi's going to go off on one of her lectures about wellness and some sort of wacky healer.*" Naomi pulled out of the parking lot, steering the SUV in the opposite direction from Walgreen's.

"All right, just go on and get it over with. I'm too drained to argue."

"Look, I'm not going to lecture. You've heard it all before. But you'll realize tomorrow morning that you're going to need help, and it's not the kind the ER or your family doctor can give. Have you ever been in a car accident before?" she asked, not waiting for an answer. "Let me tell you, accidents are always worse than you think they are. You're going to be in bad shape come morning. Plus, I'm sure damage has been done to your spine."

"But the doctor said that the X-rays were negative."

"There was nothing broken," Naomi said, "but everything's got to be out of alignment. There are also lots of little things you can't see on X-rays like ligaments and tendons that get damaged and need help in order to heal properly. I'm going to go home and pray that you heal, but I'm also going to pray that you find the right person to help you heal. And take lots of Vitamin C tonight—you have some, right? If not, I can give you—"

"Yeah, yeah, I have some," Hope lied, wondering what kind of wacko takes Vitamin C instead of professionally prescribed medications.

surgery, or have I caused my body to lack health? Do I need to follow the essentials of the Natural Health and Happiness System so that I can cause my body to produce health?

No Pain and Boredom Necessary

I have found that the major reason most people quit or simply *refuse* to move regularly for extended periods of time (aerobically exercise) is that it looks too painful, or past experience tells them that it truly *is* too painful. When you ask someone why he does not jog, walk, or bike to get healthier or lose weight, he will often tell you that he has a knee, hip, or foot injury, or some other sort of pain or problem. Even experienced exercisers will often skip the cardiovascular portion of their exercise program because it just sounds as if it's going to hurt.

If it's not the pain that keeps people away from cardio, it's usually the boredom. Nonetheless, the truth is that if you find the right activities, do them with friends and family, and perform them at a moderate, fat-burning rate, you may really begin to enjoy them.

Research shows that that brisk, moderate physical activity provides up to 50 percent reduction in your chance of forming Parkinson's and many forms of cancer and causes improved function in all metabolic activities.[43] On the contrary, avoiding movement can produce the opposite effect, or poorer function and decreased immunity.

Optimum Lean Muscle

One of the many preposterous aspects of the weight-loss phenomenon is the idea of dieting without exercise. You've seen the ads. Lounging around the house eating Big Macs, yet losing inches, sounds wonderful, but the reality is that losing weight without increasing muscle means only that you'll fit in a smaller coffin. There are a whole lot of skinny people in the cancer and heart disease wards. You do not have a weight problem just because you weigh too much; you have a weight problem because you have too much body fat.

It is not only how much you weigh that causes you to develop disease; it is how much body fat you have compared to how much muscle you have. One of the many aims of exercise is to increase the amount of real muscle and decrease the amount of loosely packed muscle, or what we call *fat*. High body-fat-to-muscle ratios negatively affect organ function, hormone balances, immune control, brain activity, and blood chemistry, and that makes you more sensitive to potentially hazardous food elements such as sugar and cholesterol.

Aerobic exercise has an impact on building lean muscle, but to really help your cause you need *anaerobics,* or "exercise without air." For muscles to become stronger, leaner, and better developed, you have to apply resistance to them. While many people put resistance only against their gluteus muscles (the ones they sit on), to create actual

They picked up Adam, who made it known that he thought his mom looked awful, and Naomi dropped them off at the Samuelses' house with an order: "Call me tomorrow morning when you can't get out of bed. Keep your cell phone on the nightstand."

Good grief! She might be the most helpful lunatic I've ever known! I'd think she was a complete lunatic if I hadn't seen with my own two eyes how competent she is at work. I'm exhausted, must be the stress from the whole thing. I wish I had gotten some of those prescription muscle relaxers. That and a glass of wine and I'd be out. Although I'd also probably not be able to wake up for two days, and I've got to spend time with Adam tomorrow. I'll give Naomi that. Besides, I feel like I can pass out pretty easily right now on my own.

When the human alarm—Adam—woke her in the morning, Hope could not move. She felt as if someone had glued her head to the bed and an elephant was sitting on her chest.

Her first thought was, *Adam—I need to feed him and spend time with him today, and it hurts to blink. How could I let Naomi talk me out of getting those prescriptions filled? That woman! And it's Sunday morning so Mom, the great socialite, won't be up for hours. That witch!* She had no choice; she called Naomi. "Medication, please! I need drugs. Lots and lots of drugs!"

Naomi, however, would hear none of it. She immediately responded, "No drugs. I'm coming to get you right now and take you to my doctor."

That nut! Hope thought. *I'm not sure what I've done to deserve all this, but I think the whole world really is out to get me. What kind of crazy doctor could Naomi be talking about?*

muscles you must adapt some sort of force. Remember, God gave you muscles that were supposed to be digging, climbing trees, and wrestling a lion from his prey, not simply cracking open a beer. If you do not regularly put your muscles under some strain, you again work against the intentions of nature and interfere with what it takes to have vital health and *real* wellness. With time and pressure, lean-muscle-mass-to-body-fat ratios go up, in addition to creating a stronger, more shapely body—which isn't bad either.

The most effective way to create pressure against the muscles and get predictable results is through a properly applied weight-lifting program using machines, weights, bands, or any other form of resistance equipment.

Some Simple, Natural Forms of Movement

Thinking of normal, natural ways of moving that are more pleasing to perform, compatible with your body, and fit well into your life makes regularly exercising—and creating lean muscle—easier. Look at it this way: children can play on a playground and get several hours of aerobic and resistance training while having fun and not even realizing they are getting a workout. What can you do to get exercise every day, the way you were created to, and enjoy yourself at the same time? Here's a starter list:

- Cut the grass.
- Walk.
- Bike.
- Paint a fence.
- Jog.

- Go hiking.
- Build a deck.
- Swim.
- Play basketball or tennis.
- Carry your own golf clubs.

The Power of Ten Minutes

One of the most encouraging discoveries in the history of exercise was one called *the power of ten minutes*. In as little as ten minutes, your body begins to function better and increase metabolic processes, with benefits that can last as long as twenty-four hours.

In addition, ten minutes twice a day—a morning power walk while praying or meditating, followed by an evening bike ride with the family—has all the benefits of twenty straight minutes of activity. Just about anyone can find ten minutes a day for physical activity.

Spend at least ten minutes in some kind of physical activity, and you will enjoyably, safely, comfortably, and easily feel better, trim down, and enhance your health. Keep moving!

For resistance training (weight lifting), there are types of workouts

Ah! A ray of light broke through the darkness of her despair: *It's Sunday! No doctor works on Sunday!*

"Naomi, I am sure that man will not be in his office today. Please, just get me to Walgreen's, Wal-Mart, Eckerd's, Kmart—any mart, just somewhere that sells pills."

"Not so fast. My doctor will come see you after he gets out of church. I called him last night and told him all about the accident and warned him about your stubborn self. He said this was very important, and he'd do everything he could to help. So there. I'm on my way over to help you get dressed and get you over there. Don't worry—I'll play with Adam in the waiting room while you're with the doctor."

Doctor or witch doctor? I need a real doctor, with lots of drugs. Great. Just great.

Barely able to hold her head up, Hope approached the doctor's office. When she looked up at the door and saw the sign, she was furious. "Chiropractor! You absolute maniac! I can barely move and I'm obviously seriously injured. I need the care of a real physician."

"As you said," Naomi said, smiling, "no doctor works on Sunday." Naomi pushed Hope through the door, knowing she was too weak to fight, and said, "Besides, not only is he a real physician, he's the only hope for Hope."

Practically stumbling through the door, Hope lifted her head up just enough to come face-to-face—or face-to-chest—with a guy wearing a fishing hat, shorts, a T-shirt, and flip-flops. Her first thoughts were, *Very unprofessional—cute, though.*

"Hi—I can tell by the angle of your head and the fact that Naomi forced you to be here that you must be Hope. Excuse my

that take only two to three minutes to do an exercise for a given body part. These programs show you how to apply steady force to your muscle groups in a way that helps them to get leaner and stronger in no time. Using these methods, you can do a three-body-part workout—in only ten minutes.

For more information on ten-minute aerobic activities and three-minute resistance training programs, ask your *real-*wellness provider, see *Body by God: The Owner's Manual for Maximized Living,* or go to www.thebodybygod.com.

You Have to Move—Make No Bones About It!

Contrary to popular outside-in, mechanistic opinions on wellness, the best way to build strong bones as you age is not through swallowing as much pasteurized dairy product as you can handle and taking estrogen, Fosamax, and other antiosteoporosis drugs every day for the rest of your life. With the chemicals and hormones present in nonorganic cow's milk, all of these recommendations are diametrically opposed to Essentials #1 and #3 for Maximized Living.

The skeleton, like the muscles, gains strength or weakness depending on how much pressure is applied. When you move, you place pressure on the bones, and they adapt by building up more bone tissue. The more pressure, the more bone.

For example, martial artists will actually spend time tapping their fists against a brick or other hard surface to build up extra bone in their hands and wrists so they can deliver a more intense blow.

Eating foods that contain more calcium, magnesium, and other minerals is important for building bone; however, it is *movement* that actually causes these elements to be laid down on the bone. Research at Penn State and Johns Hopkins was reported in *USA Today* on June 10, 2004, showing that exercise is significantly more important than calcium intake for developing and keeping strong bones.

While you do lose some bone density as you get older, the most significant reason for diminished bone mass is people's natural tendency to stop moving and to break other wellness rules as they get older. If you keep moving, bone keeps regrowing.

When women lack regular movement, this loss of bone is so severe it can be not only unhealthy but also deadly. Due to the hormonal changes women go through as they age, without exercise the bones can become so weak and brittle that they lead to fractures and even death. In fact, the American Red Cross and Centers for Disease Control now report that falling is the number one cause of injury and death among the elderly.

clothes. Naomi said you might not show up so I changed into my fishing gear. I was going to try and catch dinner, but I'm glad you got here instead. You're far more important than the fish, and I can always hit the seafood department after we're done. I'm Dr. Elijah Knight. But my friends just call me Dr. Eli."

When Eli had stood as a young boy staring at his changed X-rays, something profound happened inside him. Eli decided to be a chiropractor. His choice of that career ran deeper than mere desire; on some level, even at his young age, he knew it was his calling, his mission—a purpose for his life. Deep in his heart, it was as if God Himself had said to him, "You've been helped; now go and help others." That kind of experience was hard to deny and even harder to ignore. Even though Eli didn't understand everything about it, he knew it was real.

In his senior year of college, Eli applied to chiropractic college. He was never as happy in his life as when he received his acceptance letter.

Now, seven years later, Elijah Knight was a bona fide doctor of chiropractic, a graduate of Life College of Chiropractic, thanks to a combination of scholarships, student loans, some great mentors, and several part-time jobs. He became not just another doctor, but a selfless healer who made house calls at midnight, spent his evenings adjusting hospitalized patients, and offered free care to residents of homeless shelters and orphanages.

Eli wanted to save and transform lives, just as his had been transformed. He knew that in today's world, people needed a cutting-edge wellness leader. Unlike Doc Abe, a highly skilled chiropractor but a little old-school, Eli went through intensive "new-school"

Vestibular (balance) problems are created by interference in the central nervous system. With falls being the number one cause of death among the elderly, chiropractic care for the reduction of central nervous system interference is a true lifesaver.

Exercise—Wow!

From the moment you start to exercise, you boost the vital performance of the body. Instantly, many of the health dysfunctions occurring inside you (due to being out of shape) begin to improve. Therefore, if you exercise for ten minutes, then for ten minutes you are healthier. For some, that may be the only ten healthy minutes they've ever had. Wow!

Exercise is drug-free, true health care. It

- improves heart function
- lowers blood pressure
- reduces body fat
- elevates bone mass
- prevents brain deterioration
- slows, reverses effects of aging
- decreases total and LDL ("bad") cholesterol
- raises HDL ("good") cholesterol
- raises energy level
- enhances and balances hormone production
- aids sleep
- increases stress tolerance
- eliminates toxins
- reduces depression
- controls or prevents diabetes (blood sugar issues)
- decreases the risk of injury to the muscles, joints, and spine

At any time you decide to improve your behavior and make lifestyle changes, they make a difference from that point on. Maybe not right away. It's like slamming on the brakes. You do need a certain skid distance.

—DR. JEFFERY KOPLAN,
director of the Centers
for Disease Control and Prevention

preparation and training. He acquired a bachelor's degree in the science of nutrition before going to chiropractic college, became a certified master personal trainer, had advanced training on chiropractic for pediatrics and pregnant women, and was certified in six different chiropractic adjusting techniques.

Now, due to an emergency call from one of his patients, Naomi, he had just canceled his fishing trip and was standing in front of not just another patient, but the next life he planned to affect, save, and transform. The next step to fulfilling his dream of a better, healthier world.

"Here—sit down," he said, guiding Hope toward a chair in the empty waiting room. "You must be in a tremendous amount of pain. We can talk here. Now, tell me what happened to you when you had the accident."

"Well, I was waiting at a red light when this car came up from behind—"

"No, I mean what happened to *you*—to your body. Did your head hit the windshield? Did your chest hit the steering wheel?" he asked, gently pushing her dark brown hair aside to get a better look at her forehead. She shook her head, the hair falling back into place—or rather, back out of place.

"How about your knees? Did they hit the dashboard?"

"Not that I remember. I don't know, maybe they did. And maybe my head did hit the steering wheel. I don't know."

"Were you wearing your seat belt? Did the airbags deploy?"

"No. I mean, yes. I mean, I had the airbags disabled after I heard about all those people that were injured. And the seat belt—well, yes, I was wearing it, but it was loose. I didn't want it to wrinkle

Essential for Maximized Living #2, Maximum Nerve Supply, plays an integral and preliminary role in the amazing benefits of exercise. Without appropriate nerve supply, the organs affected by exercise will not respond appropriately and optimally. Nerve supply is completely reliant on the alignment and posture of the spine. If your spine is poorly placed and positioned (vertebral subluxation), then exercise can speed up bone and soft tissue deterioration, cause damage to the vertebrae and nerves, make you more susceptible to joint or muscle injury, and make you more vulnerable to serious spinal cord trauma following a fall or collision. Athletes or those beginning or maintaining an active exercise program should be evaluated by a chiropractor for spine and joint dysfunction.

my outfit, because I was supposed to show a house yesterday afternoon." Panicked, Hope looked at Naomi playing with Adam across the room. Naomi nodded in assurance—"I took care of that for you," she mouthed to Hope.

Relieved, she looked back at Dr. Eli, still wearing his fishing hat and still looking more like a charter boat captain than a doctor. *Am I hallucinating or what?* she wondered.

"Do you think you can hold your head up long enough to take some X-rays?"

"Can't you just get them from the hospital? They took some yesterday."

"No, Hope. I need to look at some very specific areas of your spine for the kind of damage they would not have thought to look for at the hospital. For the time being, think of me as a spine specialist, if that helps you to understand why you have to go through this again. I know you feel battered right now, and I promise I'll make this as easy on you as I possibly can. Here, hold on to my arm, and we'll go get those X-rays taken."

This is weird, way weird. This place doesn't look like a real doctor's office, Hope thought as Eli guided her down a hallway and past a series of open treatment rooms. *It's too—too—cheerful to be a doctor's office!*

"Look, I just don't know yet," Hope said the following day, in answer to yet another of Naomi's persistent questions. "I agree that he seemed to really listen to me and care about what I had to say. It was different from my hospital experience. But the jury's still out. He didn't even do anything. He said he had to study and measure my X-rays before anything could be done. And I'm still in

| 8 |
Essential #5:
Peace of Mind and Strong Relationships

Health is a state of: (1) physical well-being, (2) mental well-being, and (3) social well-being. Essential #5 for Maximized Living is composed of the second and third definitions.

A negatively stressful life will rarely lead to a healthy body. A struggling, desperate individual will be very likely to experience illness despite following other important rules of wellness. Even if you could be healthy while experiencing stress, you'd just be a healthy *miserable* person, and who wants that?

On the other hand, someone who has peace of mind, knows who he is, is gaining victory over struggles, and is experiencing loving relationships is very likely to enjoy ongoing good health. If you're not having a good time living in your body, it's hard for that body to be well or for you to call it healthy. The fact is, you cannot separate your wellness from your emotions. Every feeling you have affects some part of your body.

All feelings create physiologic change. Skin, heart rate, digestion, joints, muscle energy levels, the hair on your head, and endless cells and systems you don't even know about change with every emotion. These changes can be called the *stress response.*

Celebrations and tragedies alike cause a stress response in the body. Some stress is unavoidable. The only stress-free people on the planet can be visited at any local cemetery. On the other hand, stress becomes negative only when

- your *response* to it is negative;

- the feelings and emotions are inappropriate for the circumstances; or

- the response lasts an excessively long time.

Feeling continuously overwhelmed, overpowered, and overwrought from circumstances is not God's grand scheme for your life. Therefore, just like drugs, subluxations, a man-made diet, and a lack of exercise, these toxic emotions can radically interfere with well-being.

pain! Also, what's this about spending an hour Tuesday night at that—what's it called—the Doctor's Report meeting? I don't have that kind of time or money."

"Just give it a try—that's all I ask," Naomi said. "In fact, give it just two weeks. I can help you work your schedule around the appointments. It's not like it is at other doctors' offices—you don't have to be there very long. You can drop Adam off here on Tuesday night. My daughter can watch him, and I'll go with you to the Doctor's Report. And stop worrying about the money. He has options, and it's worth it. Besides, the Doctor's Report is free."

Well, she could hardly argue with any of that. Adam loved having Naomi's daughter babysit for him. Plus, she'd feel a whole lot less awkward if Naomi went to the Doctor's Report with her.

"All right, I'll go and I'll give it a try—for a couple of weeks. Thanks for the offer to have your daughter babysit. See you at work tomorrow," Hope said, hanging up the phone and lying back down on the bed.

What was it Dr. Eli said? Something about how some chiropractors hold these sessions so patients will be better educated about their health. I really don't want to learn more about my health as much as I just want him to take away the pain. He did really seem to be concerned, and he did cancel his fishing trip. I guess I do owe him a chance to explain what he does. He certainly wasn't a voodoo doctor the way I thought chiropractors were.

Still a committed cynic who was determined to prove that this was an utter waste of time, Hope silently critiqued Eli's every move and every word from the moment he started the Doctor's Report orientation on Tuesday night. Her mother had warned her not to

The Stress Effect

When negative stress reactions occur, the resulting systemic chaos has several very specific physical effects on your body's numerous organs and operating systems. Catecholamines, or "stress hormones," are released through emotionally traumatic incidents—like someone making you angry, your favorite team losing in the playoffs, getting dumped by someone you're dating, or getting laid off from work.

Stress is an insidious issue. The deeper you look into it, the more trouble you find it causes. It's simply impossible to have an emotion without it effecting your body. Look at the power of the placebo. One of the most frustrating facts for drug and surgical researchers is that studies almost always reveal similar or same results from placebo (fake) surgeries or drugs when compared to the actual ones. This is particularly true of mind-altering drugs like Prozac, Zoloft, Paxil, etc., where placebos tend to fair just as well.

The mechanism of stress is designed to keep you alive. Fear and anxiety are important survival mechanisms. Unfortunately, when triggered inappropriately, as is the case about 99.9 percent of the time in today's world, your own survival mechanism can be the very instrument of your own undoing.

When the feeling of stress becomes evident in your body, the pituitary launches the fight-or-flight system. This is the physiological power to fend off danger or flee from it. Stress hormones in the bloodstream constrict the blood vessels, forcing digestion energy to nourish the extremities so that you can do battle—or run like crazy. Blood flow to the visceral organs is inhibited so that your arms and legs can work at their greatest capacity. The problem is, for most people, when you're stressed you're not really fighting off a bear or a mugger, you're typically sitting at dinner or in your car. During the stress response, your organs cannot function normally because your blood's nourishment is moving away from them. You're trying to think, digest a steak, grow knew cells, or interact socially . . . and meanwhile all of your blood is in your feet.

Stress literally turns the priorities of your body upside down. Where the priority should be relaxed, healthy blood vessels and organ and cellular function, during flight or fight it becomes running and punching.

There is a direct link between negative stress and the dysfunction of various parts and systems within the body. Stress reactions alter the digestive system, overstimulate certain glands while understimulating others, affect heart function, and change breathing patterns. As a result, stress has an actual, measurable negative impact on physiologic entities such as blood pressure, cholesterol, electrolytes, brain chemistry, sleep cycles, muscle tone, joint function, blood sugar levels, and hormone balance. Abnormal changes can lead to all kinds of unwanted side effects such as

get sucked into anything, and her words echoed in Hope's head as she found a seat in the "classroom"—a converted part of the waiting room whose walls were lined with inspirational artwork and technical posters outlining the specific needs of chiropractic.

Yeah, I know that—tell me something I don't *know,* she thought as Dr. Eli began talking about diseases that kill Americans prematurely, such as cancer and heart disease, and statistics, such as diabetes quadrupling, and so on. Somehow, though, after a few minutes, he started to get to her. Her thoughts drifted momentarily to Bill Simons at work, who had just been diagnosed with lung cancer. What a shame. And Martha Anderson, her mom's friend who just had a mastectomy; and Aunt Betty, who called last week to tell Mom she found a lump.

Hope suddenly realized Dr. Eli wasn't just talking about statistics. He was talking about *people,* just like the people she knew: her cousin, who had been on insulin all her life; her grandmother in Colorado, now in the advanced stages of Alzheimer's; countless people she had known who died following a heart attack or a stroke. *Disease certainly does seem to be raging out of control. Something's not adding up.*

Hope sat up a little straighter and began paying closer attention. But still, what on earth did all this have to do with her back? Or her accident? Both Naomi and Dr. Eli had assured her she'd understand by the time the meeting was over. She couldn't exactly say she was convinced, but she had to admit she was becoming intrigued.

"What do you think the number three killer of Americans is? Anyone have an idea?" Dr. Eli's voice interrupted her thoughts as he asked the twenty or so patients a question that clearly had them stumped.

weight gain, depression, advanced aging, heart disease, arthritis, cancer, intestinal dysfunction, and any number of neurological or immune-related conditions.

Stress of all kinds zaps nutrient storage by sending your glands and nervous system into hyperdrive. This can lead to the depletion of certain key vitamins, such as B and C, along with other antioxidants. This will affect the immune system, leading to common outward side effects of stress, such as flu symptoms, cold sores, skin problems, pain, and illness. *Additionally, as with all deterrents to good health, like drugs, subluxation, and a toxic diet, stress causes an unacceptable internal environment for cellular survival.*

From an outside-in paradigm, doctors would call these bad results of stress "sickness" and write prescriptions. The best prescription, however, would be one for dealing with the cause of stress rather than taking something for the side effects.

Prozac Nation

The challenges of surviving on earth are numerous and often overwhelming. When the pressure becomes chronic and coping gets more and more challenging, it's now common to seek the help of a physician. A physician that recommends drugs, not Maximized Living.

When people face hopelessness and despair, nothing could be more appealing than a diagnosis and a quick chemical solution. Millions of anxious, chronically unhappy people have found sanctuary in antidepressant medications. To even suggest to someone who believes his life has been "saved" by antidepressants such as Zoloft, Paxil, Wellbutrin, or Prozac that these drugs are dangerous, or that there are alternatives, is to take your life in your own hands. This is completely understandable for someone who feels that his past misery has been finally pacified due to the miracles of modern medicine and what has been labeled a "chemical imbalance." No one wants his life preserver questioned when he truly feels it's keeping him afloat in rough waters.

More than thirty million Americans—one in every ten—have taken Prozac, Zoloft, Paxil, or a similar antidepressant.[44] Very few of these patients are aware of the dangers these drugs cause as a result of the brain's reaction to artificially boosting serotonin levels. These side effects include neurological disorders, such as disfiguring facial and whole-body tics that can indicate brain damage; sexual dysfunction in up to 60 percent of users; debilitating withdrawal symptoms, including visual hallucinations, electric-shock-like sensations in the brain, dizziness, nausea, anxiety; and a decrease of antidepressant effectiveness in about 35 percent of long-term users.[45] In addition, investigation and research are beginning to shed light on the direct link between these drugs and suicide and violence, particularly among children.[46]

"Traffic accidents?" an older woman asked after an uncomfortable silence. No, it wasn't accidents.

"Probably other accidents, like fires or drowning or poisoning, right?" someone else suggested. Nope, not those either.

"Old age!" a white-haired man shouted. A few people chuckled.

Naomi raised her hand but didn't wait to be called on. "Medication and medical mistakes," she said confidently.

"That's right," Dr. Eli said. The audience was visibly impressed with her knowledge. "Hey, don't feel bad. She's a veteran member of this office. She'd better know the right answer!"

Hope watched as the expression on Dr. Eli's face suddenly turned serious. "In fact, some studies show that medication and medical mistakes are the number one killer. As many as a million patients a year die prematurely due to medications and medical error, some because they were given the wrong medication, but many who were given the right medication as well. And it's not always prescription drugs; some people are slowly poisoning themselves with over-the-counter drugs."

Dr. Eli paused to allow all that to sink in. Hope looked over at Naomi, who was blinking back the tears; Naomi and her mother had spent the last ten years grieving the early death of Naomi's dad, Charlie, the love of her life. Charlie's death had been caused by a medication that had just recently been pulled off the market.

"Let's get back to the issue of drugs for a minute," Dr. Eli continued. "Where do doctors learn about the medications they prescribe for you?"

"At medical school," Hope said, surprised at the sound of her own voice speaking out in a public meaning. "I mean, doctors

Like all drugs, antidepressants are necessary for some percentage of the people who take them. Dr. Elio Frattaroli, famed psychiatrist, psychoanalyst, and author of *Healing of the Soul in the Age of the Brain*, explained, "Modern Psychiatry's theory that mental illness is a chemical imbalance and that all inner [mental and spiritual] experience is a byproduct of brain activity—the so-called Medical Model—views human beings essentially as biological puppets, controlled by the strings of DNA and brain wiring, without free will or higher consciousness. Focusing exclusively on brain and behavior, it denies the spiritual element in humans . . . not only as if it didn't matter, but as if it didn't even exist. It promotes the delusional expectation that we can eliminate suffering and achieve a state of contented normalcy simply by taking a pill. It subverts our ideals of moral responsibility by encouraging us to rationalize anything that disturbs us within ourselves as the accidental product of an abnormal brain state: My neurotransmitters made me do it."

What biological psychiatry says today is that "if my brain chemistry makes me do it, then everything wrong with me has a solution that lies outside me." This may be the most dangerous kind of outside-in thinking that exists in our culture today. When diagnosed with a chemical imbalance, you're told you are damaged goods with no hope of ever being normal. Your personality and your character are permanently flawed, and mind-altering drugs are your only way out.

What's worse, that sends a message opposing perhaps the noblest of human efforts: overcoming your problems by the strength of the human will, which always seeks higher ground and an improved mental and spiritual outlook on life.

In the past, no doctor treated the kinds of common anxiety and depression we see today with medication. Counseling from a mental-health professional or clergy was the primary modality of care. According to psychiatrist Peter Kramer, author of the best seller *Listening to Prozac*, since the advent of Prozac and Prozac-like drugs, "the bar has been lowered for what constitutes an emotional disorder that needs drugs, and it has been raised for what constitutes successful treatment." Where the measure of successful treatment was once alleviation of debilitating pain, today patients want to feel, as Kramer phrases it, "better than well."

Antidepressants are another case of medical science using a simple quick fix to cover the symptoms of a complex problem. A comprehensive program—including a healthy nervous system, exercise, sound nutrition, strengthened relationships, natural supplementation geared toward these concerns, and increased self-knowledge through counseling and study should certainly be of primary consideration with or over the use of drugs with this kind of track record.

Incidentally, studies have shown that counseling and even placebos are as effective as antidepressants.[47] Nevertheless, counseling doesn't pack the quick-fix punch for which doctors and patients are looking.

Looking to and believing you can get mentally/emotionally healthy and overcome is always the first step and should at the very least be part of, *real* emotional *wellness.*

know the best medication to give for a certain problem from what they learned in school. Like Prozac is the best drug for depression and that kind of thing."

"Well, not quite," he said. "It's unlikely your doctor learned about Prozac at Harvard. In fact, Prozac and many of the other new drugs that are regularly prescribed today may not have even existed when your doctor was in med school. What actually happens is that the pharmaceutical companies provide literature, seminars, and salespeople to educate the doctors on the newest drugs, often offering incentives for doctors to then prescribe these medications. I mean, don't you always walk out of a doctor's office with a prescription of some sort?"

Heads nodded all around the room.

"Understand this, though—it's not necessarily the doctor's fault. Patients don't feel as if they've gotten their money's worth, or that the doctor is really doing anything for them, if they don't walk out with a prescription. Patients want answers and solutions—*now*. They don't want to be just sent home and told not to worry about it and that things will get better in time on their own."

Pretty much everyone in the room let out a sigh as Dr. Eli took another long pause. "We have it backward in this country. In other countries, drugs are given as a last resort. In this country, drugs are given as a first form of treatment."

Eli told his story of how many drugs and visits to emergency rooms he had when he was a child. Hope almost felt as if she was going to cry when she thought of little Eli gasping for his life. He then shared how a chiropractor had restored his health and saved his life.

FOUR STEPS TO OVERCOMING STRESS, ANXIETY, WORRY, DEPRESSION, AND FEAR:

1. Anger Management

2. Peace Management

3. Reprogramming Perceptions

    a. The Art of Overcoming

    b. Moving from Pain to Purpose

4. Time Management

Anger Management

We've all been there—unfortunately, some more regularly than others.

The *Journal of Circulation* reported in May 2004 that people with normal blood pressure and with higher scores on an assessment of their anger traits (with the resulting negative stress and anxiety) are nearly three times more likely to have a heart attack. Even those whose anger is moderate face a significant risk of illness and death from coronary heart disease. In other words, even if you're healthy and routinely test in the normal blood pressure range, if you've got an anger management problem, you put yourself at high risk of not only emotional explosion, but also valve explosion.

Where Does Anger Come From?
The A, B, C, and Ds of Resentment

Hint: it's not from your wife's aunt Maude, your competition, a slow driver in front of you, or even the incompetent kid at the Wendy's drive-thru. Take a look at these different anger "inspirations" and responses.

A. Low Self Esteem

What really is self-esteem? It's confusing because typically "self" has nothing to do with it. Sadly, who you are is usually not based on who you really feel you are, but how others around you perceive you.

When you were and infant and a toddler, you assumed you were loved. As a result, you focused your day on play and screaming or crying to demand what you wanted. You acted as you pleased and fearlessly sought all you desired. Eventually, however, as you began to recognize the judgment of others and what was considered "popular" or "appropriate" in the world, you began to paint a self-portrait of who or what you believed to be you.

"Seriously," Dr. Eli said, pacing back and forth across the front of the room, now looking and sounding very intense, "does anyone here think that the more drugs you take, the healthier you are?"

Everyone laughed. Except Hope.

"What about another form of health care: surgery? Does anyone here think that the more useless organs you can remove, the healthier you are?"

Everyone laughed. Even Hope this time.

"People take drugs because they're scared—very scared. We've been taught that we're feeble, weak, susceptible to getting sick from everything around us, and that we're completely incapable of healing ourselves. But I'm here to tell you that nothing could be further from the truth. God created you to be well, not to be sick.

"Sometimes drugs are absolutely necessary. However, they shouldn't be part of a regular lifestyle, and it's important to understand that while in emergency cases drugs may be vital to keep you alive or get you out of intense suffering, they shouldn't be a regular part of your lifestyle. Not if you want to be healthy."

No wonder Naomi got on my case about all those drugs I'm taking. She's heard all this before. She wouldn't have been much of a friend if she hadn't tried to stop me from filling those other three prescriptions. I feel like a jerk. Hope nudged Naomi: "I'm sorry I gave you a hard time about going to Walgreen's last week," she whispered. Naomi just smiled, obviously happy that Hope was actually listening.

"After all, what is health? Is it an absence of symptoms? Of course not! If it was, then lots of healthy people drop dead of heart attacks or find out they have cancer. Health is when you are not only feeling good; it's when your body is working well. Health is

Suddenly, it was no longer just okay to jump around and speak up for yourself at any time or go for whatever you wanted. As others seemed more capable, more confident, more accepted, and better looking, then you most likely quietly became unhappy with certain parts of yourself.

When we begin no longer accepting ourselves for what we are and want to change anything up to, and even including, becoming someone else entirely, you stop trusting your own opinions and capabilities. To fit in, you do what you should, ought, or must because you no longer feel your own wants and natural behaviors are okay. If you don't trust or like yourself enough, you may even act in such a way as to not be seen at all.

When you don't love you and you're not all right with who you are (low self-esteem), and someone appears to attach or challenge you, you guard and react—or in other words, you get angry. Should you be confident in who you are and accepting of all that is you (high self-esteem), you do not feel threatened or bothered when others judge you. In fact you begin recognizing that most who judge you really are aggravated with something they see in you that reminds them of themselves.

True self-worth comes from a feeling of being unconditionally loved. This love is often measured through the kind of love that God has for you. This type of love is not based on your actions but on your essence—who you really are. Unfortunately, we often feel we're loved only for A's, B's, homeruns, good looks, tight thighs, ripped abs, money, and the other things we accomplish rather than just for who we are. We then work at achieving acceptance. Yet, when we finally get the bank account or the big car, we still feel empty, always wanting more but never having enough. Self-esteem issues are a part of all of the causes of anger. Until you feel loved for who you are and equally love yourself as you are, anger and emptiness will be an ever-present, unwelcomed companion.

B. The Immature Emotional Response

When someone does something to get you angry or stressed out, usually he is in your way; disrupting your schedule; generally not agreeing with your brilliant ideas of how all homes, relationships, and businesses should run; or somehow foiling your plans to rule the world. The truth is, however, that stress and anger do not come from a person, place, or airline. They come from your reaction to them. Therefore, an emotionally mature person does not say to a spouse, friend, fellow employee, waitress, or bank teller, "You made me angry!"

A mature person, who does not want his heart to explode at any minute says something more like this: "Something you did triggered something within me that has caused me to get upset." Then you do the best you can to discuss it so that the other person can become aware of how he's triggering your emotions, and you can

when your body is functioning as close to 100 percent of its God-given potential as possible.

"Drugs, surgery, and doctors try to get you well from the outside in. This may get rid of symptoms or even save your life in the case of emergencies, but it doesn't make you function any better. Really, you function worse. You can truly get well only by doing things to restore normal function—from the inside out."

Dr. Eli continued, "There's only one healer. It's not a pill, a drug, a knife, or a doctor of any kind. It's your body itself, and the God-given intelligence within it. The goal is not to treat the symptom or the disease or to cure the disease. Your body doesn't need any help to get well or to stay well. It just doesn't need any interference to normal function. Chiropractic seeks to remove this interference."

The rest of the evening passed by in a blur. Dr. Eli brought out a model of a spine and explained how it functions and what happens when it doesn't function properly. He talked about his experience as a personal trainer and nutritionist.

"By aligning your spine and your lifestyle with what was the ultimate intention for your body, you begin to move as close to 100 percent function and have your best chance of not only feeling better, but reaching and maintaining your optimum health potential. This is everything you were created to be!" he said.

But Hope had trouble focusing on all he had to say, as her mind kept thinking about all of the chemicals coursing through her veins at that moment. Never had it occurred to her how much damage she might be doing to her body by putting all those drugs into it, not even when Naomi gave her that talking-to after the accident. Despite her distraction, she managed to get the gist of Dr. Eli's talk: the spine

learn a little about yourself as well. This will allow you to eliminate unresolved issues in your life and the constant presence of people around that make you *angry*.

C. Value Judging

A young, single mother is doing everything she can to work and put food on the table. In addition, she goes to church twice a week and attends occasional conferences to build her spiritual foundation and gain new skills to help her succeed in life. When she is at work or church, her mother or best friend watches her kids. Her mother and several members of her family feel she needs to spend more time with her kids and focus less on work, "going to that church," and attending those "useless seminars." As a result of her family's value judging, she feels guilty for being a lousy mom and stays angry at her family. Rather than getting the most out of work, church, and seminars, she is almost constantly in a state of turmoil and stress.

Seeking acceptance is a good way to remain miserable. Your desire for acceptance may not be as obvious as a teenager's; you may not be smoking pot in the bathroom at school or getting your tongue pierced just because all the kids are doing it. But even as adults, we often base the way we measure our self-worth or value on what other people say about us or how the world values us. Many of our decisions come from whether or not we feel our behavior will be deemed socially acceptable or will make others happy.

For those who know you, no explanation is needed. For those who don't, none is possible. Be more concerned with your character than your reputation. Your reputation is who people think you are. Your character is who you really are. While accountability is important, beware of mentors who are really just critics.

D. Unforgiveness

Here is an illustration of the poisonous heart of unforgiveness: a Holocaust survivor once said that if you licked his heart, you'd die from the poison. The truth about refusing to forgive, thinking hateful thoughts, and judging others is that such actions are like drinking poison in an effort to kill your enemy. Unforgiveness hurts only you. No matter how bad the offense against you was, not forgiving the offender causes only yourself—not the guilty party—an early death. So give yourself a gift by giving someone who needs forgiveness a gift he or she doesn't deserve. This will add years to your life and life to your years. It may just change the previously unforgiven person as well.

Essential #5—peace of mind and strong relationships—is critical to good health. Fit, angry people aren't really fit. Whether or not you are a jogger may not matter as much as how you'd like to run someone over. If you're not nice, you're not healthy. Master your emotions so they are no longer your master.

protects the nervous system, which controls the whole body. How all that was related to cancer and heart disease was starting to make sense, but her brain was pretty much on overload by the time the hour was over and she had seen how bad her X-rays really looked.

"Okay, I admit that a lot of what he said made sense," Hope said as she gingerly slid the seat belt across her torso once she and Naomi made it back to the SUV. "I'm convinced enough to go for my adjustment in the morning. But I'm not *completely* convinced. He's got me going three times a week for ninety days and saying it could be twelve to eighteen months before I'm back to a preventative maintenance level. I signed up for the plan, but I still don't know if I can or will do all of that. I'll try. I'm not promising anything. Just don't nag me about this, okay?"

"Okay," Naomi said, smiling, knowing something that Hope did not know—that an amazing transformation was about to begin.

"Good morning!" The man's full head of white hair was a shocking contrast to his dark skin and wiry body. He held the office door open for Hope when she arrived at Doc Eli's for her adjustment the following morning. "There is much wisdom on the whiteboard today," the man said.

"Pardon me?"

"On the whiteboard—right there." He pointed to a dry-erase board hanging on the wall facing the door.

"Oh. Right. Yeah, that is a good saying."

"That is no mere saying," the man said. "That is straight from

Stress Management from the Outside-In, Peace Management from the Inside-Out

Stress management is an outside-in, mechanical concept. The idea of managing stress is similar to the idea of managing or treating symptoms and illness. The outside-in, mechanical disease model treats unwanted health or disease with pills, vitamins, weight loss, surgery, magic potions, leeches, and the like. Stress management involves treating stress with positive thinking or Prozac.

Real wellness through Maximized Living is disease treatment. That's why rather than calling it "stress management," we should call it "peace management." Don't look to fight stress; instead build and manage peace so as to overcome and/or prevent stress.

You attain peace through better managing your life. Life management includes getting control of your time, gaining new perspectives on life, and building strong relationships. Peace is not something you find when your latest crisis is over. In a stressful life, what usually follows stress is the *next* stress. When you manage your life better, stress is more likely to be followed by peace.

Creating peace and strong relationships does not begin by changing everyone and every circumstance surrounding you. Switching locations, jobs, or spouses is typically *not* the answer. While the grass always seems greener (in this case, more peaceful) in someone else's yard, occupation, or relationship, once you get over there, over *there* becomes over *here*. As the adage says, "Wherever you go, there you are." Peace of mind and better associations start (and end) with you. When you change, the atmosphere around you changes. *(Remember, you're not controlled by your genes or fated for anxiety, depression, and stress—you control them.)*

The fact that you are responsible for your mind, your relationships, and your emotions is good news. The easiest thing in the world to change is *you*. People, jobs, and situations may be impossible to change. But you can change right here, right now—in *one minute*. The change starts when you intentionally reprogram your outlook on life.

For more information on peace management, see "The 10 Instructions for Peace by God" in *Body by God: The Owner's Manual for Maximized Living* (page 239).

Are You Programmed for Stress, Depression, and Low Self-Esteem?
Reprogramming Your Perceptions—In One Minute

The way you look at the world and the people who live in it has, in many ways, been programmed. That's why when five eyewitnesses are interviewed following

the Word of God, the prophet Hosea. You have a blessed day!" With that, he left the office and started down the sidewalk, whistling a hauntingly familiar tune that Hope couldn't quite place.

What an unusual man. I wonder if he works here, Hope thought. *Strange accent. The "Word of God"? Must be the Bible. This is weird, Doc Eli talking about God last night and this guy talking about God today. There's a lot of God talk around here. Are they going to expect me to get all religious? My mom said this could be some kind of cult.*

"Good morning, Ms. Samuels," said Caroline, the chiropractic assistant.

"Please, call me Hope." *Might as well get on familiar terms if I'm going to be here three times a week.* "Caroline, that man who just left—does he work here or is he a patient?"

"Oh, him. That's Benjamin," Caroline said. "He beats us here to work every morning. We love it. He always says something to brighten up our day. I wouldn't know how to start a shift without him. I think he's become a kind of spiritual mentor to Dr. Eli."

"But he's a patient," Hope said, accustomed to the standard and distant doctor-patient relationship. "Isn't that unusual?"

"No, not for Dr. Eli," Caroline said, obviously reading Hope's expression. "Dr. Eli loves all his patients. Although I do suspect that Eli may be the son Benjamin never had, and Benjamin may be a father figure for Eli as well."

"Oh. Okay," Hope said, rattled from this whole new experience. Fidgeting with the strap on her shoulder bag, she looked away from Caroline and back to the whiteboard:

an accident, they may describe five different versions of what happened, and it's difficult to determine who's at fault.

That programming has caused you to label things as *good, bad, important, insignificant, fun, boring, safe, dangerous, "It's me," "It's totally not me," worthy, unworthy, popular, unacceptable, right, wrong*—whatever. We're all prone to making these judgments, which on one level are necessary for good decision making—and even, perhaps, our very survival. This natural response, however, can also lead to a miserable life of judging and alienating the people around you. Then you miss out on opportunities that God designed to lead to fulfillment, health, and all that God created you to do.

You've probably seen this scenario on television, which was for a long time a staple story line for sitcoms: a crazy relative from California comes for a visit and drives the family nuts by forcing them to drink carrot juice, eat oatmeal, and practice yoga. To this day, many people carry that image over into real life and label nutritionists, chiropractors, naturopaths, and massage therapists "quacks"—no different from those crazy Californians. Meanwhile, that judgment keeps them from seeking the kind of care that could very well alleviate much, if not all, of their suffering. Many of your failures tomorrow will be due to today's labels.

Labeling has caused people to feel shamed, defeated, or inadequate because they've been judged and now have been programmed to think of themselves as bad, unacceptable, unfair, abnormal, incapable, irredeemable, or less worthy of blessing than the other people on the planet. This low self-esteem, this poor self-image, this mind-set that marks you as "unworthy" is a lie. It's faulty programming. God is not a past-performance God; He's an unconditionally loving, past-forgotten, "Let's step boldly together into the future" God. If you take just *one minute* and change the label you and others have placed on you, you can begin to change your life in that same minute.

A parent who loses a child faces one of the worst tragedies imaginable. Few people would be surprised if that parent ended up clinically depressed or addicted to drugs—prescription or otherwise. By contrast, though, many people who have faced that kind of heartbreaking loss have used their experiences as a catalyst to establish some of the greatest charities, foundations, and support groups in the world today. Those people turned their stress-inducing tragedies into life-changing missions.

Abuse victims, families and loved ones of alcoholics and illegal drug users, severe burn sufferers, ex-convicts, abortion-trauma sufferers, people who have gone bankrupt or failed in business—so many people who have been made to feel like failures have gone on to lead victorious lives and have a positive impact on other people's lives. They were able to do this because they stopped judging and labeling. They stopped viewing their circumstances as tragedies that ended their

> *My people are destroyed for lack of knowledge. (Hosea 4:6 NKJV)*
>
> People do not perish from a lack of information. There are plenty of Bibles, books, tapes, CDs, and DVDs out there.
>
> Biblical knowledge = information + action. It's taking action on what we learn that will improve and even save our lives and change our world.
>
> —Dr. Eli

> Keep your appointments.
> Send a friend.

"Hope? You can come in now," Dr. Eli said, motioning her toward the treatment room and the adjusting table. "I was glad to see you at the Doctor's Report last night. Is there anything you want me to clarify?"

"Well, I think to understand so far," Hope said, lying facedown on the table, once again marveling at the fact that she didn't have to change into one of those awful paper gowns. *This sure beats a regular doctor's appointment in that respect,* she thought. "I guess my main question is why I have to come back three times a week. I know you explained that to me before, but then I got home and started thinking about how hard that's going to be."

"Remember, Hope, correcting your spine with a chiropractor is like going to an orthodontist after your teeth have grown crooked. It takes months for the teeth to move and years for them to be

lives and began seeing them as opportunities to change lives. Yet most of us who suffer stress and depression have not been through such extreme circumstances.

To live in congruency with your God-given nature is to be an overcomer—an overcomer with a purpose and a mission. Moses, David, Joseph, Jesus, Paul (the apostle, not the Beatle), Abraham Lincoln, Ludwig van Beethoven, Ray Charles, Helen Keller, Franklin Delano Roosevelt, Winston Churchill, Martin Luther King Jr., and countless people you've never heard of turned personal tragedy into triumph. Some lived with searing pain and suffered intense moments of loneliness, regret, and despair, and yet they *chose* to not go "quietly into that good night." They *chose* to not give up without a fight. They reprogrammed failure into purpose and setback into mission.

Purpose and mission are the hallmarks of the overcomer.

THE ART OF OVERCOMING
Purpose-Driven: A Human State of Being

by Dr. Patrick Gentempo

Webster's defines purpose as "the object for which something exists." Short and powerful. So, what is the object for which you exist? This can be applied in a broad or a narrow context. You may want to consider why you exist at all. What is your purpose as a parent? What is the purpose of your business?

Defining a purpose is like setting a compass. It gives you direction. The more time you spend checking your compass, the more assurance you have that you will stay on the selected path and get ever closer to your selected destination. Without a compass, you find yourself at any given point by chance, never going in a straight line, never being on any particular course.

I have heard many self-help gurus describe an axiomatic concept referred to as the "pain/pleasure principle." Indeed, famous psychologists have used it to describe human behavior. One psychologist stated, "Man lives in the seeking of pleasure and the avoidance of pain." Some self-help gurus try to categorize their disciples as being either pain-driven or pleasure-driven. Pleasure-driven people make changes in their lives because it is fun and brings them pleasure. They don't like to wait for things to become painful. Pain-driven people will change when the pain of not changing outweighs the pain of changing. All of these concepts relegate humans to the level of the animal—subhuman.

settled into their new position permanently. Your spine didn't get this way overnight—it came from a lifetime of poor spinal health. Having someone ram into you with their Buick didn't help, either."

Seemingly never at a lack for inspiration, Dr. Eli said, "The only thing worse than the pain of discipline is the pain from a life that lacks discipline."

"Is that another one of your Bible verses?" Hope asked, instantly regretting her snippy tone. Trying to save herself, she said, "I saw the other one on the whiteboard. I'm not very religious."

"No"—Eli smiled—"that's an Eli-ism. I'm a Christian, but I don't like to get too religious either."

With that, Eli adjusted her spine and said, "Your power's on—see you in forty-eight hours. And don't forget to do the exercises I showed you before you leave today. And read your newsletter!" Quickly, he walked out of the room.

Naomi had alerted Hope to the newsletter routine: she could expect the staff to hand her a new inspirational newsletter every week. "That's where I draw the line!" Hope had told Naomi. "I've got enough reading to do between work and studying for this impossible real estate license. Besides, I'm a realist. I don't go for positive mental attitude stuff."

Now, however, even though she thought Eli was a combination of a bishop and a boat captain, she had begun to sense that she needed to pay attention to what he had to say. In the privacy of her newly repaired car, she sat in Dr. Eli's parking lot and began reading portions of his most recent newsletter.

Animals roam the earth and instinctually seek pleasure and avoid pain. When they see something good to eat, they eat it. When the weather gets cold or brings rain, they seek shelter. They cannot form abstract concepts and cannot think beyond the range of the moment. By their very nature, they must be pain- and pleasure-driven, and as a result, morality is not an issue with them. It is not immoral for a shark to attack a fish. It is its nature, without choice. Where there is no choice, no morality is possible. What distinguishes humans from all other animals on the earth is that we can form abstract thoughts and think in terms of a lifetime or longer, not merely the range of the moment. We can therefore choose our actions and assess the consequences. Where choices are present, morality is inescapable.

Humans are unique in that they can form the concept of and actualize a life's purpose. It is therefore obvious to conclude that if one is going to live a human experience, then one will have to formulate a purpose. People are not pain-driven or pleasure-driven; they are purpose-driven.

Let's say that you set your life's purpose compass to northwest. As you head northwest, you may encounter some sunny days and some rainy days. You may come face-to-face with a huge mountain or a beautiful meadow. You may walk into a wide and raging river, or take time to sit by a reflecting pond. All of these things may exist along the northwest path. Some of them will bring you pain. Some of them will bring you pleasure. All of them will take you toward your purpose.

If you were pain- or pleasure-driven, you would find yourself heading in a different direction every time you came across a mountain or a river, making no real choices, having no real direction, thinking in terms of the range of the moment, which will usually lead to moral depravity. Anybody can lose sight of his compass once in a while, but people with a purpose will check it and get back on course every time they stray from northwest—or whatever their course might be.

What makes a human being different from any other form of animal on the planet is the ability to choose a purpose. If a cow could choose a purpose for its life, there would be no such thing as McDonald's. Anyone living without a conscious purpose is having a subhuman experience. Be purpose-driven.

The Mission Mind-Set: Moving from Pain to Purpose

History books are filled with stories of people who faced life-threatening illness or injury yet lived into their eighties and nineties too bound to their mission to leave the

> Turn Frustration into Inspiration
>
> *Put an End to Complacency*
>
> . . . frustration causes people to begin dropping out of the race. Enchantment turns into disenchantment, and most people finally just sit down and begin watching life and all the other runners pass them by . . .

"That's me!" Hope cried aloud, quickly looking around to make sure no one heard her. *My fairy tale has been destroyed. It's like I'm in the most important swim meet of my life, and I've dropped out of the race as everyone I know has passed me by.*

> . . . Something occurs that turns a youthful, idealistic, uncompromising dreamer into an old, pessimistic, compromising realist . . .

I'm definitely pessimistic. I'm becoming my mother.

> . . . Once you have tasted freedom, you will never again be content being a slave . . .

Sounds good for people who haven't ruined their lives the way I have, Hope thought. *A kid, no money, no education, and no support—face it—I am a slave. That's what I hate about this positive mental attitude stuff; it works for pie-in-the-sky dreamers like Dr. Eli who had normal parents and were probably born with silver spoons in*

planet. There's something about a purpose that keeps you not just alive, but kicking.

On the other hand, I've heard it said by many people that there is an eerie and common occurrence among people who retire: a tremendous percentage of these people die within the very next year. Perhaps they've left not only their careers but also their missions.

It's hard to imagine someone on a mission chronically unhappy and in need of mood-altering medication. The phrase "on a mission" conjures up an image of someone fired up, energetic, and ready to take on the world. It certainly doesn't paint a picture of someone depressed, fatigued, and hunched over on a bar stool or in a medical waiting room.

While *purpose* is defined as the "object or aim," *mission* is defined as "the sending or self-imposed charge to *perform* a specific duty or service [object or aim]."

Purpose is of critical importance. Your God-given purpose is what you were born to do—*the object or aim for which you exist*. Mission, then, is the performance of that aim or purpose. I generally don't like war-related metaphors, but in this case, such a metaphor works particularly well. A military mission is a sworn duty. There are no intentions or aims, only results—or you die trying. It's not just high calling; it's high commitment. It's not just purpose; it's sworn and lasting purpose. There's focus, there's excitement, and there's a never-stop, never-quit attitude that causes you to learn, adapt, and persevere no matter the circumstance. It's the virtual baby atop a burning building, whom you will stop at nothing to save. Either two lives or none are coming down.

Anytime your life's focus turns to serving yourself, you will find that you are highly susceptible to a lack of motivation, disorder, and sometimes even despair. But when you choose to focus your energy on your mission—your duty to serve others—you will quickly watch your mood elevate along with your energy and enthusiasm.

No one is without their moments of fear, self-pity, and regret. But, sooner or later if you recall that God and others are counting on you to move and function at your best and your attention turns back to those who really need you, you will become inspired and disciplined, and the stress will begin to fade.

From a life perspective, your mission and all of the goals, training, and activities that support it should serve God, family, and whatever it takes to make this a better world. When this encompasses the majority of your waking and dreaming hours, to use more war terms, you will abolish depression, annihilate despair, and be taking a shock-and-awe approach against dis-ease.

Some people think they'd like to be Bill Gates, Tom Cruise, Dan Marino, a rock star, or some other celebrity or famous billionaire. But I would not want to be any of those people until I had a chance to spend some time in their skins, to see the purposes they live for, the missions they're attempting to fulfill, and the evidence of genuine peace in their lives.

their mouths. Hope started to crumple up the newsletter but then smoothed it out, folded it, and stuck it in her purse.

———————

Like clockwork, Benjamin Karume appeared at the door to Eli's office three mornings a week at 6:30.

"So, we have a lot to pray about today?" Benjamin asked as Eli entered the conference room where they met each morning before the other patients arrived. "I hear you have many new patients. We will pray for a partner for you."

"I can handle it. I've moved my sessions at the nursing home to Saturday mornings before visitors get there and before I go to the office, so that frees up an extra hour on Wednesday afternoons for more new patients."

"As I said, we will pray for a partner for you."

"Pray if you like, but I don't need a partner. I'm doing fine. I like keeping busy."

"Kila jambo na wakati wake."

"Is that another one of your Swahili sayings?" Eli's impatience with his friend surprised even him.

"Yes. *Kila jambo na wakati wake:* there is a right time for everything. Do not play when it is time to work. Do not work when it is time to play. Very much like Ecclesiastes. Eli, when will you ever play?"

"I told you I was going to spend the afternoon fishing last Sunday, but something came up."

A One-Minute *Real* Wellness Approach to Fatigue and Depression

Seek, find, and develop your purpose. Follow that up by recognizing that this is a mission God has sent you here to fulfill; then self-impose a sense of duty to fulfill it.

All that's left to figure out is the time. Without time management, there is no stress management, functional family, nutrition, fitness, or trips to the chiropractor. With all of the rushing, there may be time only for medication. Now, however, on a do-or-die mission from God, we accept no excuses, only results. You adapt; you overcome; you start managing your time and stop your time from managing you.

Time Management: The Key to Maximized Living

Managing your time is perhaps the most significant aspect of managing your life. If you had forty-eight hours a day to get things done instead of twenty-four, your stress would already be reduced, you'd eat less fast food, and you'd probably even exercise more. Although it may not appear that way right now, this *is* possible. The time is there; all you have to do is get twice as much use out of your time.

Much of your time is probably centered around handling all the issues and "emergencies" you face with your relationships, your health, your work, and your stressful outlook on life. In a life like that, you end up so focused on just getting *through your day* that you forget about getting *from your day*. The result of that kind of focus is more issues and "emergencies" that use up even more time.

Good time management is what allows this health and happiness system to never fail. Stress management, relationship building, financial increase, appearance enhancement, and stable health are things you attain and maintain only as you do what is necessary to reduce the amount of stress that you experience and to develop a body that doesn't get sick, tired, or out of shape in the first place.

Time management is working from the inside out on your life, instead of working on your life from the outside in. Over time, this will create fewer and smaller issues and emergencies, allowing you to continue focusing more of your time on what you are passionate about and what and who are important to you.

Typically, *you are not managing your time; it is managing you.* You are getting *through* the rush of the day instead of *from* the day. The rushing manages your time as well as controls how you take care of your body and your relationships.

When you woke up this morning, it is likely that the very first things you thought of were not exercise, better nutrition, peace, and stronger relationships. Instead, from the moment you opened your eyes, you were probably thinking of those things that were so urgent they had to be handled *immediately*. Then you rushed on.

"My friend, you work too hard. You tell me it is because you care so much about your patients. I believe you do care for them. But you do not care for yourself. You've never taken a vacation, much less a day off the entire time you've been in practice.

"You do not know yourself and what you really want. I am speaking to you in this way because I care for you. God cares for you. He wants you to enjoy all of the life He has given you. He does not want you to be so—what is the word you use?—so driven. Particularly if you are not driving in the right direction. I know you want to save the world, but who is going to save you? We will pray for a partner for you."

With that, Benjamin prayed for Eli, who knew better than to object. Like clockwork, at 7 AM Benjamin said the final amen and headed out the front door for the Grace of God Community Church two blocks away. Not to pray—though he would do that constantly for the rest of the day—but to begin his workday as parish handyman.

"Good morning, Hope! Are you ready to have your power turned on?"

"I'm not sure if this is going to work. That last adjustment made me pretty sore."

"That's great!" Dr. Eli said.

"Great?" Hope returned. "Why would that be great? I'm here to get rid of pain, not get more pain."

"Hope, no one wants you out of pain more than I do. I know that

A better way to live is to administrate your life and your time so you can do what is necessary to fulfill your mission and not interfere with your health. You have to draw the lines—the Solid Yellow Lines.

Why is it that no one wants to die, but everyone wants to rush through life? Things like fast food equal fast life.

— DR. PATRICK GENTEMPO

Painting Solid Yellow Lines

If you've got a full-time job, family, a higher aim in life, and a desire to maximize all the essentials of the Health and Happiness System That Never Fails, you have to become a black belt in time management.

There is always enough time to get the important things done. The problem is never the lack of time; the problem is the lack of time *management.*

Our lives are complex. You probably have a lot of rows in your garden. Any row that is left unwatered and unattended is going to fail to flourish—or die altogether.

Let's count your lives:

1. Spiritual life

2. Relationship life

3. Parent life (If you have more than one child, there is more than one life here.)

4. School life (Learning continues throughout your life, long after "school" is over.)

5. Work life

6. Health and fitness life

7. Purpose and mission life

Kids have a bunch of lives too, if you consider school, relationships, family, and extracurricular activities such as sports, cheerleading, or music.

If you and/or your children have any chance of thriving in each of these areas, organization and planning are vital to making it work. You do this through compartmentalizing your lives by a system called Painting Solid Yellow Lines.

When you are driving, if there is a dotted yellow line, you can pass or cross over into the other lane. If, however, there is a solid yellow line, you cannot (legally) pass and you cannot (legally) cross over. Others cannot pass or cross over either. If

subluxations not only cause pain, they destroy futures. Remember, we're working on causes, not just symptoms. But the beginning is like going to the gym. As the changes we desire occur, there can be soreness.

"There's always darkness before dawn—don't give up before you see the light."

"Yes, O great and wise Dr. Eli. I just hope the light at the end of the tunnel isn't a Greyhound bus."

"Are you sure your name's really Hope? Just kidding! Face down so we can take the next step toward wellness."

She sure is an ornery one, Eli thought. He wasn't sure what it was about Hope, but for some reason he looked forward to her visits. "See you in forty-eight hours—and we need to get Adam checked out, too."

———————

"You need to slow down—that's what you need," Miriam told Eli as she passed the platter of leftover Thanksgiving turkey to him. "I hear you at work, telling everybody else to slow down and take it easy. You ought to practice what you preach."

"I do. You just don't realize that I love what I do. I'm relaxed when I'm working. Mom, we go through this every week. Can we just eat dinner together and not talk about this again?"

"No," Miriam said, drenching her reheated mashed potatoes with reheated gravy. "Why do you think we go through this every week? It's because you do nothing but work. Even on Thanksgiving!"

"I wasn't really working yesterday. I was serving dinner to my

you paint solid yellow lines around each of your lives, other lives and activities cannot pass or cross over. That way, the important activities within those solid yellow lines stand a better chance of actually getting accomplished.

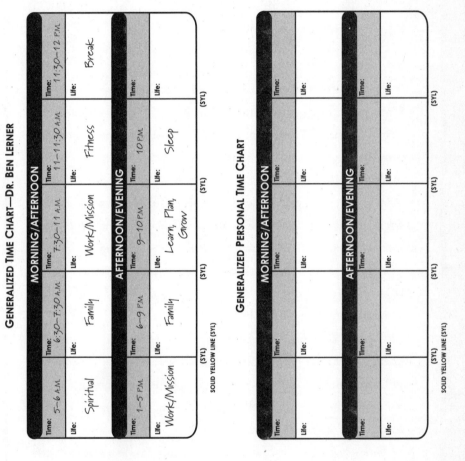

Adult Solid Yellow Line Example

6:00 AM to 6:30 AM: Spiritual Life. You draw a solid yellow line next to that life so that you are not a doctor, accountant, landscaper, secretary, or whatever you might be at other times. During this period of time, you are a student of the Bible and a prayer warrior and nothing else. It's a time for you to avoid calls or getting distracted by your family or e-mail or anything else that could draw your attention away from what you're doing.

hospice patients and visiting with them." Miriam could never understand what it took to be truly successful, Eli had figured out long ago.

After a couple of hours alone in his apartment, Eli flipped open his address book for the third time. "Lots of good this is going to do," he said out loud. "There's not a woman left in here I can date." He scanned the names one more time, just in case he missed someone the last time through.

Becky: ah yes, the psychologist. Told me she could have fallen in love with me if I hadn't been so insensitive and "emotionally distant." Says I fear intimacy. Well, she's a shrink. Always overanalyzing.

Deborah: reminds me too much of my mom. She couldn't get a babysitter this late anyway. I don't know if I'd be a good father figure to someone's child anyway.

Elizabeth: now there's a piece of work. Calls me up and reads me the riot act just because I didn't call her for a week.

Eli continued thumbing the pages, all the way through to *Z*, even though he knew full well that the last entry was on the *V* page. *Victoria: told me to go adjust myself.*

I hate when I get like this. I know I shouldn't, but maybe I'll call Michael. I swore I wouldn't hang out with him again, but I've got to do something. He never misses a Friday night happy hour and rarely misses the corresponding hours on Monday, Wednesday, or Thursday either.

Eli had met Michael at the gym. Eli wasn't into the club and bar scene, but sometimes he let temptation get the best of him. In his

This means you can't hit the snooze button—that would be an illegal crossover. You also can't quit at 6:24 because your pager goes off—also illegal.

6:30 AM to 7:30 AM: Family Life (assuming that you are married and/or have children). There is a solid yellow line between Spiritual Life and Family Life. Once the clock hits 6:30, Spiritual Life time cannot cross over 6:30, and Family Life cannot cross over 7:30 into Work Time.

7:30 AM to 11:00 AM: Work (Mission) Life. There is another solid yellow line drawn between Family Life and Work Life. You drive to the office, do your job with excellence, and focus on it from 7:30 AM to 11:00 AM. At 11:00—you guessed it— another solid yellow line is drawn and you begin another life. Sometimes it's Nap Life—but it's still scheduled. Just as in kindergarten. From 1:00 PM to 5:00 PM is Work (Mission) Life again, with new lives starting at 5:01 PM.

Each day has Spiritual Life, Family Life, Work Life, Health and Fitness Life, and School Life (again, you never stop learning). All other lives are strategically placed throughout the week so that everything you need to accomplish, you do *well*.

Obviously, it doesn't always work out so perfectly. Sometimes a child wakes up during times designated for reading, or an urgent issue pops up that you have to handle. At those times, you have to practice flexibility. You do not want to become massively stressed when something or someone tries to get by you in the no-passing lane.

If lives cross over into other lives, as they occasionally will, try to remember the admonition "That's life." Work to get past the issues and try to get everyone and everything back in their lanes as quickly as possible, before there is an accident!

Unfortunately, a few times a year there are some traumatic, stressful life pileups. But by getting back to proper compartmentalization through the painting of solid yellow lines and proper delegation, you will usually manage to escape with only some minor damage.

Child's Solid Yellow Line Example

If a child has baseball, homework, piano lessons, and loves video games, you allow a specific time or times for all of those during the week.

4 PM to 5:30 PM: School Life, including schoolwork, reading, and educational videos

8 PM to 9 PM: Play Life (video game time)

3 PM to 4 PM (Mon., Wed., Fri.): Sports Life (baseball practice)

Thursday Nights, Saturday, and Sunday Afternoons: (times vary) Family Life

12 PM to 1 PM (Sat.): Hobby or Music Life (e.g., piano lessons)

lonely hours, Eli secretly wondered what it would be like to be Michael—all fun, no responsibility, and most of all, companionship.

"Get on over here," said Michael, shouting into his cell phone so Eli could hear him over the din. "I'm flying solo—but not for long. I suspect even you may find a date here—this place is packed."

I've got to be the only guy in town who goes to a club all night and drinks one beer, Eli thought as he headed for the club. *I hate it when I get like this. I need to get a girlfriend, or at least a date. What am I saying? I need to get a life.*

Maybe this is the night God will finally bring "the one" into my life. I've prayed long enough for that, every day for about as long as I can remember. I know He has the perfect woman for me. I might meet her tonight. I could. I really could. She could be sitting at the bar right now, feeling just as uncomfortable as I do, just waiting for Mr. Right to walk in and take her away from all this. That, of course, would be me.

Three hours later, leaving the nightclub very much alone, Eli slipped on a patch of ice on the sidewalk and nearly fell—caught at the last second by a guy heading for the door.

"Thanks, man," Eli said right before he found himself staring into the face of one of his newest patients.

"You're lucky I caught you, Dr. Eli. A fall like that, and you'd be the one needing a chiropractor!" Slapping Eli on the back, the young man helped him steady himself. "See you at orientation next week!"

Oh, no. That guy is going to hear me talk about healthy lifestyle choices and purpose, and he sees me falling down leaving a bar. This is not good. No, this is definitely not good.

He knew a relationship would happen in God's time. He just wished God would hurry up, because he also knew loneliness could

Do the same with your life, and you can begin watering and fertilizing every plant in the garden of your universe. Commit to this, and soon your life will reap a harvest even in places you thought you never had space to grow anything.

Also, remember: your child will never be more organized than you are!

He who takes his time generally takes other people's time too.
— ANONYMOUS

The Power of Prayer and Healing

A health-care revolution is under way—a dynamic transformation in the way people view the healing of their bodies. Today, health-care methods that were once ridiculed, considered unscientific, fringe, bizarre, or even cultish not only are being embraced by the general public but also are being incorporated as normal practice in most health-care institutions.

Take prayer: an estimated one-third of adults use prayer, in addition to conventional medical care and complementary and alternative therapies, for health concerns, according to an article in the April 26, 2002, issue of the *Archives of Internal Medicine,* one of the *JAMA/*Archives journals. A special project at Duke called MANTRA, headed by cardiologist Dr. Mitchell Krucoff and nurse practitioner Susan Crater, produced results that showed heart patients who receive prayer have 50 to 100 percent fewer side effects than those patients not prayed for.

A study published in the October 25, 1999, issue of the same journal looked at the widespread use of prayer and its application to health concerns. Of the 2,055 people ages eighteen and older included in the study

- 35 percent used prayer for health concerns.
- 75 percent used prayer as a way to seek recovery from a health condition.
- 22 percent directed their prayer for specific medical conditions.
- 69 percent of those praying for specific medical conditions claimed they greatly benefited from the use of prayer.

Heart patients whom others prayed for, but who were not aware of being the object of prayers, had an 11 percent reduction in medical complications or the need for surgery or medication while in the hospital, according to the investigators. The authors examined the medical charts of nearly one thousand heart patients, following their health histories between hospital admission and discharge and noted:

get the best of him and he'd probably be back meeting Michael at the bar again.

————

Flicking on the windshield wipers, Hope looked at the ominously steel-gray sky with dread. *That* color meant only one thing in Ohio in December: snow. And lots of it. By the time she got home, the icy rain that was falling would have turned to sleet and then to snow. Snow that had to be shoveled. Snow that Adam would want to play in and track all through the house.

Yikes! Where did he *come from?* Hope slammed her foot on the brake pedal and hoped the car wouldn't skid. Just like that, a man in a dark wool overcoat had appeared in the intersection right in front of her car. With his head bent low and a black baseball cap on his head, he was barely visible amid the sheets of rain. Hope's car just missed him.

Rolling down the driver's side window, Hope didn't know whether to yell at the guy or make sure he wasn't shaken up by the near-miss. Hold it—Hope knew that white hair and overcoat. That had to be Benjamin!

"Benjamin! Get in the car—it's me, Hope Samuels!" If he was that hard to see, she figured he couldn't see her face very well, either. "It's got to be freezing out there!"

Benjamin slid into the passenger side and buckled his seat belt before saying a word. "I am sorry. I have made your car all wet inside."

"No problem—hey, are you okay? You came out of nowhere. I could have hit you."

Today, we are as baffled by the remote effects of prayer as Newton's critics were by the distant effects of gravity. But, just as the dispute over gravity gradually abated, the debate surrounding intercessory prayer may also diminish with time, even though our ignorance about the mechanism involved may remain. The truth remains, in light of all current scientific and medical research, that prayer absolutely works. If there ever was a drug to show the same level of findings as prayer, it would be the drug of the century.

Unfortunately for many, prayer can't be patented. The greatest aspect about this type of healing is not only is it free of charge, there are no harmful side effects.

— DAN YACHTER

Stepping into Greatness:
Painting Solid Yellow Lines Around Time Thieves

"If you want something done, give it to a busy person." Or better, "If you want something done well, give it to a busy, successful person." Busy, successful people have learned how to compartmentalize their time and delegate responsibility so that they can get *multiple* things done better than some people can get *one* thing done.

Distractions are time thieves. They will rob precious time from you, your family, and your mission. Voracious time thieves include worrying about world events; news; other people's behaviors, problems, opinions, and personal challenges; reading and responding to mail, e-mail, cell phones, pagers, and beepers; watching TV; attending to fringe businesses, amusing hobbies, regrets, worries, or concerns; and allowing yourself to get sick and need visits to the medical doctor. You cannot afford to be robbed by these thieves of time on a regular basis.

While certain distractions can be entertaining, and some distractions and downtimes are necessary to give your brain a break, these time thieves can steal countless important hours from your week and severely stunt your emotional and personal growth and prosperity if they are not contained.

For your protection and for the good of humankind, you must treat time thieves with extreme prejudice, eliminate them, or compartmentalize them between solid yellow lines—then forget about them until the next time they appear.

When determining your solid yellow lines, put in place activities that create better performance and an ever-advancing future. Do not confuse contentment with complacency. It's easy to get comfortable. Because of this, many have lost jobs, lost families, and gained large waistlines. You're either growing or dying, so to keep the mission alive, plan daily and weekly growth.

The discipline of doing work that serves your mission sounds tough. Many people look at guidelines for living as a lawful, dry, and boring existence. But they

"I am sorry. It is my fault. I was lost in thought and did not see your car. Thank God. He protected you."

"Me? It was you He protected," said Hope, startled to find herself talking about God as if He really had anything to do with what just happened.

"Yes, He protected me. But He also protected you from having your day ruined," Benjamin said as he looked her way and chuckled. "I believe I am right about that."

"Yes, you are," Hope answered, amused at this strange man's way of thinking. Time for a change of subject. "Where can I take you?"

"To the Wild Oats health food store on Maple, if it is no trouble."

"So, Dr. Eli has you eating Food by God and following the Undiet too." Hope laughed. "No trouble at all. I'm trying to listen to what the doc says about Food by Man myself, so I should probably pick up a few things there also and skip the pizza tonight. I'll take you there and home as well." Because it took her forever to get her car back after the accident, she knew what it was like to be rideless.

Curiosity about Dr. Eli was also getting the best of her, and Benjamin knew him better than anyone else she knew. Was Eli for real, or a crook and a quack as her mom and her boss's secretary had said? She also had a funny feeling that Eli's mentor could give her some insight into her own life as well.

"Have you been to one of Dr. Eli's classes on nutrition or one of his private consultations?" Benjamin asked.

Hope turned up her stereo to reveal Dr. Eli's voice. "No time for a class and no private help yet—just a tape. That's why I was planning to get the pizza. Figured it may be my last good meal."

"Oh, no," said Benjamin, "you just haven't heard about Vacation

are not. Far from it! The life that is inspired by and obedient to God is the blessed life. It is a life that goes beyond simple happiness into an inner sense of peace and fulfillment. It is the embodiment of Maximized Living.

Only the artist who's disciplined to practicing his violin is free to have harmony and beautiful music in his life. Schedule your time—and become free!

For more information on time management, visit www.thebodybygod.com.

Strong Relationships Start with Moment Management

There is a story in the Bible that describes the new millennium person to a tee. In this parable the man works and works to fill his barn, never making time for what is important. The judgment God makes and the question He asks: "You fool! You will die this very night. Then who will get it all?" (Luke 12:20 NLT).

There is a very common, modern-day example of this story: a man works hard at his business to get ahead, often working seven days a week and long into the night. Although he rarely spends enough time with his wife or children and they all go to church and school events without him, he convinces himself that he is doing it all for them. He will give them more time as soon as he reaches his goal.

His waistline starts getting bigger; if he takes the stairs at work, he is breathing hard at the top, and his neck and back hurt after about three or four hours at the computer. His wife starts bugging him about his weight and telling him he needs to go see a doctor for a checkup or visit a chiropractor. *Who has time to eat well or go to a doctor?* he says to himself. *But I'll start exercising and going back to the chiropractor as soon as I reach my goal.*

Eventually his business is doing well and he tells his wife, "We are finally about to be able to do a lot of the things we dreamed of doing: buy that bigger house, get the nicer car, take a Caribbean vacation, and put the kids in private school." But there is one more move he must make. He is about to do a total business model makeover at the office, and if he works nights and weekends, he can get it done before the New Year. *Then* he will have reached his goal.

Unfortunately, one night at work, he has chest pains and is rushed to the hospital. The doctor tells him he has to slow down and start exercising. He does that for a few weeks, but soon he's back to his old habits. One night, working late on his laptop at home, he tells his wife he'll be up in a few minutes. When his wife awakens at three in the morning, he's still not in bed. She finds him slumped over his computer. She tries to wake him up, but his body is already cold. He's had a massive heart attack.

At his funeral, everyone talked about what an "innovator" he was, a "leader in the industry," and a "great husband and father." But, according to Luke 12:20, God had only one thing to say about him: "You fool!"

Meals yet. You definitely have to make time to have a meeting with the doctor about how, as he puts it, you 'fuel your body.' The Un-diet isn't about depriving you of your favorite things; it's about adding better things. You'll see when we get to the health food store. They've got healthy pizza. It's my favorite Vacation Food!"

"But can you really lose weight that way? I've tried everything and nothing seems to work."

"That's because you're trying to diet," Benjamin explained. "But when you eat the way God created you to eat, you cooperate with your body. When you are considerate of your body, it always finds a way to look and feel its best."

The way God wants me to eat, Hope thought. *What's God got to do with eating?* "I hope my best includes my high school swimmer's body," she said sarcastically. "You know, Benjamin, I see you all the time at Dr. Eli's and around town, but I don't know a thing in the world about you. Where are you from? I know you're not American!" Hope tried to make sure that she sounded as if she was interested and not just making small talk.

"Tanzania. I left there in 1958 when it was called Tanganyika. My family is still there."

"Tanzania? Isn't that where that devil-thing is?"

"You are thinking of Tasmania," Benjamin said, suppressing a laugh. "That is a common mistake. Tasmania is in Australia. I am from Africa. You are familiar with Kenya and Mount Kilimanjaro?"

"Sure," said Hope, convincing herself that since she had at least heard of both, she was "familiar" with them. High school geography class suddenly seemed a lifetime ago. She eased the Honda into a parking spot at Wild Oats, which was already filling up with

In developed countries, on average, women live five to seven years longer than men. In underdeveloped countries there's a smaller difference but still a difference. It has been well documented that this is not due to the wellness benefits of shopping but the fact that all doctors and shoes that sell health care books and products will tell you that women spend 75 percent more time, effort, thought, and money on their well-being. Remember that family and people are not managed. Your goal is not to be efficient with those around you; your goal is to be effective.

The true peace of Maximized Living comes from maximizing the moment. Too often we're with our families and thinking about the office or at the office thinking we should be with our families. Often, to get ahead, we skip what appear to be small events with our loved ones only to realize sometime later that all of those small events amounted to a lifetime.

Tuesday, June 26, at 6 PM, with your five-year-old, is the only Tuesday, June 26, at 6 PM with your five-year-old that you will ever get. The old cliché is not exactly true: no one ever dies wishing he had spent more time at the office, but many people have failed important missions out of procrastination and complacency. No one has ever wished he missed more school plays, canceled more date nights with his spouse, skipped more opportunities to put his child in his lap and read a book, or passed on more time with his elderly parents. These are important moments to manage, to manage with nonnegotiable, unerasable, very definable solid yellow lines.

Eight Characteristics of Muscle-Bound Relationships

by
Dr. Lise Cloutier and Dr. Michael Reid (husband and wife)
and
Drs. Tony and Marty Nalda (husband and wife):

1. Love Yourself

You can't possibly love and accept others without first having a relationship with yourself that includes flaws and all. Self-care is not being selfish; it is really about being selfless in order to be a better, happier mom, dad, spouse, and/or career person.

2. Develop Your Listening Skills

When everyone is speaking at the same time, no one is listening, and what happens is a major family feud—which is really based on a misunderstanding due to poor listening skills.

shoppers desperate to stock up on essentials before they got snowed in. This quick stop looked as if it might become more of a long ordeal.

"Tanzania is near Kenya, in East Africa," Benjamin explained, pushing the car door open against the gusty wind. "We must run now!" he said, taking off like a man half—no, make that a third—his age, laughing like a child, and delighting in the driving rain.

"So what brought you here?" Hope angled a shopping cart through the crowd of people huddled by the door, waiting for their rides—or a break in the weather, which didn't appear likely to occur.

"God and a girl."

"Really? I didn't know you were married. I don't think I've ever seen your wife."

"You haven't. She died many years ago."

Good job, Hope. Bad remark. "You must have been a young man—what did you do in Tanzania?" That ought to do it—steer the conversation away from God and Benjamin's dead wife.

"Do you know what tanzanite is?" Benjamin asked, gesturing toward the bakery and raising his eyebrows to see if it was all right to head in that direction. Hope nodded.

"It's kind of like amethyst, right? Amethyst is my favorite gem. Tanzanite is also purple, isn't it? I never thought of it in relation to Tanzania." *Not that I ever remember hearing of Tanzania.*

"Tanzania is the only place in the world where it is found," Benjamin said. "My family owned a tanzanite mine. I worked with my family until I came to America."

"So you must have been a miner here."

3. Invest Quality Time Through Present-Time Consciousness

One afternoon, it was particularly busy in my office. It was so hectic, I didn't have time for outside thoughts, and as a result I was very focused on every patient as he or she lay down on my table for adjustments. I was making sure each and every adjustment was perfect and precise. After about three hours of this, I learned a patient—someone who had already received his adjustment—was waiting for me. He was a very successful businessman and had been one of my patients for some time. When I met with him, he told me that the adjustment he received that day was absolutely the best he had ever received. He commended my focus and attention to each patient, even for the brief period of time each was physically with me.

Then it hit me: it wasn't the amount of time I spent with each patient; it was what I focused on during that time. I then realized that during the time I was with my family, I wasn't really focused on them or even conscious of the fact that they were not getting 100 percent of me. I was thinking of my office, or the fact that I didn't get to golf last week, or some other thing that I couldn't do anything about at that time anyway. From that day, I made a conscious effort to focus on the present. I can't even describe what a difference that made.

No matter how present-time conscious you are, it will not help a relationship where respect and giving are not factors. Devoting specific one-on-one time to one another is also important. Sometimes you must realize that your loved ones may not share every interest that you have, but respecting what they love and trying to find common ground are ways to learn more about each other.

4. Pick Your Battles Wisely

You have to decide what's more important: winning the argument or keeping the relationship. When choosing battles, decide if the issue is a hill worth dying on.

5. Forgive Quickly

Whether it's a hug, a kiss, a note, or a hand gesture, let the other know you forgive and forget quickly. Forgiveness is a gift that you don't always feel the other deserves. But it always contains reconciliation at the heart of it.

"No. There is not much gemstone mining in Ohio," Benjamin said, the laugh lines creasing around his eyes once again. Momentarily distracted by the sight—and scent—of a tray of freshly baked whole-grain bread, he continued, "The family of my wife lived in Ohio. We came here to be near them until Doris got her next assignment."

"Assignment?"

"She was a missionary. Africa Inland Mission wanted to reassign her after we were married. We were to be relocated to a place where I could be trained as a missionary and where she could continue to work."

"So I take it you got to Ohio and both decided to leave missionary work? I don't blame you!"

"No. We arrived in Ohio, and that is when Doris died."

Think! Think! Think of something to say—now! "So why didn't you go back to Tanzania? If your family mined tanzanite, they must have been very rich." *Come on, Hope! You can do better than that! "I'm sorry" would have been nice, wouldn't it?*

"My family would not have me, and I did not want to return and upset them. Besides, my purpose is here."

"Your purpose is here, but you're stuck cleaning a church."

"I am not stuck," Benjamin replied calmly. "I repair God's house and clean it so people may worship Him in comfort. And occasionally, I get to speak with some people in need of God's help while I'm at it."

Benjamin was indeed an unusual man, thought Hope. But he seemed to have a wisdom and a contentment that she'd never known—and that she'd like to know.

6. Create a Common Purpose/Mission/Vision Statement

It's been said that couples and families that develop a common purpose, especially one that is outside of just serving themselves, have much better family dynamics and tend to stay together much longer. The reason is simple: you're moving in the same direction.

7. Routinely Give Yourself Some Breathing Space and Time Away

A relationship is made up of two, not one, strong pillars holding up the building that is the relationship. By stepping away at times, you not only miss each other, but you have time to step outside your issues; take responsibility for your own thoughts, actions, and emotions; remember how great you have it; and refocus on what's really important.

8. To Be a Great Mom or Dad, Be a Great Husband or Wife

It's been said, if you want to do something really great for your kids, love their mother. The husband/wife relationship must take priority over all other relationships. What typically happens in most families is that once children enter the family, parents tend to put their relationship on the back burner. Someone also once wisely said, "The greatest overall influence we have on our children does not come from our roles as moms or dads but rather as husbands and wives."

Without love, an infant dies. Therefore, it stands to reason that love is essential for good health, and the better its quality the better its effect on health. All eight of these secrets reveal what it takes to really love. No one is perfect. Especially you. In *one minute*, you can change flaws in people into the very things you love about them. Like health, which requires a lifestyle that is in alignment with how you were intended to live, strong relationships require love that is in alignment with how you were created to love. God loves unconditionally—so should you. Knowing you're loved unconditionally by God is the key to your own self-love/self-esteem, and loving unconditionally your spouse, children and the important people around you is a critical key to theirs.

To love is not to be better than others and love them despite themselves. Love is not recognizing that you're better, but that you are the same, that if you can be loved with all of your shortcomings, how much more do others deserve to be loved by you despite theirs.

The love you were created to have is the love your Creator has for you. It's

"So, Doc, what do you think? Am I ready to cut down to once a week?" Hope asked as she climbed on the adjusting table for the twenty-sixth time, by her rough calculation. "I'm feeling a whole lot better. I think once a week is enough."

"Ah, Hope, do we have to go through this every time you come in?" Eli asked, obviously enjoying Hope's efforts to provoke him. "You know the drill: three times a week for ninety days. Remember, we're not just repairing the damage from the accident. We're correcting twenty-six years of spinal abuse."

"Twenty-five."

"I know you've got a birthday coming up."

"I'm twenty-five, not twenty-six. I thought you chiropractors tried to help us avoid premature aging. You're not doing a very good job of it."

"Touché. Okay, let's go over this again to make sure you understand it: remember, less than 10 percent of the nervous system feels pain. I'm glad you are feeling better. But when a subluxation— pop-quiz time—what's a subluxation again?"

"A misalignment in the spine, like a dislocation or something, right?"

"Close enough. When a subluxation causes pressure on a nerve that connects to an organ, that organ nerve will rarely feel pain. It's great that you are pain-free, but you still need to correct those very important silent subluxations.

"I want you well, Hope. Maybe more than *you* want you well. Trust me: you don't want to just get out of pain, you want to get

unconditional, patient, encouraging, supporting, self-sacrificing, and understanding while still holding its recipient accountable—carefully.

The most frequently read Scripture in weddings says it best: "Love is patient, love is kind. It does not envy, it does not boast, it is not proud. It is not rude, it is not self-seeking, it is not easily angered, it keeps no record of wrongs. Love does not delight in evil but rejoices with the truth. It always protects, always trusts, always hopes, always perseveres" (1 Cor. 13:4–7 NIV).

healthy and off as many of your medications as being healthy will allow. Don't sell yourself short. Let others lead small lives, but not you. Don't go for just freedom from pain, go all out—for full freedom. Don't just go for okay—go for your full potential.

"Health is not everything, but everything is nothing without health. The problem is that all too often, by the time most people learn the truth of that statement, it's too late."

"That sounds like something I read on the whiteboard. I think you're reading from a cheat sheet," Hope said, enjoying the banter today.

"Speaking of which, it sounds like it's time for another quiz: what did it say on the whiteboard today?"

Hope had done her homework. The last time Dr. Eli had asked, she fumbled and stammered and said she didn't have time to memorize it while she was in the waiting room, only to find out that the message that day was "God is love." ("Too much for you, huh?" the doc had asked.)

"Hah! You thought you could trip me up again," she responded. "I remember it. The board said: 'The path of least resistance makes rivers and people crooked—Dr. B. J. Palmer.' And, yes, I know who Palmer is—the guy who started all this chiropractic stuff. So there," she added.

"Good job, Ms. Samuels. So go home and think about it, and the next time you ask me about cutting down on your visits, I'll quote Palmer's comment back to you until I'm sure you understand it. I tend to think you won't be asking me, 'How long do I have to do this?' again."

"Don't count on it. All done?"

| 9 |

Maximized Living in a Minimized-Living World

The integrity of the upright will guide them.
—PROVERBS 11:3 NKJV

Many people today have seen far too many wars: two world wars, wars in Korea and Vietnam, wars in the deserts of northern Africa and the Middle East, as well as wars on terrorism, crime, cancer, AIDS, hunger, homelessness, abuse, illiteracy, drunk driving, and more. For a culture that seeks peace, preaches happiness, and spends billions on medical "advancement," we sure find ourselves in a whole lot of conflict, in an ever-diminishing emotional and moral condition, and with an ever-increasing number of sick people and new illnesses.

Now that your eyes have been opened to the enormity of the problem, you can begin to make decisions that embrace God's design for your life. Unfortunately, common sense isn't real common, so while you use knowledge, others will continue to make their decisions based mostly on traditions and conventions. Nevertheless, in times when others are embracing failure, do not follow the path others take. At those times, go where there is no path . . . and leave one.

As you try to break free from the suffering masses, as Einstein said, "you will face violent opposition from mediocre minds." Living with a new set of rules takes living with principle. Men and women of integrity are not swayed by the masses. What you may find, however, is that principle will not always appear to pay off at first. But, it always pays dividends in the long run. God has always been on the side of and, more important, stays on the side of, principled men and women.

Principled men and women are those who

- trust in and rely on their bodies' own resources first for getting and staying well.
- cannot be bought at any price.
- are conscious of how they treat their bodies.
- do what is right, not what is expedient.
- have a word that is a binding contract.

"Yep. Power's on."

"See you next year, Doc." Hope rolled her eyes, wishing she hadn't said that; that cutesy remark ran its course in grammar school.

"You mean on Monday."

"But Benjamin tells me you're going to Mexico on some kind of mission trip over Christmas, right?" she asked as she picked up her purse. "You're going to be closed over the holidays, aren't you?"

"You and Benjamin seem to have become friends."

"I don't seem to have much choice. No matter where I go, he materializes before my eyes. That almost got him killed once. Anyway, he said you had a choice of trips, either to Bali or Mexico. So the great Dr. Knight chose the poverty-stricken area over the beach. No surprises there."

"I like to do everything the hard way. But there's no way we'll be closed for that long. We're off Friday for Christmas, I'm in Mexico until Sunday, and I'll be right back here on Monday."

"So your office won't give me a break over the holidays either?"

"Subluxations and poor health don't take breaks. Particularly when complicated by Christmas cookies. Enjoy your Christmas, and I'll see you on Monday. Remember, another month of adjustments three times a week, then we'll scale back to twice a week for two to three months, depending on what the X-rays tell us.

"What are you doing for the holiday?" Eli asked, his face reddening when it occurred to him that he hadn't asked or wondered what anyone else was doing and had been with Hope much longer than he had to be.

"Studying for my real estate exam," Hope shot back. *Wonder why his face is so red?*

- are honest in every transaction, no matter how big or small.

- make decisions that always take into account the well-being of others.

- look for a way for everyone to win.

- believe God is always watching their steps.

- see past what is important in this world and into what is important in God's world.

- never pay their expenses at the expense of others.

- passionately desire to be successful in their missions but will not use deception, cunning, or other people to get there.

- do not fear rejection, failure, or swimming upstream against popular opinion.

- are willing to do what has never been done.

- are inspired to consistently do God's work.

- are faithful and hopeful.

- are uncompromising in their leadership.

- are willing to endure hardships and the tests of time and do whatever it takes for as long as it takes to see their missions accomplished.

- put God and family before absolutely everything.

I love America, and what's more, I love everything it stands for. Yet its culture does not always embrace many of the things for which it stands. So it's time to stop simply floating with the current. As Jefferson said, it's time to stand like a rock.

It's amazing how a small group of committed people can change the world. In fact, it's never happened any other way.

> *Finally, brethren, whatever things are* true, *whatever things are* noble, *whatever things are* just, *whatever things are* pure, *whatever things are* lovely, *whatever things are of* good report, *if there is any virtue and if there is anything* praiseworthy—*meditate on these things. The things which you learned and received and heard and saw in me, these do, and the God of* peace *will be with you.*

> —PHILIPPIANS 4:8–9 NKJV, emphasis added

"Oh, okay," Eli stammered, trying to regain his composure. "You're going to ace it this time, now that your spine-brain connection is starting to work again. Just make sure not to miss Monday."

"I guess you're the boss. See you then."

As Hope left, Caroline told her that she'd be praying for her. *Amazing,* thought Hope. *With all of the patients they see, everyone makes it seem like they've been waiting all day to see just me. I thought it was strange at first, but I'm not just a name on a clipboard or another paying customer here—even though I've acted like nothing but a jerk.*

"Thank you, Caroline. Really, thank you. Hey, I'd also like to bring my son, Adam, in with me next time. Can I get an appointment for him? He's having trouble with his ears, and from what I've learned here, I don't want another round of antibiotics or to do risky ear surgery."

"Of course Adam can get in. We will roll out the red carpet for him." Caroline smiled.

"I'll bet you will," said Hope. She turned her head as she felt like she was going to cry. It suddenly hit her like a shovel. *They care. I don't think anyone's ever really cared before.*

———

Christmas—a whole week. Because there was not a whole lot going on in the real estate market during the holidays, Hope had the week off. She treasured the thought of spending most of the time at home with Adam and really getting ready for her real estate exam this time. She had already failed it twice. Somehow, since meeting

Remember the Alamo

by Terry Rondberg, president of the World Chiropractic Alliance

Early in the battle at the Alamo, one patriot wrote the people of Texas: "Fellow Citizens & Compatriots: I am besieged by a thousand or more of the Mexicans under Santa Anna. The enemy has demanded a surrender at discretion, otherwise the garrison are to be put to the sword. I have answered the demand with a cannon shot & our flag still waves proudly from the walls. I shall never surrender or retreat. VICTORY OR DEATH! P.S. The Lord is on our side."

The brave men at the Alamo knew they were defending the future and the freedom of America (and Texas). Looking at their odds of survival and the opportunities they had for surrender, many may say they made a mistake. Why stand for something if you're just going to get mowed down? What fools!

However, quite the contrary, these were not foolish men at all. They lived in a time when people stood firm for what they believed in, even to the point of death. They knew one day that we would "Remember the Alamo," so they risked absolutely everything for the principles by which the Alamo stood. They laid down their lives so future generations could thrive, and they knew, alive or dead, God was on their side.

As doctors of chiropractic, we know and understand the Principles of Life, and we accepted and have vowed to defend the Sacred Trust handed down to us by God through our chiropractic forefathers. We will guard this with our lives if necessary, knowing the fundamental truth that has existed throughout all of the ages: "we must stand firm, or we won't stand at all!"

Dr. Eli and Benjamin, and yes, even with Naomi's constant nagging, she had a renewed confidence. She knew she was going to pass this time.

I haven't felt this way since getting ready for a big swim meet in high school. "No more excuses, only results," she said to herself. Just like the old days. "What did that whiteboard say? '*Make today the good old days.*'" She remembered thinking that sign was hogwash when she first saw it. "I still don't know about all that—but on to better days anyway."

Naomi had invited them to attend the midnight service at Grace of God on Christmas Eve. Naomi had made several not-so-subtle attempts to get Hope to remember "the reason for the season," but no way did Hope intend to spend a special evening like this with the "God people" at church, especially not with Adam begging her to stay home so they could watch holiday videos together.

"Adam, go get your pajamas on while I make the popcorn," Hope said as she pulled a bag of microwave popcorn from the cupboard. She began reading the ingredients, a habit she'd gotten into since she had listened to Eli's nutrition tape. She planned on getting her exercise program going over the holidays as well, but she wasn't sure she was quite ready for that to happen. Naomi was always quoting Eli, "For some people exercise is more of an annual event— God made you to move." *Blah blah blah. I promised her I'd do my three-minute body-part program and my Power of 10 Minutes exercise routine I got from the* Body by God *book she brought from Dr. Eli's office for me for Christmas. "The gift of health," she called it. For some reason, I'd still rather have buns of cinnamon than "buns of steel."*

Darn, hydrogenated oils. Not entirely Food by God, but close

| 10 |

The Chiropractic Advantage

Real Wellness, Real Health Care

While people commonly go to a chiropractor for pain or injury, that's not the primary purpose of chiropractic care. Pediatrics, obstetrics, geriatrics, trauma, immune boosting, degenerative disease, and sports injury and performance care are just some of the many known areas of life and health to which chiropractic and Maximized Living care adds incredible value and safe, natural, and effective results.

Chiropractic care is necessary from your first breath until your prolonged last. Following are ways, some you may find surprising, that chiropractic can make life better.

> To read a few of the tens of millions of testimonies that have been written by patients experiencing what appear to be medical miracles but are really chiropractic normals, go to Appendix C. It's been results and not belief that have gotten chiropractic where it is today.

Chiropractic and Human Potential

One of the most interesting discoveries relating to the benefits of chiropractic came to light in recent years through a number of studies relating to the activity of electrical impulses in the human body. Of particular importance is a 2000 book by James Oschmond called *Energy Medicine*. One chapter is devoted to the work of a Harvard orthopedist, Joel Goldthwaite, whose studies revealed how the body works electrically and how the components of electricity can change the way the entire body functions.

Goldthwaite was able to cure many chronic problems by getting people to exist and function more symmetrically within a gravity environment—to exist more "vertically" within gravity and move more symmetrically with gravity.

These, of course, are primary components of chiropractic. Chiropractors want their patients' bodies to be more balanced and to function equally on both the left and the right sides. They consider subluxations to be the primary culprit when bal-

enough. I'll try and remember to get some from the health food store next time. It's more money, but I guess it's worth it.

"Bring your quilt—we can snuggle up on the sofa and stay nice and warm while we wait for Santa to come," she called to her son. Santa would not be all that good to Adam this year. In addition to Hope's being alone again for the holidays, the financial problems had not been helping her depression. *Just wait until next Christmas. A couple of big real estate commissions, and by this time next year I'll be able to buy him the whole store.* Most important, all that extra work and studying had really cut into her time with Adam and made her feel like the most negligent mother in all the world. *The best thing he'll get this year is having his mother back—if I can ever get my head and my body back together!*

Hope glanced at the day's mail piled up next to the microwave. On top was Dr. Eli's holiday mailer—she could skim that while waiting for the popcorn. One item immediately caught her eye, one of those one-minute-wellness reads that Dr. Knight was so fond of:

Knight Chiropractic Wellness
Disease Is Like Divorce

Your health is like a marriage. It's not a good idea to wait all year until your anniversary to express your love to your spouse. This is something you need to be doing daily, not annually.

It's the same way with your health. If you wait until the new year to begin caring about your body enough to make a resolution to eat better and be more active, what kind of message does that send to your body—especially when you fail to follow through on that resolution?

---

ance and function are lacking, and they attempt to correct imbalance and poor function through adjustments, exercises, and other treatment. All of this work relates to the central nervous system, the command center of every electrical impulse in the body.

That brings us to a concept known as *cerebellar plasticity*. *Cerebellar* refers to the cerebellum, the portion of the brain that in part regulates posture and balance and collects mechanical information—data related to the activity of muscles, joints, and the like. *Plasticity* refers to the ability of the central nervous system to create new electrical connections. The two words combined refer to a condition that has been shown to be the foundation of human potential—everything you're capable of being.

How does that relate to Goldthwaite's study? If you are not properly aligned, improper information is sent to the cerebellum. If you impair cerebellar development, or cerebellar plasticity, then you reduce human potential.

One of the terms used in relation to this is one you may have heard or read about in recent health-related news reports: *synapse*. A synapse is actually a small gap between two nerves (called neurons) through which information is transmitted; we speak of "firing" or "activating" the synapse, or the pathway between the neurons. What researchers have discovered is that mechanical activity—movement—creates more and more of these connections, and that in turn increases efficiency. The cerebellum contains more neurons than all those that exist in the rest of the body combined. Anything that increases mechanical activity—and remember, that data is collected in the cerebellum—increases cerebella plasticity and human potential. Likewise, anything that reduces mechanical activity reduces human potential.

The chiropractic concept is that if the joints don't move correctly or if the body is asymmetrical in relation to gravity, then there is interference with cerebellar plasticity and the way the entire body works—all aspects of spine and visceral functions through the nervous system.

Two books discuss one of the most serious indications of the dangers of reduced cerebellar plasticity: *Endangered Mind* and *Failure to Connect,* by one of the country's best-known educational psychologists, Jane Healy. In both books, she discusses the harmful effects of television on children, because television is a passive activity that provides input into the brain but requires no mechanical activity. She also chides those school systems that fail to require physical education classes. The combination of increased passive activities such as television viewing and decreased physical activities such as gym class is reducing our children's human potential.

The American Academy of Pediatricians went even further in a 1999 article published in the journal *Pediatrics,* which concluded that no children two years old or younger should ever watch television—period. They meant that literally—

No doubt about it, your body will want to divorce you and will show it by becoming diseased. Disease is the equivalent of divorce, as far as the body is concerned.

So I don't have a husband, but I bet there are days when Adam wants to divorce me. Heck, there are days when I want to divorce me. I've got to start working out, for him and for me. I got myself into this mess, and I'm bored, sore, and tired just thinking about exercise, but I'm going to make a better life for my son. If I get in better shape, I'll look better, have more energy, and probably get off these nasty antidepressants. I'd also have a shot at getting a husband.

Just because we can't see air doesn't stop us from breathing. Just because we can't see God doesn't stop us from believing. . . . That's what we call faith.

More God stuff. All this God talk is making me nuts. Good, here's one I can sink my teeth into:

. . . By interfering with God, we created things like depression and all kinds of new diseases. He created health; interference created disease. There should be signs that say, "Save the Humans . . . Stop interfering."

The sun is always shining; it's just that clouds get in the way. If it is dark in your house, you need only lift the shades—remove the interference . . .

no *Barney*, no *Sesame Street*, nothing that would even be considered educational TV. That's because television puts information into the brain while bypassing the mechanical aspects of the cerebellum.

Television is the bad guy. Activity and chiropractic are the good guys. You can create connections in the cerebellum only with mechanical function. Again, this is a goal of the chiropractic: to improve mechanical function.

In 1985, researchers from the University of California at Berkeley published a study in a journal called *Experimental Neurology.* The study was based on an examination of the brain of Albert Einstein—arguably one of the most brilliant people who ever lived. They compared his neurons with the neurons from eleven other adult males to see what differences they might find. The first thing they noticed was that Einstein had the same number of neurons as everyone else. But then they found that his neurons had more synapses.

Most people would agree that Einstein exemplified the higher end of the scale of human potential. More synapses plus more cerebellar plasticity equals increased human potential. Today, you have the opportunity to see that potential maximized in your own life through the benefits of chiropractic adjustments—and greater physical activity in your daily life.

— DANIEL MURPHY

Chiro-Pediatrics and Pregnancy

On February 25, 2004, *CBS News* aired a report on fighting infertility in women. The problem of infertility has climbed significantly in recent years, affecting millions of women and their partners in the U.S.[48] The medical solutions are extremely risky, involving an extensive use of drugs and hormones, and result in only moderate rates of success. This problem is so common that if you haven't struggled with it yourself, the chances are good that you know someone who has.

Startling new research shows a possible link between spinal adjustments and increased fertility in some women. "It lets couples who have been infertile or couples who are planning on having a family, [have] hope," explains Dr. Madeline Behrendt.

Dr. Behrendt led a study of fifteen women who struggled with infertility, some for more than a decade. Each of these women went to see Dr. Behrendt for a variety of problems, not for infertility. Of the fifteen women, fourteen became pregnant.

"The chiropractor identified spinal distortions, which are called subluxations, and once they were detected and corrected, the fertility function improved," Dr. Behrendt explains.

She says there's a link between chiropractic care and fertility because the nerves to your reproductive system run through your spine. And she says when the back is misaligned, the nerves misfire and cause a hormone imbalance, which can prevent a

CHIROPRACTORS REMOVE INTERFERENCE

Beep . . . beep . . . beep. The microwave interrupted Hope's thoughts. *Let the popcorn sit for a minute. Maybe that's true. Have I been interfering with God?*

An Aspirin Tree?

If God thought we needed aspirin, He would have created an aspirin tree. Humans keep trying to outsmart God by creating things they believe He has overlooked. We do not need aspirin to keep us healthy. What we need is God's power working through us at 100 percent capacity.

Aspirin cures headaches and kills aspirations.

—Dr. B. J. Palmer

Okay, so I've definitely interfered with God by using aspirin. I'll admit that. An aspirin tree—if I could have grown one of those a few weeks ago, I would have—which reminds me—I haven't taken my Norflex.

Hope couldn't remember the last time she took Norflex, a muscle relaxer that helped ease the pain of her fibromyalgia. How could that be? She hadn't taken Norflex in maybe two weeks, now that she thought about it—but she hadn't had any pain. *That's weird. I wonder what made the pain go away? I can't believe it—this chiropractic thing may be really working.*

"I'm all ready, Mommy! Can I start the movie?"

A short time later, an excited but exhausted Adam had drifted off to sleep, hours before Santa was expected to arrive. Hope lowered

woman from getting pregnant. Dr. Behrendt is now on a mission to see more research dollars spent on the benefits of chiropractic care to infertility.

Note: Chiropractic is also important for expectant mothers. Nerve impulses into the womb will play an integral role in the child's progress. Structurally, the child is at rest inside the pelvic cavity. Spinal distortion, pelvic rotation, and subluxation can all have a negative effect not only on the likelihood of conception but also on development and delivery.

In studies conducted within the medical profession, it was shown that women who received chiropractic adjustments in their third trimester of pregnancy were able to carry and deliver children with more comfort, and that those incorporating chiropractic adjustments during their pregnancy needed half the amount of painkillers during delivery.[49]

Newborns and Infants

Birth is a normal, natural process that's been around since almost the beginning of humanity. As with any other task the body was created to perform, when you support normal function, you have your best chance at success.

The road down the birth canal and out into the world can be a trying one, particularly in the case of medical intervention and high-tech births. (Recall the *JAMA* study showing that the U.S. ranked last for neonatal mortality, infant mortality, and for the health of newborns.) As a result, there has been an ever-increasing occurrence of traumatic birth syndrome.

Traumatic birth syndrome describes the presence of trauma-induced skull and spinal damage and spinal misalignment as a result of the birth process. As tough as birth is, going through it with the woman lying on her back, working against gravity, on medications to increase the intensity of labor, numb to the delivery muscles, and often accompanied by surgical interventions, makes it exponentially more traumatic. When you think about this, it is no surprise that vertebral subluxation in infants is a common reality.

During the pushing stage of labor, the spine may be injured as the fetus is compressed and pushed down the birth canal. The most frequent cause of subluxation in infants is the pulling, twisting, and compression of the infant's spine during birth. If something alters normal birth, you will frequently have subluxations occur at the point of greatest stress (upper and lower cervical vertebrae). While in severe cases these can result in more obvious, clinical nerve damage, such as paralysis, more frequently subluxations remain unnoticed by physicians and parents, with health issues arising at a later time. These issues can be colic, sleep disorders, symptoms of lowered immunity, poor development, and more. Pediatric expert Dr. Maxine McMullen states, "Subluxations should be analyzed and corrected as soon as possible after birth to prevent these associated conditions."[50]

the volume on the television and sat stroking Adam's hair. But the more she stroked, the guiltier she felt. Watching *The Grinch Who Stole Christmas* was one of the few pleasant activities they'd shared all week, and it was over all too soon.

What if Jacob and I had married—if he'd turned out to be a decent guy and done the right thing way back when? I might even have my degree right now, if he'd been supportive—and honorable. Seems he's done all right for himself—married, kids, successful career.

But me: twenty pounds overweight, even though everyone tells me it's only ten; haven't had a date in months; the one or two decent guys I've met haven't really hit it off with Adam; on three medications— wait, make that two. Guess I don't need the Norflex anymore, but who knows? Maybe it's just a fluke that I don't have any pain right now. It'll probably come back.

Hope took another sip from her glass of supermarket-brand eggnog, being careful not to disturb Adam. *It would be so nice to share Christmas with someone special, someone my own age, someone who would love me and love Adam. I have to admit, I* would *like to be married. What would it be like if I had married Eli?*

Eli? What? No, no, no, I meant Jacob . . . Jacob. What would it be like if I had married Jacob, that's what I meant. Eli? Where on earth did that come from? Hope shook off the thought with a shudder. *Oh, no. I hope I haven't been sending out some kind of signal to him. What made me think of Eli?*

She put the eggnog down. Suddenly she felt like having a little Food by God and doing some exercises.

These subluxations have been found to be severe enough to lead to Sudden Infant Death Syndrome (SIDS), due to the pressure they cause upward toward the lower brain,[51] as well as creating numerous other disorders common to newborns, infants, and young children. Reports show that chiropractic care can be helpful in such diverse disorders as cerebral palsy, seizure disorders, ear infections, the prevention of SIDS, and others.[52]

While chiropractic care is not a treatment for anything, the benefits of adjusting subluxation to remove interference have been particularly telling in the case of small children.

The facts show that young people need chiropractic care as much as or more than anyone to maximize proper development and minimize the advent of common infant symptoms and disease.

One of the most interesting studies, based on examination and adjustment of one thousand infants, was done by Dr. Gutmann, a German medical doctor.[53] He concluded that blocked nerve impulses at the level of the first vertebra can be the cause of central motor impairment and lower resistance to infections, especially those of the ear, nose, and throat.[54]

Dr. Gutmann's research showed that the one thousand children treated had success, almost without exception, for a variety of ailments by spinal adjustments at the atlas (top vertebra in the neck). Symptoms to have responded favorably include: congenital torticollis, disturbed mental and especially linguistic development, recurrent rhinitis, bronchitis tonsillitis, enteritis (inflammation of the intestine), persistent conjunctivitis, restless sleep, unmotivated central seizures, cerebral spasms, disturbed motor responses with repetitive falls, infantile scoliosis, distortion of ilio-sacral joint, "growing pains," appetite disturbance, and inability to thrive.

"If the indications are correctly observed," states Dr. Gutmann, "chiropractic can often bring about amazingly successful results, because the therapy is a causal one. With developmental disturbances of every kind, the atlanto-occipital joints should be examined and in each case be treated manually in a qualified manner. The success of this treatment eclipses every other attempt at treatment, including especially the use of medications."[55]

Early Childhood

by Drs. Jennifer and Palmer Peet,
Chiropractic for Kids and Adults, Shelbourne, Vermont

Doctors of chiropractic have included children in their wellness practices for more than a hundred years. Go to just about any chiropractor's office

"What is up with you today? I've never seen you so nervous!" Naomi pulled into a parking spot at Knight Chiropractic Wellness Center. She turned to face Hope. "Are you nervous about Adam getting checked out today? He'll be fine. Dr. Eli takes care of hundreds of kids, and they do great!"

"Real estate exam! I've got my exam today."

"Well, you're about to get adjusted. You'll relax, get your brain moving, and you'll be fine. Look how hard you studied!"

"I know. It's just hard to be comfortable about your next dive when you did a belly flop the last time. At least I don't have to worry about Adam—he isn't afraid at all. He loves it here. He calls this 'the toy-room doctor' and asks me to come here practically every time I pick him up from day care. He can't wait to get adjusted. Somehow Adam is convinced this is what his ears need. I'd almost swear he'd been reading Eli's newsletters."

"Why don't you explain today's whiteboard to Adam while I go get his paperwork from Caroline?" Naomi said as she held the door open for Hope and her son.

Hope read to Adam:

> *Rather than searching the world for remedies, you must realize the*
> *cure is already in the person ailing.*
> *There is no disease the body has not cured because . . .*
> *"each patient carries his own best doctor inside him."*
> —*Dr. Albert Schweitzer*

"What does that mean, Mommy?" Adam asked.

"It means you're the doctor, because God put an amazing healing

in the world who adjusts children and you'll find that, in addition to the research, parents report that their children with ear infections, colic, bed-wetting, asthma, hyperactivity, and other conditions have improved with chiropractic adjustments.[56]

Through the years, chiropractic techniques have evolved, improved, and been measured for effectiveness. It has been estimated that more than twenty-five million adjustments are given to children each year in the United States.

Considering all the falls, accidents, jars, jerks, and jolts the average child faces, it's no surprise that such a massive amount of children have faulty postures or curvature of the spine, which may cause headaches, auditory problems, dizziness, motor problems, and other disturbances.[57]

In fact, a comparative study of kids raised under chiropractic versus those raised under medicine showed that chiropractic kids are less prone to infections such as otitis media (inner ear infections) and tonsillitis and that their immune systems are better able to cope with allergens as compared to children raised under traditional medicine. The chiropractic kids also used less antibiotics and recovered more rapidly from injury or illness.[58]

While findings in different areas of the world and inside the chiro-practic profession clearly show the need for chiropractic care for children, unfortunately today, many U.S. patients continue to be harassed by their medical doctors for seeing a chiropractor. Some parts of the medical establishment are coming around and beginning to report on the impor-tance of pediatric chiropractic for wellness.

One medical study wrote: "For many families in the U.S., chiropractic care is no longer an alternative, but an integral part of regular health care, both for health promotion and the treatment of common diseases."[59]

Every child from birth onward should have access to chiropractic care to correct vertebral subluxations, which interfere with the ability to be as healthy as possible.

Making the Right Choices for Your Children

by Drs. Theresa and Stuart Warner
Children's Health and Wellness Strategists and Spokespersons
Founders of Kids Day America and the Childrenswellness.com newsletter

All good parents want to maximize their children's health, and the best way for them to do that is by developing a proactive approach in keeping

power inside your body that allows you to heal yourself." *Goodness'
sake*—Hope sighed—*I think they've got me brainwashed. I don't think
I've ever used God's name in a sentence before . . . Unless it was in vain.*

Dr. Eli walked into the waiting room. "Welcome, Adam! Today's
a big day. A very big day."

"You mean Dr. Adam—right, Mommy?"

Eli laughed and looked at Hope, both impressed and disbelieving.
"Well, that is right—Dr. Adam. Right this way. We're going to take
just two quick X-rays of your spine and if we find anything, as I
expect we will given your unhappy ears, then tomorrow we're going
to turn your power on for the very first time."

"Don't I get an adjustment today?" complained Adam.

"No, buddy, we're going to study these pictures so that you get
the best adjustment that's ever been given to any kid on the planet.
You deserve the best!"

After the X-rays, Dr. Eli went into one of the treatment rooms
to adjust Hope. "You are a mess today!" he said. "What have you
done to yourself?"

That triggered something in Hope that made her lose it. "What
happened? Well, let's see. Ten hours of studying a day, I started
working out, battled fits of depression from being alone again for
the holidays, chased a little boy with endless energy, and on top of
all that, I'm quite certain I'm going to fail this test and I can't go
through this again, and—"

"Hope, I know you hate when I do this, but let me quote you
something. There's a Dr. James who once said, 'Consider it pure
joy, my brothers, whenever you face trials of many kinds, because
you know that the testing of your faith develops perseverance.

their children healthy. But between getting conflicting information from various sources such as books, health reports, and pediatricians, and the rapidly changing medical protocols, health-care decisions have become confusing. As a result, the incidence of childhood illness is skyrocketing. The 2002 Centers for Disease Control Summary of Health statistics for U.S. children found that the number of young asthma patients has doubled over the last ten years, while the incidences of allergies, ear infections, obesity, and diabetes is also increasing in children.

As a result of all this, many children have had to undergo unnecessary treatments. For decades, a tonsillectomy was considered a routine procedure, even for healthy children. Parents were not told that tonsils are part of the immune system and that removing them placed their children in danger of numerous complications. Today, fortunately, tonsillectomies are not the norm that they used to be.

Another standard procedure was prescribing antibiotics to children with ear infections. In 2004, however, the American Academy of Pediatricians reversed its guidelines, pointing out that in more than 80 percent of the children with ear infections, symptoms would subside on their own, without the need for antibiotics. Research showed that antibiotics have no value in treating the majority of otitis media cases (inner ear infections), because most are caused by viruses and not bacteria. The overprescribing of antibiotics yielded a host of problems, ranging from the development of drug-resistant bacteria to gastrointestinal and skin problems to immune system deficiencies. The millions of unnecessary prescriptions of antibiotics have resulted in millions more recurrences of ear infections.

Drugs such as Zoloft and Paxil are given to millions of children every year, even though research has not proved them to be effective or safe for children. Other studies show that family physicians are not only untrained in but also uncomfortable prescribing these drugs; still, they prescribe them. Fortunately, the FDA is forcing drug manufacturers to place warning labels on the containers stating that these drugs can cause suicidal tendencies in children, among an array of other side effects.

The best way to avoid unnecessary drugs and procedures is to have a good understanding of what your child's symptoms mean. A common misconception is that symptoms such as a runny nose, cough, fever, or diarrhea indicate your child is sick. A more empowering understanding is that the symptoms might actually mean your child is healthy and responding the way the body is supposed to under different stresses in the

Perseverance must finish its work so that you may be mature and complete, not lacking anything' [NIV]."

"What if you don't have any faith?" she said, choking back the tears.

"Hope, do you even know what your name means?"

"Yes, like I *hope* I'll pass the test."

"Not exactly. Hope is a confidence that comes through faith. A confidence that no matter what the outcome of life's challenges are, God's going to take care of you so you never have to beg."

"I don't think I could go through this test again. I have to pass."

"Hope, you're one of the toughest, most successful people I've ever met."

"'Tough,' 'successful'—what could you possibly mean?"

"Success isn't measured by wins and losses. It's not what you own; it's who you are. Success consists of being tough enough to get up just one more time than you've fallen down. You've been getting up from knockdowns all your life. I know you'll succeed, because you're not a quitter, and nothing is more certain than the success of someone who will never quit."

"Who's Dr. James?" Hope asked. "Another chiropractor you know?"

"Kind of. He's a guy from the Bible I know."

"I knew it. Maybe I'll read the Bible before my test. Couldn't hurt to hedge my bets, you know."

"No, Hope, it couldn't hurt. Let's get your power on and get you ready."

Hope didn't feel like reading anything else before her test, but

environment. The body is smart; God designed it with a nervous system and an immune system to help it survive and thrive in all types of situations.

Is a fever part of the problem or the cure? We as chiropractors would say that the fever is part of the cure, because your body is intelligent and recognizes that a virus is present. The body then raises the temperature high enough to kill the virus. The fever indicates a healthy response. If you use drugs to lower the fever, you are doing more harm than good in most cases; the virus can lie dormant in the child's system, perhaps even mutating to cause more problems.

Is a cough part of the problem or the cure? We say it is part of the cure, because the body recognizes the presence of a toxin or an infection in the lungs, forcing the body to cough until it rids itself of the problem. If you suppress the cough, your body has no opportunity to heal itself. Aside from the side effects of the medication, you may develop additional problems.

Mucus from a runny nose contains and destroys the bacteria. Diarrhea rids the body of poisons. By now, you should be getting the idea. The best way to react to a child with a runny nose, a cough, or a fever is to say, "Great! Thank God—the body is healing and becoming stronger." In otherwise healthy children, symptoms are beneficial because they help activate and mature the immune system, which is also how a child becomes immune to chicken pox, measles, and whooping cough.

When a healthy child's body faces these stresses or symptoms and processes them naturally, the child becomes a healthier adult with a stronger immune system. When the symptoms are treated with drugs, the children develop weakened and suppressed immune systems and often end up with such chronic diseases as allergies, asthma, and eczema.

Of course, if a child's symptoms worsen over time and the body is not responding normally, you need to seek a medical evaluation. If fever and other signs of a bacterial infection elevate or persist, the child could be facing a potentially life-threatening situation. In our family's experience, however, the body has had the potential to heal itself in approximately 99 percent of the cases.

To maximize your child's immune system and brain function, lead your child into the wellness lifestyle, which includes being well informed and being cared for by a chiropractor.

Contrary to what you may have been thinking, children are actually more and not less likely to be candidates for chiropractic care. Between standard childhood mishaps, trauma from the birth process, and the reality that when a child is learning to walk, he or she falls enough times in

Naomi said it would be a good one for Adam, so she let Naomi read it to her.

> ARE YOU A DIRTY GARBAGE CAN OR A CLEAN ONE?
>
> . . . Simply put, the reason many of us become sick is because our bodies are like dirty garbage cans that have opened themselves up for invasion. If you keep your garbage can (body) clean, the bugs don't show up.

"I'm doomed", said Hope. "Better keep Adam away from me. I'm a walking, talking dirty garbage can."

Naomi snapped back, "Not with your power on!"

———

"I'd like to tell you how wonderful you look! But I cannot. You look weary, my friend. I am certain your trip was beneficial to the people who needed you in Mexico. But I am not so certain it was beneficial to the chiropractor." Benjamin looked over his reading glasses, awaiting a response.

"It's just jet lag. I'm fine."

"Jet lag? You've been back for a week. Your normal eighty-five-hour workweek." Benjamin's eyes remained fixed on Eli.

"I'm fine. I know my limits."

"That is good. Then you must know you have reached them."

"Could we just pray today? No sermons?"

"Ah. You make a good point. God has not seen fit to give me a pulpit from which to deliver my sermons. He has given me just

an hour to hospitalize an adult, it is highly likely that a spinal condition, including vertebral subluxation, would exist.

The following are facts about a child's spine:

- The joints and bones in children are not yet fully formed and are very fragile.
- The spinal joints in children need to function properly in all ranges of motion.
- Ligaments, tendons, and muscles are in an ever-growing state and very sensitive to trauma.
- If unequal pressure on the growth plates of the bones exists due to vertebral subluxation, poor posture, or concussive forces, this can lead to improper function and maldevelopment of bones in the spine and the extremities.
- If the spine is bent, shifted, or imbalanced in any way, this creates unwanted nerve stress and could grow into scoliosis or other spinal abnormalities.
- The sensitive nervous system of a child is responsible for not only organ system function as in an adult but also normal growth and development. Therefore, in many ways, central nervous system interference in children has the potential to have a much more hazardous effect on their futures than on an adult's.

The only people who have a complete chance of attaining and optimizing their true health potential are children. By the time a person has reached adulthood, areas affected by vertebral subluxation will have some level of permanent impairment. Many of these problems will go unnoticed for years or even decades, and all the while the person is functioning below his or her potential. Then, as the person ages and health problems arise, the truth will be revealed: those problems started long before, and there may be no going back.

What parents wouldn't want to do everything possible to help their children have the best chance at maximum physical, mental, and social health?

Aging and Its Symptoms

Following a car crash, sports injury, or other situation in which the body has sustained a significant amount of force or trauma, the potential for damage to the spine and the central nervous system is so evident that even skeptics are willing to give chiropractic

this"—his arm swept through the air over the table in front of him—"this table in this conference room in this doctor's office. I must deliver my sermons here, it seems." Benjamin's eyes sparkled with delight as he surveyed his sanctuary.

"Benjamin, you're my friend and maybe the wisest person I know spiritually, but when it comes to giving me advice on how I run my life . . . I can't say I'm sure you're the right guy for the job. No offense, but look how your life turned out."

"And how is that? How did my life turn out?"

Eli wasn't sure he should say any more. He knew he was just tired and not in the mood for the "you work too hard" thing. "It's nothing, Benjamin. I'm just a little out of it this morning."

"Tell me how my life turned out."

"Come on, Benjamin! You gave up everything—your family, your wealth, your country, your future—to follow a woman. A woman who died less than six months after you married her. You couldn't go home; you had no one here except her family, whom you hardly knew. You couldn't raise the support you needed to go to school, you never remarried because no other woman could equal Doris, and you ended up doing odd jobs until you started working as a custodian at Grace of God. And that was years ago!"

"You are right. I gave up everything most people would ever want. But I gained things few people every truly have. I spent many precious months with the woman I love, and together we realized the power of our first love—our love for God. Few men have had so much. Yes, you are on a different path. Are you sure it is ending up exactly where you want to go?" Benjamin continued staring straight at Eli.

a try. Through their advertising, some chiropractors inadvertently perpetuate the assumption that this is the only reason chiropractors exist in the first place. What many people fail to understand is that the long-term effects of traumatic injury can be far more significant than they first appear to be. When, for example, people blame old age for the fact that they have arthritis in one knee, that begs the question of why they don't have it in the other knee. Aren't both knees the same age? When questioned, people often get around to mentioning an old injury from a fall or a car crash, but they usually add, "But that was a long time ago." The truth is, however, that it's our old falls and accidents that cause much of our arthritis today.

Maximized Living at Forty and Beyond: Chiropractic for the Ageless

by Dr. Robert Hoffman
Foundation for Chiropractic Education and Research

The Keys to Longevity

Facts:

- Longevity is only 25 percent genetic; 75 percent is socioeconomic and lifestyle, or, in other words, living to one hundred is mostly up to you.
- Genetics does not hold the answer, as no centenarian has ever been recorded as having a centenarian parent.
- Many superagers live well past ninety without the disabling symptoms of heart disease, diabetes, pain, or Alzheimer's.

Centenarians have maintained ten important characteristics and traits. (All of these are found in the Five Essentials of Maximized Living.) They

1. are conscious of drug use;
2. maintain strong social relationships;
3. practice good stress management;

4. have purpose and passion for life;
5. welcome the challenge of learning;
6. follow a healthy diet;
7. exercise;

"But the tanzanite! You could have been a multimillionaire—a billionaire, even! Think of how many people you could have helped with that. Instead, you're cleaning toilets in a church building for less money than I made when I was working part-time during college."

"Ah, but who is always telling us to find our purpose and work for God? You are! How many men can say that they work for God—literally? His name is on all of my paychecks: Grace of God!" The custodian chuckled.

Eli decided that sometimes Benjamin was right-on, and sometimes he was clueless about real life. He didn't say anything else.

"Perhaps you should not listen to me. Perhaps you should not listen to my advice. But I must tell you this: *Hata ukinichukia la kweli nitakwambia*—even if you dislike me, I will tell you the truth. Now let's pray and get you back to saving lives."

"Up on the table, Ms. Samuels! It's your lucky day. I have good news. You don't have to look at my ugly mug three times a week anymore. I've reviewed your reexam and that one new X-ray we took of your neck. You've graduated to twice a week. We can put you and Adam down for Mondays and Wednesdays."

"Lucky me," Hope said.

"Hey, you don't sound too excited. Aren't you the patient who bugged me for three months to cut back on the adjustments?"

"Yep, I'm the one," Hope said. "I'm glad. I really am. Twice a week—that's good. I'm glad." *Am I falling for this guy? No way, I just like coming in here. I must sound like an idiot!*

8. are spiritual or religiously active;

9. are optimistic and gracefully adaptive to change; and

10. get chiropractic care (elderly patients under chiropractic care report better overall health, fewer chronic conditions, spend fewer days in nursing homes and hospitals, are more mobile in their communities, and are more likely to report regular levels of exercise).

There is actually a proven fountain of youth found by receiving chiropractic care. A study done in February 2005 called "Surrogate Indication of DNA Repair in Serum After Long-Term Chiropractic Intervention" showed that serum thio levels in wellness subjects under chiropractic care were higher than patients with active disease and patients who had been under short-term chiropractic care. Serum thiols are a measure of human health status from DNA repair. The patients under care the longest had the greatest level of DNA repair.[60]

When you have an accident, the impact causes tiny soft tissue tears and small spinal and/or extremity misalignments. If these go uncorrected, the small dysfunctions turn into large damage. Similar to an automobile tire that is slightly out of place or brakes that are squeaking slightly, time causes further damage. Saying that an old fall off your bike when you were five or the car accident when you were sixteen has nothing to do with today's knee pain or lumbar-disk herniation is like saying to the mechanic, "Yes, the brakes squeaked, but that was weeks ago."

Following are some conditions related to aging where chiropractic care can make a difference.

Degenerative Arthritis

The good news about degenerative arthritis is that outside an extreme genetic circumstance, it can be avoided and even reversed. Common medical wisdom is that if you have arthritis, you are doomed. This could not be further from the truth. The body heals.

Arthritis is due to a physical or chemical irritant in a joint or the system. If the cause of this irritation is avoided, removed, or corrected, your body has a chance to heal. There are endless stories of athletes and people who assumed their activity level was destined to be compromised only to see the effects of arthritis reversed through a change in lifestyle or help from a chiropractor. Then they went on to be champions.

Chiropractic care can be the key. Through a change in diet that supports a

"If that's the case, I don't think I want to see you when you're sad."

"Actually, I really am happy. I'm just distracted today," she said, hoping he wouldn't ask what was distracting her. *Think of something to say—quick!* "Hey, you know what I forgot to tell you? I think my fibromyalgia went away, just like that. It happened over Christmas, while you were out saving the world."

Eli ignored the sarcasm. "What makes you think it went away?"

"Well, I don't need to take Norflex anymore. I realized I had been forgetting to take it, but I wasn't in pain the way I used to be. I still haven't had time to go to my real doctor—"

"Oh, your 'real doctor,'" Eli joked.

"Well, the one who gives medications," Hope said, trying to pull her foot from her mouth.

"Hmmm," he said. "Let's think this through. Hope is on Norflex for—how many years? Three?"

Hope nodded.

"Hope visits a chiropractor—three whole times a week. Hope no longer needs her medication. If the one who prescribed the Norflex was your 'real doctor,' then I'd rather be the fake one who helps get you well."

"Hey, I'm still on medication. You're not such a wonder-worker." *Back off, Hope. Sounds like you're flirting.* "I mean, chiropractic isn't such a wonder. I'm still on Prozac and Synthyroid."

"For now," Eli said.

"My doctor says I need these drugs."

"He may be right," Eli said. "But wouldn't it be smart to give the body a chance to reduce or eliminate these medications? Your body is always the best doctor."

more alkaline system (includes a large amount of good fats and green vegetables and minimal amounts of flour, grains, caffeine, sugar, and pasteurized dairy products), increased hydration, spinal alignment, posture restoration, and muscular balancing, degenerative joint and muscle conditions can be overcome—they are not a permanent sentence.

Other Degenerative Diseases

Cancer, heart disease, diabetes, and other types of conditions associated with aging are called *degenerative diseases*. They develop through the breakdown of cells and tissues along with the accumulation of fat and toxins in the body that occurs due to lifestyle and the wear and tear that is normally associated with aging. While a great deal of time and money have gone into research treatments for these conditions, the only solutions that continue to ring true are in the area of wellness. What we often blame on aging and genetics apparently has different sources, as many who've been stricken with these conditions get well.

If you live long enough, eventually you're going to die—from something. To protect yourself from the aging process the best you can and prolong degeneration, follow the path of *real* wellness.

We must stop looking at health as something that goes bad in a day, a week, or a month. If your heart is functioning at 100 percent normal and you are living in a manner that is conducive to cellular survival, then you are not going to die from a heart attack in five minutes, tomorrow, or in five weeks. If, however, the heart is operating at only 90, 80, 70, or 60 percent normal function and you're ignoring various essentials of Maximized Living, then even though you may feel well right now, disease or even death is on the way. People who think they are healthy because they feel good have a nasty habit of dropping dead.

Health is not all or nothing. There are percentages. You have to work toward normal function every day. It's the only way to live life at your full potential. Removing the interference to good health stops the breakdown and disrepair that lead to degenerative illness. You are either healing or dying. Live as though you want to cure disease right now and never get the disease. In this way, you'll be saved and you won't even know it.

Cancer and Chiropractic

You already have cancer cells in your body. As Dr. Michael Williams, professor of medicine at Northwestern University Medical School, says, "Everyone has from one hundred to ten thousand cancer cells floating in [his or her] body at all times. If the immune system is strong, they are destroyed before any damage is done. However, new cancer cells develop every day, so you must keep your

"It's no big deal," Hope said. "Everyone's on medication of some kind."

"Not me and hundreds of my patients. But that's beside the point. The point is, just because something is popular doesn't make it right."

"Well, there has to be something to it. It must help people or doctors wouldn't prescribe it, and half the world wouldn't be taking it."

Someone once said, "'When five hundred million people believe in a bad idea, it's still a bad idea.' Expect to see that on the whiteboard someday soon," Eli said.

"So why doesn't everybody go to a chiropractor, if chiropractic is so great?"

"Just because something isn't popular doesn't mean it's wrong. Expect to see that, too," he said.

> *Real Wellness: If the principle is right, then everything in tune with that principle is right.*
>
> *Traditional Medicine: If the principle is wrong, following it is disastrous.*

"Don't you think people are smart enough to know what's good for them and not to follow a wrong principle straight into a disastrous situation?" she asked. Hope realized she had just hit a hot button as Eli suddenly appeared very serious—as if she had just gotten to the core of everything he lived for.

He looked at her as if he were looking right through her. "No, Hope! A person is smart, but people as a group are often stupid,"

immune system in top condition. If it weakens too much, that's when cancer can establish itself."

What causes cancer cells to become a problem is a poorly functioning immune system, the very condition that chiropractic care works to correct.[61] Some of the signs of a weakened immune system are frequent colds, infections, and bouts with the flu, allergies, and asthma. People with those illnesses and disorders are more vulnerable to becoming cancer victims and need to do whatever it takes to strengthen their immune systems.

In America, you are taught to fight cancer by early detection. Men and women are taught to begin checking for cancer regularly once they get older. This way of dealing with cancer is counterproductive. In order to prevent cancer, it is something you must be concerned about from the moment you are born.

Researchers at the University of Maryland Cancer Center found that interleukin-10, a substance that occurs naturally in the body's immune system, fights and destroys cancer even at sites where cancer has spread. If you are functioning well, interleukin-10 and the rest of your immune system can keep you well.

Dr. Ronald Pero of New York University studied the immune systems of cancer patients, noncancer patients, and noncancer patients who had been under chiropractic care for five years or more. The noncancer patients had immune systems that were 200 percent stronger than those of the cancer patients. The chiropractic patients had immune systems that were 200 percent stronger than those of the noncancer patients and 400 percent stronger than those of the cancer patients.

Once again, chiropractic isn't a cure for cancer. However, maximum nerve supply, along with the other essentials of Maximized Living, is worth ten pounds of cure.

Chiropractic and Degenerative Neurological Disorders

Aging isn't a problem. Aging with vertebral subluxation, constant medication, and a poor lifestyle is. The longer you pour chemicals and junk food into your body and allow your spine to go uncorrected, the older you get. While genetics play some role in the aging process, the reason most people do not age like fine wine is that they've minimized their genetic potential with a poisonous lifestyle and subluxation degeneration.

One of the more common effects of a degenerative lifestyle is not just a wasting away of the knees and your throwing arm; it's deterioration of the brain, spine, and spinal cord.

The benefits of spinal correction and lifestyle direction for degenerative neurological disorders, such as multiple sclerosis and Parkinson's, make a tremendous amount of sense. Multiple sclerosis is a gradual breaking down of the spinal cord.

he said. "People follow the current conventions, not wisdom. That's why some suffer through such desperate, depressed lives. It's sad, because people have so many opportunities to thrive and succeed. But the masses are huddled on an island of pain, surrounded by a sea of wellness."

Suddenly, Hope realized she and Eli had been talking for far longer than he typically talked with any of his other patients and had actually walked out of the treatment room together. They were now the center of attention in the waiting room. And across the room stood Benjamin Karume, arms crossed, head nodding, looking from Eli to Hope and back to Eli again, wearing a smile as big as the room could stand.

Uh-oh, Hope thought. *If my face is as red as Eli's is right now, I'm in trouble.*

"Well, thank you, Dr. Knight. See you Friday." *Dr. Knight? Nobody* called him Dr. Knight. *Could she be any more obvious?*

––––––––––––

Twice a week, as it turned out, was about all Hope could handle. She had done it: she had passed her test. Spring brought a resurgence in the real estate market, and with it even greater demands on her time. Even so, things were looking up: a class of Dr. Eli's and the book Naomi had given her as a Christmas present had taught her how to better manage her time. She worked more hours while doubling the time she was spending with Adam. With reading food-label ingredients, getting her diet up to 75 percent Food by God, and the ten to twenty minutes of exercise she was squeezing in four

Who could benefit more from a healthy spinal column than an MS patient? And midbrain stimulation is one of many leading technologies in the medical system for treating people suffering with Parkinson's symptoms. This is done in an effort to stimulate further brain chemical output, which will allow a reduction in the horrible effects of this potentially crippling illness.

For nearly a century now, the leading research in chiropractic has had to do with the upper cervical spine. This area of the spinal column consists of the top three vertebrae—C1, C2, and C3. The higher up the spinal column you move and the closer you get to the brain, the more dense in functional neurons the spinal cord becomes. As we mentioned, the very upper part of the spinal column is there to protect not only the spinal cord but also the lower part of the brain. This is why, if you were to significantly damage the spinal cord from C3 to C1, you would most likely die, since vital functions such as breathing are controlled from this area. When you see a ventilator-dependent paralyzed person who became that way due to trauma (as Christopher Reeve did), you know that the person's spine was damaged at C3 or higher.

Upper cervical vertebral subluxations are menacing. Because of the tension they create on the vital upper cord, along with the brain stem pressure they can cause, one can conclude that the midbrain, the area researchers are now most concerned with in the treatment of Parkinson's, will not function optimally.

A study evaluating the care of forty-four MS patients and thirty-seven Parkinson's patients who received treatment of upper neck subluxation over a five-year period revealed that 91 percent of MS patients showed improvement and 92 percent of Parkinson's patients showed improvement. These findings led researchers to believe the spinal misalignment in the upper cervical spine could activate a reversal of MS and Parkinson's symptoms. For a long time, head and neck injuries have been thought of as contributing factors to the development of MS and Parkinson's. These results are the first to confirm the relationship between the two.

As that study showed, relieving pressure through a measured, scientifically applied, gentle chiropractic adjustment would reduce spinal cord and brain stem pressure. Anatomically, this would relieve the midbrain of some stress as well as result in better function and maximum brain chemical output. The research makes sense, as these events could only help and provide another level of symptom relief or even recovery for MS and Parkinson's patients.

As people who are in the over-forty category could have untreated and undiagnosed vertebral subluxation for years and even decades, they are the most susceptible to subluxation degeneration and degenerative neurological conditions.

From a *real* wellness prospective, it would be far more important to check to see if an upper cervical misalignment exists prior to finding out you have arthritis,

or five days a week, she had lost ten pounds since Christmas, without a whole lot of effort and in most of the right places.

"Call me crazy, but between getting Adam adjusted and cutting back his Food by Man, he seems to have calmed way down and hasn't had a single ear infection in months," Hope told Naomi over lunch. "Would you believe that just a few months ago his teacher talked to me about putting him on Ritalin? Ritalin! I think every child in his class is on that! No way would I let him take it. Now look, he's doing amazing."

"So Eli's been having an effect on you, I see," Naomi said, just barely managing to stifle a knowing grin as she drizzled olive oil on her salad.

"Well, I'd have to be pretty stupid not to pay attention to him, when it's all there right before my eyes," Hope said.

Naomi choked on a tomato.

"I didn't tell him this—I didn't want to give him the satisfaction of always being right—but I've been 'forgetting' to take my thyroid medication," Hope continued. "And look at me: I haven't even died or anything yet! I feel great, in fact. Don't tell him I said so, but he's going to make a believer out of me yet."

"I sure hope somebody does!"

"Wait—I didn't mean it that way. I mean a believer in chiropractic. The God thing, I'm still not so sure about," Hope said.

"You've come a long way, though, I'll give you that. I can remember when you couldn't even say the G-word without flinching," Naomi said. "And when I saw you at Grace of God on Sunday, I nearly died. Like I said then, it was as if a whole new you walked in the door that day."

Parkinson's, MS, Alzheimer's, or some other nervous system disorder we've written off as a sign of "old age."

Allergy, Infection, and Communicable Diseases

The best way to fight communicable diseases such as colds and the flu is to keep your immune system strong. That is enough to get you well and keep you well. But that's easier said than done in a society bombarded with commercials and advertisements informing you of the many products available that promise to relieve your symptoms and your discomfort. But if you've read this far, you already know that the use of antibiotics and fever-fighting medications weakens your immune system—exactly the opposite of the outcome you want. Other medicines considered to be safe, such as over-the-counter cold and flu remedies, have been linked with strokes and colon problems.

The Essentials of Maximized Living offer maximum immune system function. Some chiropractors even recommend being checked for subluxations every day while you are ill. Remember, even when you are sick you are in a constant state of repair and regeneration, morning, noon, and night, in every cell and system of your being. Working with that nature and the getting-well process rather than against it will bring about your healing much more quickly.

> *Coughs, sniffles, sneezes, and fever are good for you. Coughing and sneezing clear the airways of harmful irritants and allergy-causing substances while fevers actually fight virus and bacteria. Our body raises its temperature on purpose. Robert Mendelson, M.D., stated, "Unless there are additional symptoms such as extreme listlessness, abnormal behavior, and other indicators of serious disease such as meningitis, your doctor should tell you there is nothing to worry about and send you and your child home. Diseases are shortened by letting a safe fever run its course. Taking fever-reducing drugs or cough suppressants can lead to pneumonia or more serious respiratory infection.*
>
> —Dr. William B. Greenough,
> professor of medicine, Johns
> Hopkins School of Medicine

Sports Performance and Durability

Other people who continue to benefit enormously from chiropractic care are Olympic and professional athletes. Today, nearly every sports team and the vast

"I went because I thought it would be good for Adam. I guess I've always had this belief in God, or a Creator of some sort, way deep down inside. I just couldn't admit it—not to myself, and certainly not to anyone else. If there is a God, I wouldn't blame Him if He didn't like me very much. The one thing I have been thinking a lot about lately is that something supernatural was involved in my life even when I didn't know it. When I think of Adam—"

At his name, Hope's voice broke. Assuring Naomi with her wordless gestures that she was okay, she took a minute to compose herself. "When I think of Adam, I know more than ever that something was guiding me. I mean, every girl I knew at that time who got pregnant went out and got an abortion. So why didn't I? At the time, I thought I was trying to get back at my parents by shaming them with my very obvious pregnancy. Later, I realized that I just wanted someone to love, someone who actually might love me back. I didn't get that from Adam's father, but I got that in Adam. Do you think that was a miracle?"

"I'd go with 'miracle,'" Naomi said. "How about God? Are you convinced He's there and He loves you—and is the One that helped you and keeps right on helping you?"

"I'm working on it," Hope said, self-consciously looking at her watch. "Sorry, Naomi—gotta go. I have a house to show," she continued, picking up the check. "Your treat next time!"

———

"Hey, buddy, how are you?" Eli called out to Adam from the adjustment room. "Where's your mom?"

majority of top athletes interested in optimum performance and career longevity are under chiropractic care.

Olympic and professional-level competitors depend on improving their performance and avoiding injury, says Nick Athens, former team chiropractor with both the San Francisco Giants and the San Francisco 49ers. Now exclusively in private practice, Athens counts among his patients two superstars who live in the Bay Area: New England Patriots quarterback Tom Brady and San Francisco Giants slugger Barry Bonds.

More than most other people, professional athletes recognize the importance of dealing with injuries—and their causes—immediately, Athens says: "By giving them regular adjustments, we're realigning their spines, taking pressure off the central nervous system, and taking care of injuries as we go, rather than having them accumulate." Athletes see such care as an investment not just in their careers but also in their future earning potential; every year of better health that they "buy" with chiropractic is another year they can play professional sports and make millions of dollars.

That wasn't always the case, though. It's only been in recent decades that teams have recognized the value of having a team chiropractor. Even at that, it's largely been the athletes themselves who have fully appreciated the benefits of regular chiropractic care. As in the medical industry as a whole, doctors in the field of sports medicine are reluctant to acknowledge the overwhelmingly positive results from regular chiropractic care. But today's younger athletes are more inclined to seek out alternative care than previous athletes were, and those players want to continue getting the kind of care to which they've become accustomed. Often, that means chiropractic care.

To Athens, a chiropractor is like a mechanic for the body. Every patient is like a car—a Porsche or a BMW, he's quick to note—and you want to keep that car tuned up. By adjusting the spine and the extremities and taking the pressure off the central nervous system, chiropractors get the body to run more efficiently.

"The thing is, most people don't know what that feels like because they've never had their bodies worked on," Athens says of those who aren't professional athletes. "You don't know how well a car can run unless you tune it up. It's like the Indy 500 cars. They go around the track at two hundred miles per hour and keep stopping at pit stops so they can keep going at that pace.

"Some people choose to live their lives at that high pace, and chiropractic helps them continue that. If they want to play sports and make sure their bodies hold up, adjusting their spines and their knees and ankles helps them have fun in their sporting activities and also play the sport more effectively," Athens said.

"Getting something from the car."

"Come on in. You want to see something really cool?" Eli's stage whisper sounded nothing short of conspiratorial. "Just don't tell your mom." Eli lifted his index finger to his lips as Adam scrambled out of his chair.

"Look at this!" Eli brought a skull down from a shelf in the adjusting room and mimicked a creepy corpse as he worked the jaw. "Whoops! Looks like I forgot the rest of him!" He steered Adam toward the spine in the corner and pretended to try to attach the skull to the top of the spine. "Uh-oh. He's gonna get me now. It won't fit. Guess I have the wrong skull."

"Are we having fun?" Hope stood in the doorway to the office. "Dr. Eli, I do think you've been playing almost as much as Adam has lately. I heard you were a hit in the science classes at Adam's school last week."

"We chiropractors have many hidden talents."

"I don't get you. I've been coming here for, what, seven or eight months now, and you haven't once taken a vacation. If you're gone, it's for a seminar or a mission of some sort. So are you looking for the big payoff so you can retire early? Or what?"

"There is no payoff. I don't look for any kind of return on all this. I love serving other people."

"You get something in return. You get paid."

"Not for a lot of the work I do."

"There's still a payoff."

"Like what? What makes you think I have some ulterior motive?" Eli asked, becoming more agitated the longer Hope spoke. "I serve people for the sake of serving them."

Chiropractic Patient Satisfaction
by Dr. Robert Hoffman

In a recent survey, chiropractic patients were asked how their lives had changed since they began chiropractic treatment:

- 71 percent take less medication.
- 87 percent experienced an improvement in their overall health.
- 92 percent are living healthier lifestyles.
- 98 percent saw an improvement in physical problems.
- 99 percent experienced a decrease in physical pain.

I couldn't agree more with what Dr. Athens said. The thrill I've had working with two Olympic teams and the Orlando Magic had nothing to do with the fact that I was working with superstars. What I enjoy about working with top athletes is their desire to be the best. I believe the pastors, teachers, single mothers, doctors, and garbagemen I take care of every day are the real celebrities. They have real roles to play in life, and they, too, should work to be their best.

For further information and research on chiropractic for performance and disease, see Appendix A.

Choosing a *Real*-Wellness Chiropractor

While some chiropractors choose to limit their scope of care to short-term pain relief, today's *real*-wellness chiropractor focuses on overall health through Maximized Living. There's nothing wrong with short-term pain-relief doctors. They don't use drugs, and you will typically see relief very quickly. There's just so much more you can have.

Health- and wellness-oriented chiropractors provide a care plan designed to reduce or eliminate the problems they discover using precise measurements of the spine. They work to help your spine to return to as normal and healthy a level as possible, using specific, scientific chiropractic adjustments, along with pinpointing therapeutic techniques to help restore normal spinal curves, reduce abnormal lateral curves (scoliosis), strengthen the spinal musculature, balance posture, and even allow for certain levels of regeneration of the bones, disks, and other soft tissues.

Once you are at your optimum state, these wellness leaders will then have

"Your purpose is to serve others. The people you serve allow you to fulfill that purpose. That's getting something in return."

That stifled Eli. Baffled, and not quite following Hope's train of thought, Eli grumbled, "Why don't we just get your power on?"

———

The weekend proved to be a monumental disaster for the Samuels family, thanks to Thomas, Hope's dad, who dropped into town, toyed with everyone's affections, and left as quickly as he came.

The wounds still fresh from his second divorce, Thomas Samuels had come back to Ohio for one purpose and one purpose only: to wreak as much havoc as he could, in as little time as possible. At least, that's how Hope saw it.

He blows into town saying he wants to see his grandson and his only daughter. He actually made me believe he was sincere when he promised Adam he'd take him to a Reds game in Cincinnati. But what does he do? He goes over to Mom's to get a box of some old junk she had in storage, says he has an important business meeting that "suddenly came up," and disappears. Probably ran into an old girlfriend.

He crushed Adam and infuriated Mom, but he can't hurt me anymore. That man will never hurt me again—ever. And neither will any other man.

———

Eli sat at the desk in his condo surrounded by papers. Where was that article? He just printed it out last night, but it had already

you follow a solid spinal hygiene program, establish an ongoing schedule for wellness adjustments, offer lifestyle workshops, and provide personal lifestyle guidance.

When you're ready to choose a *real*-wellness chiropractor, here are some important things to note:

Purpose of Adjustment

- Positive indicator: The practitioner applies a very specific, gentle force with the intent of removing interference from normal nerve transmission.

Objective of Care

- Positive indicator: The practitioner helps create and maintain optimum position of your spine based on scientific norms as well as aligning your lifestyle with what it takes to produce health. The practitioner doesn't work to alleviate symptoms alone (this would not be *real* wellness).

Assessment of Improvement

- Positive indicator: You see actual change in objective findings: X-rays, posture, EMGs, computerized range of motion, muscle testing, and so forth. The practitioner is not merely looking at symptoms and doesn't judge the frequency, duration, and type of treatment on whether or not insurance covers it.

Proper Evaluation

- Positive indicator: The practitioner tests posture and takes X-rays, EMGs, and computerized tests to create an accurate measurement of your spine and other important indicators of good health. He or she doesn't just work where it hurts.

Ongoing Evaluation and Care

- Positive indicator: The practitioner remeasures within a 90- to 120-day period to see changes in initial measurements.
- Positive indicator: The practitioner creates a plan for correction and not just pain relief.
- Positive indicator: The practitioner offers an ongoing wellness care plan and does not only have you come back when it hurts.
- Positive indicator: The practitioner offers continual lifestyle education and counseling programs.

gotten mixed in with research he had printed out for the presentation he was giving at next week's regional chiropractors' meeting. The printout he was looking for was a great article about how many chiropractic patients were discovering that they no longer needed to be on Prozac. He just had to give it to Hope Samuels. Funny, it hadn't occurred to him to give it to several of his other patients who had been on Prozac. But there was something about Hope made him want to make sure she got better.

And he was thinking about her more and more. *Don't go there, Knight. She's a patient. You can't even* think *about her in any other way than as a patient.*

Besides, she's not the perfect girl. Yet, she is amazing—strong, caring, independent, insightful. No, no, not your type, though.

Eli gave up the search for the article on Prozac. He wanted to do the June newsletter on Peace Management to help get Hope—people—over depression and anxiety.

One thing Elijah knew for sure: the next time he saw Hope, he would make sure to keep the conversation brief. It was time to go back to treating her just like all his other patients, to bring things back to a purely professional level. *Her health and growth are my responsibility. I don't want to let my occasional loneliness and infatuation confuse that and interrupt her healing.*

———

"God morning, Ms. Samuels"—saying "God" instead of "good" was Eli's favorite way to greet his patients in the morning. It kept him focused. "How's your nutrition coming along? You look like

Why Do I Have to Keep Going?

One of the many questions people ask about going to a chiropractor or any wellness provider is, why do I have to go for the rest of my life? The easy answer is: you don't. You only have to go for as long as you want to stay healthy!

When do you stop drinking clean water? When does exercise stop being important? When do you stop building loving relationships? The answer is, of course, never, unless at some point you stop caring about your life.

It's the same with your spine. The level of physical, emotional, and chemical stress your body is under will determine how often your spine needs to be evaluated and adjusted. Because of the trouble most people's spines are in when they start care and the ongoing stress most of us face regularly, we typically need to start with multiple adjustments per week for several months[62] and then, as or more important, continue with some sort of weekly or biweekly maintenance/wellness care.[63] Examining posture and using EMGs are two safe, effective, and practical ways to regularly determine how much stress your central nervous system is under and how frequently you need ongoing care.

Insurance companies do not consider corrective, rehabilitative, preventive, or wellness care to be necessary. They pay only for people who are sick. It's not "health" insurance; it's really "sick" insurance. While prevention would save them billions, they have not as yet gotten the picture, so ongoing care is something that is paid for through reasonable wellness programs found in most chiropractors' offices.

Fortunately, caring doctors will typically create corrective programs and family wellness plans that are cost-effective. This makes care affordable for those with limited or no insurance to still receive all the treatment they need—really need.

The Clear Difference Between Your Doctor and Your Chiropractor

The medical community is not completely ignorant of the concept of wellness. In fact, medical practitioners have tried to jump on the wellness bandwagon not by changing their practices but by tweaking their jargon, with early detection of disease increasingly being called "wellness services," according to Dr. Christopher Kent, president of the Council on Chiropractic Practice. To make clear the distinctions between the allopathic (traditional health care) and chiropractic approaches to wellness, Kent developed this table:

you've lost several inches," commented Eli in his most professional manner.

"Yes, your information has worked well." Hope was glad he noticed, but he seemed awfully serious. *I'm sure he meant his comment from a nutritionist's perspective, since he didn't say I looked good, just thinner.*

Eli planned to say nothing—just make the necessary corrections and move on to the other patients. But Hope seemed uneasy; her nose was obviously stuffed up, and her neck was inflamed.

"You don't sound too well, and your neck is so swollen it feels as if you swallowed a water balloon," Eli said before he adjusted her neck.

"I know you're not into medications, but you'd have to admit, this is a good time for an antibiotic and an aspirin."

"I suppose it is if you're trying to destroy any chance of digesting food ever again. Really, Hope, there is a time for those things. If this was a raging bacterial infection, I'd be the first person to recommend that you go see a medical physician. But in this case, your body should handle it just fine. Why don't you give your own immune system a chance to heal this one? You'd be surprised at how powerful you really are, with a little patience and perseverance. If you don't start improving or if things dramatically worsen, then go to your MD."

"This time you might be right, Doc. I'm just stressed out over my father. He was in town this weekend spreading his usual joy, peace, and merriment."

Suddenly Eli was very thankful for the newsletter he had just written. This was not the kind of problem you answered in a one-liner,

Wellness Paradigms

	ALLOPATHIC	CHIROPRACTIC
GOAL	Prevention and early detection of disease	Maximize the expression of innate potential
STRATEGY	Passive	Active
MOTIVE	Fear	Empowerment
PRACTITIONER ROLE	Dominant	Partner/Coach
HOW DELIVERED	Event	Process
TEMPORAL PROFILE	Episodic	Lifetime
CRITERIA	Based on "normal" values and epidemiologic data	Goals set by the individual

Among other equally good definitions of wellness, Dr. Kent likes this one from the National Wellness Institute: "Wellness is an active process of becoming aware of and making choices toward a more successful existence."

The institute expands on the key words in that definition:

- *Process* means that we never arrive at a point where there is no possibility of improving.
- *Aware* means that we are by our nature continuously seeking more information about how we can improve.
- *Choices* means that we have considered a variety of options and select those that seem to be in our best interest.
- *Success* is determined by each individual regarding his or her personal collection of accomplishments for his or her life.

These definitions, Dr. Kent points out, embrace a vision of *real* wellness grounded in patient empowerment, which contrasts sharply with the fear-driven, patient-passive strategies of early detection, prevention, and maintenance.

and the office was packed. "Have I got a newsletter for you. Guaranteed to remove all your stress, cure your sinus problem, and there are no side effects. Pay careful attention to Rule Number 7."

"Thanks. This will give me something to read instead of filing for a restraining order against my father."

Noticing how down Hope looked when she came out of the treatment room, Caroline called her attention to the sign over her desk.

> **If you're less than a B+, let us know—**
> **we'll give you a hug!**

"Oh, yeah, that's me. A solid C-minus," Hope said.

"Well, then, you just come right here," Caroline said, opening her arms wide.

The two women embraced as Eli looked on. For a moment, he wished he could trade places with Caroline, but he quickly shook it off.

———

Benjamin sat in the front pew at Grace of God and continued the conversation he had begun with God earlier in the day. "Lord, I do believe it is time. It is time for my friend Eli. It is time for my new friend Hope. It is time for my little friend Adam. Open their eyes. Open their hearts. Lord, open their mouths! Give Elijah the power to speak. Give him the courage that he tells others they must have."

The quietness of the cool, cavernous sanctuary soothed Benjamin

Chiropractors study all these areas of wellness so that they truly can build awareness, lead people through a legitimate healing process, give them good choices to make for their health that go above and beyond a simple pill or shot, and give people real hope for success in body, mind, and spirit.

Chiropractic: The Foundation of the *(Real)* Wellness Movement

by Dr. Fabrizio Mancini, president of Parker Chiropractic College

Why do we believe chiropractic is the foundation of the wellness movement? It's the one profession that does not compromise on its commitment to promote drug-free and surgery-free health. By allowing a chiropractor to be your main health-care provider, you choose a professional who will not override the wisdom and healing potential that your body has; who will inspire, educate, and encourage you to be a participant and not just an observer in your health; who will not just treat a diagnosis or disease but serve the person; who will guide you and coach you to make better decisions for a healthier lifestyle; who recognizes that you have a greater potential for performance than even you realize; who will take into consideration your emotional and spiritual nature; and who has dedicated his or her life to be of service to you when it comes to your well-being.

The choices you make today will have a direct impact in the quality of your life. Don't you want to get started now? If you have developed bad habits, there's a tremendous reason to be optimistic, because you can reverse most of them within a month if you make a conscious decision to replace the negative habits with positive ones.

Chiropractors spend a lifetime studying the human body. What continues to amaze us, though, is the potential for a healthier life that is already inside each person's body. If you simply apply the lifestyle habits of healthy people, you, too, can achieve optimum health.

as he focused on Eli—successful, ambitious, caring, compassionate, utterly miserable Eli. Always giving, always serving, always alone.

Benjamin closed his eyes and gave silent thanks to God for handling the situation. For giving Eli and Hope and Adam to one another, though they could not see it yet. For giving Benjamin a glorious life. For the privilege of cleaning and polishing and neatening every square inch of this house that belonged to Him and Him alone. For each person who would walk through those doors and into this sanctuary. And for the many others who would not.

The heavy oak door leading from the street slowly opened. Benjamin heard the door close quietly and the sound of soft footsteps on the center aisle, but his eyes remained closed. He did not know the name of the cologne, but he knew the name of the one who wore it.

Hope gently touched the custodian's arm as she slid into the pew and sat next to him. "I'd ask if you were praying, but I've never seen you when you're not." She smiled as Benjamin opened his eyes. "I'd also apologize for disturbing you, but I have a feeling this is the kind of interruption you don't mind. I need to talk to you."

"I know." Now they were both smiling.

After reading Eli's June newsletter, Hope felt she had to talk to somebody. A great article on "peace management" listed ten biblical instructions for achieving genuine peace. The last two really struck her: *Thou shalt be faithful* and *Thou shalt be hopeful.* "Needing evidence for faith is *not* faith," Eli wrote. "Even when there are no miracles or magic tricks, God is still there." Wow! Hope never thought of it that way. In the section about hope, he wrote that hope helps you take risks and try the impossible, overcome fears and pursue

| Appendix A |

Further Information and Research on Chiropractic for Performance and Disease

Dr. Christopher Kent reports on a treasure trove of facts about the success of even the earliest chiropractors with regard to drug-free health care, documented as early as 1925 in a book titled *Chiropractic Statistics,* before the full advent of "modern medicine":

- 83.6 percent of 408 cases of gonorrhea: recovered or very decided improvements
- 99.4 percent of 4,193 cases of influenza: complete recovery
- 98.8 percent of 673 cases of measles: complete recovery or very decided improvement
- 98.7 percent of 149 cases of scarlet fever: completely recovered
- 100 out of 101 cases of smallpox: completely recovered

Another study was conducted by Dr. Henry Winsor, a medical doctor in Haverford, Pennsylvania, who was intrigued by chiropractic and osteopathic claims that there was a relationship between the shape of the spine and the health of internal organs. In his study, there was nearly a 100 percent correlation between "minor curvatures" (misalignment or subluxation) of the spine and diseases of the internal organs.

As Dr. Kent points out, these statistics are historically fascinating and serve to underscore the body's ability to heal itself when interference is removed. Chiropractic is not a treatment for a specific disease, but it's clear that the nervous system is involved and more research should be done to look at the effects of chiropractic and disease.

Immunity*

Significant increase in circulating B-lymphocytes and immunoglobulins in 63 to 75 percent of patients with skeletal conditions following chiropractic.

goals, have the freedom to fail and have the confidence that things will work out.

She rescheduled all of her real estate appointments and ran straight to the church, hoping to find Benjamin. She realized she was faithless and hopeless. She resented her father, and yes, she hated him. How could she possibly forgive him after he had physically and emotionally deserted her—his only daughter?

"I've told you a little bit about my father," Hope said.

Benjamin nodded.

"And about the problems he caused."

"Yes." Benjamin smiled and nodded.

"Well, I realize I'm supposed to forgive him and be hateless, but how can I after all he has done? How can I love or trust a man like that ever again? He should really be doing the apologizing."

"Have you perhaps been reading the works of our young genius, Dr. Knight?"

"I felt like that whole newsletter was written just for me," Hope said.

"Perhaps it was," Benjamin said, enjoying his private interpretation of that notion. "First I will tell you what I told my friend Eli: *Hata ukinichukia la kweli nitakwambia*—even if you dislike me, I will tell you the truth."

"Go ahead—shoot."

"Why do you think your father left and doesn't come to see you?"

"He obviously doesn't like me."

"What about God—does He like Hope?"

Hope wasn't sure what this had to do with her father. "No. I

B-lymphocyte changes were as high as a 200 percent increase, and immunoglobulins increased concurrently with the patients' improvement in their spinal condition. *(Vora and Bates and Alcorn)*

Labor Times*

Sixty-five women under chiropractic from at least their tenth week of pregnancy through labor and delivery were found to have 24 to 39 percent less labor time than the statistically averaged mean labor. *(Fallon)*

Seniors*

Senior citizens using maintenance chiropractic care made approximately half the visits to a medical provider compared to the national average, only 36 percent of patients reported frequent use of nonprescription drugs, reported fewer depressive symptoms, were more likely to report having strenuous levels of exercise, and 73.9 percent had not been hospitalized in three years. *(Rupert and Coulter)*

Diabetes*

Spinal adjustments and interferential therapy on thirty-one diabetic patients revealed that 87 percent demonstrated increased circulation. *(Dickinson)*

Athletic Performance*

Twenty-four athletes had a 6–12 percent increase over a control group of athletes not under chiropractic in the areas of agility, balance, kinesthetic perception, power, and speed reaction. *(Lauro)*

Further research documents the positive effect of chiropractic care on pulmonary function, ulcers, visual acuity, anxiety, cognitive brain function, strength, cardiac output, metabolism, optimizing blood lipid (cholesterol) levels, and the nervous system response.*

*Compliments of Dr. Matt McCoy, editor, and Dr. Terry Rondberg, publisher, *Journal of Vertebral Subluxation Research,* 2950 N. Dobson Rd., Suite 1, Chandler, AZ 85224. To learn more, go to: JVSR.com.

mean I'm trying to be the kind of person He would like. But with all of the mistakes I've made and how much I doubted Him, there's no way God would like me. Who would?"

"Hope, God does love you. He is not like other people. There's a saying *munotindaisle*. It means 'The Lord loves us; He *really* loves us.'"

"I know what you're trying to do, Benja—"

"No, Hope, really; God does love you."

"You're going to say He forgives, but—"

"No, really—God loves you."

Tears began to stream down Hope's face. "I know, I'm working on it, I'm—"

"No, no, Hope, God loves—you, just as you are."

"He can't. No one would."

"He is not like other people. He loves you, the Hope who is here right now. The Hope you have always been. With all the mistakes, with all the frailties, with all your lapses of faith, He loves you. He loves you.

"He sees the good, the resilience, the love you have for your son. He recognizes how hard you are trying to make your life better. He not only loves you, He even likes you, and He's proud of you."

"Oh, God, I love You, too. I love you too!" Hope said, falling into Benjamin's lap and crying as she hadn't cried since she was a little girl. As she lay there she felt affirmed, as if everything was going to be okay. As if somehow she had crawled into her father's lap the way his lap should have been. Like God the Father's lap.

When she could finally listen, Benjamin spoke softly. "You have come to a turning point, a crisis, which is a moment to make a

Food by God, Food by Man

*Note: these lists do not take into account food sensitivities
or other health issues you may have.*

Food by God

Good Carbohydrates

Cream of brown rice
Oats
Grits
Other hot whole-grain
  cereals (barley, quinoa,
  rye, spelt, millet, flax)
Brown, jasmine, and
  basmati rice
Rice cakes, rice noodles,
  puffed rice cereal
Barley
Buckwheat
Rye
Unprocessed soy
Spelt
Millet
Quinoa
All-natural, whole-grain,
  chemical-free, sugar-
  free breads, flours, and
  cereals
Gluten-free bread and
  sprouted-grain breads

Starchy Vegetables

Potatoes
Sweet potatoes
Corn
Peas
Squash

Vegetables

Alfalfa
Artichokes
Arugula
Asparagus
Bamboo shoots
Beets
Broccoli
Brussels sprouts
Cabbage
Carrots
Cauliflower
Celery
Collard greens
Cucumbers
Eggplant
Escarole
Green beans
Kale
Lettuce: all kinds
Mesclun
Mustard greens

Onions
Parsley
Parsnips
Pea pods
Portobello mushrooms
Radishes
Radicchio
Scallions
Seaweed
Shallots
Swiss chard
Snap peas
Snow peas
Spinach
String beans
Tomatoes (also
  considered fruit)
Turnips
Watercress
Wheat grass
Zucchini

Fruits

Apples
Bananas (high blood
  sugar effect)
Blackberries

decision. And you have made a decision. You decided that the Hope you have known up until now has to die. She has to die to her inadequate self-concept, and she has to die to low self-esteem and to the seemingly endless cycle of rejection and pain in her life. The old chapters are part of an old book, and Hope has come through a long downtime not realizing that when she was out of sync and out of sorts, she was exploring things deep within.

"Hope, you withdrew from God and the outer world, and like the caterpillar you began to reinvent yourself from the inside out. You are now emerging as a new creature with wings to fly because you let go of the need to crawl in the lowlands of frustration and disappointment any longer. You're going toward where God wants you to be.

"You love God."

"Yes."

"You want to please God."

"Yes."

"Forgiveness pleases God. Why not give your father as well as your mother a gift they do not deserve? It will be the best thing you have ever done for . . . you."

———

Early summer in Ohio proved to be its usual hazy, hot, and humid self. But the humidity broke during the first week of July, bringing in temporarily cooler temperatures and much drier air. Hope closed her eyes and breathed in deeply as she sat at an outdoor café with Naomi. She smiled, sipped her herbal iced tea, and said to

Blueberries
Cantaloupe
Currants
Grapefruit
Grapes
Honeydew melons
Kiwi
Lemons
Limes
Mangoes
Nectarines
Oranges
Peaches
Pears
Pineapple
Plums
Prunes
Raisins
Raspberries
Strawberries
Tangerines
Watermelon

Good Proteins

(All animal proteins are
   best when raised
   organically and fed
   their natural diet.)
Eggs
Fish (limit due to mer-
   cury toxicity)
Grouper
Halibut
Mackerel
Mahimahi
Rainbow trout
Salmon
Sardines
Sea bass
Snapper

Swordfish
Trout
Tuna
Whitefish
Chicken/turkey breast
Red meat
Beans (protein and
   carbohydrate)
   Chickpeas
   Kidney
   Lentils
   Lima
   Navy
   Pinto
   White
   Fresh or fermented
   soy (no processed
   soy products)
Nuts (fat and protein)
   Almonds
   Walnuts
   Hazelnuts
   Macadamia nuts
   Pine nuts
Seeds (Fat and Protein)
   Pumpkin
   Sesame
   Sunflower
   Flax

Good Fats

Olives (olive oil: cold-
   pressed, extra-virgin)
Extra-virgin coconut oil
Crushed flaxseed (cold-
   pressed flaxseed oil
   can be used, although
   it breaks down like
   other seed oils)
Fish oil capsules

Organic fats in grass-and
   vegetable-fed beef, egg
   yolks, and chicken
Almonds and almond
   butter
Avocados
Walnuts
Tahini (sesame and
   olive oil)

Bad Fats—Not Food by God

Non-grass-, nonorganic-
   fed animal fats
Palm oils
Hydrogenated oils (trans
   fats)
Milk fat/cream
Vegetable oils removed
   from original source
Nut and seed oils

Beverages

Water: reverse osmosis,
   distilled, fresh spring,
   filtered
Fresh-squeezed fruit and
   vegetable juices
Almond, rice, or oat
   milk
Herbal tea

Condiments

(Condiments are not
   used in heavy
   amounts, so they can
   do little damage unless
   they are from a chemi-
   cal source.)
Sesame seeds
Ginger

Naomi, "With all of the great things that have been happening, I've really felt like there was more for me. Maybe even in a different place. On my last visit to Eli, I asked him how he knew chiropractic was his purpose. He said he loved it and he just knew he was put here to save the world the same way his world was saved. But then he asked me what my purpose was.

"Well, I—really didn't know. I know my purpose is to serve God and be a good mother to Adam and help other people and all that. But I don't know. There's got to be something more, you know?"

"I guess so," said Naomi. "I'm not really sure where you're going with this."

"I wasn't sure either until he asked, 'What would you do if you knew you couldn't fail?'"

"Wow! What did you say to that?"

"I said I had no idea, but that I was pretty sure I'd mess it up, whatever it was. Of course, you know Eli. He said, 'Wrong answer, Ms. Samuels. Remember, you can't fail at it, no matter how hard you try to. Never be afraid of making mistakes. The only thing you need to be afraid of is not learning from your mistakes.'

"My response was that it was easy for him to say—Mr. Fearless, save the world, Superman."

"Was that it?" questioned Naomi.

"Would the Answer Man let me have the last word? He said, 'Superman doesn't have courage—no one could hurt him. He's the man of steel. I'm not Superman, and I'm not fearless. Courage doesn't mean you're not afraid. It means you're afraid and you do it anyway.' After thinking about that, I remembered how I always wanted to build things, not just sell them. And you remember

High-quality vinegar
All-natural hot sauce
Spices without MSG or
hydrolyzed vegetable
protein
Basil, curry, dill, garlic,
ginger, horseradish,
mint, miso, mustard,
paprika, parsley,
rosemary, tarragon,
and thyme

Olive oil–based and low-
fat, chemical-free
dressings
Lemon juice
Natural soy sauce or
tamari
Natural mustards
Butter Buds

Sweeteners
Honey

Stevia
Unrefined maple syrup
Brown rice syrup
Almond butter
Fresh fruit and fruit
juice
Unsweetened, all-natural
fruit jellies and syrups

Food by Man List

Some primary examples:
Pork products
Shellfish
Sugar substitutes
(Aspartame, Splenda,
Saccharine, etc.)
MSG and hydrolyzed
vegetable proteins

Hydrogenated oils
Additives, colorings,
flavorings, and
preservatives
Fast, refined, and fried
(convenient) foods
Regular use of animal
products

Pasteurized, nonorganic
dairy products
Caffeine
Refined sugar and salt

when I got that great job offer in Detroit to work with that real estate development company? Well, I've decided that may be my purpose. Besides, I'd get to see more of my dad."

"Are you sure you're not jumping into this? I mean, you've only just started to have a relationship with him," Naomi said.

"Oh, but it feels so *right*. It will be a big change for Adam and me, but I'm ready to take the plunge," Hope said.

"I don't know. I think you ought to take this slower."

"Aren't you one of the gazillion people who keep telling me that I need to take more risks? Allow me to quote you: 'If you want something you've never had before, you've got to do something you've never done before.' So here I am, wanting something I've never had before, and to get it, I'm doing something I've never done before. You ought to be supportive!"

"I can't. This isn't exactly what I was talking about when I said that. Look, I just don't want you to get hurt. Give this some more time."

"Well, I can't exactly do that. If we're going to move to Detroit, we have to do it before school starts. I don't want to transfer Adam after the school year starts."

"I know, I know. But still, you've just gotten on good terms with your father after all these years."

"But I've lost so many years with him. My mom's hopeless, but I'm okay with that. I know I've told you this a hundred times, but if only you could have been there when I asked him to forgive me for being such a brat all these years! He just crumbled. I'd never seen my dad cry. He's carried this guilt around for so long, and he never even felt worthy of our love. He assumed he had ruined his life and everyone's around him. Naomi, we *forgave* each other—

Appendix C
Testimonials

Finally Free

By the time I was nine years old, I had realized that the occasional difficulty I had breathing was not normal. Because both of my parents had suffered from asthma, my family doctor determined I had inherited the same disorder. For the first few years, I was placed on a succession of different medications, all of which failed after a while. At the age of twelve, I was on four medications, including two different inhalers.

Christmas was a particularly miserable time for me, since the arrival of colder weather always brought on a bad spell. A hurried trip to the emergency room would result in an immediate shot of adrenaline, a round of Prednisone and antibiotics, and an admission ticket to a room upstairs for at least a week.

That routine continued until I was in my early twenties, when a doctor recommended that I have regular allergy shots. Every shot—for three full years—resulted in an asthma attack and another round of medication to prevent hospitalization. The shots did nothing but drain my bank account.

I am now forty-one years old. My entire family and I have been seeing a chiropractor regularly, at first because of my husband's back pain. I was hopeful that undergoing treatment might help improve my breathing, but I found there was much more healing in store for me. I am now off medications completely, have a normal breathing pattern, and can even exercise without any breathing problems. That is a miracle in itself!

I attend as many workshops as possible to learn more about what I can do to allow the body the Lord has given me, which is His temple, to breathe freely and be healthy. We give thanks to God, for His ways are far better than what man thinks and does.

—ROSE MOYER,
patient of Dr. Roger Romano,
Sarasota, FL

really, truly forgave each other! He's transformed. He's like ultra-Grandpa now."

"Look, I'm not saying you shouldn't spend time with him—as much time as possible even. But moving? I don't know. That's pretty radical."

"But the real estate market in the suburbs around Detroit is really booming right now. I have a great offer to work at the leading real estate company in the area. I'll be making malls, mansions, and skyscrapers. I will not only be making a killing there, I'll be making a difference."

Naomi paused. "What about Eli?" she quietly asked.

"Oh, I'm on maintenance now, once a week. He's going to refer me to a chiropractor in Detroit."

"Hope, I'm not asking about *Dr.* Eli. I'm asking about Eli the man. The man you're in love with."

"Naomi!" Hope sat up straighter and glared at her friend. "He's my doctor. I'm his patient. He's only interested in me as a patient. I admit I have some confused feelings for him sometimes, but maybe that's just because he's done so much for me. I've never felt better. I have more energy than I've had since Adam was born. I've lost all that weight, and I'm the same size I was in high school without even dieting. I'm off all my meds—I haven't even been on Prozac since the breakthrough with my father!

"Even that was Dr. Eli's doing," Hope continued. "My nervous system healing, the tapes, all those whiteboards about God, the newsletters, and all of his one-minute quotes and Eli-isms that he'd say to me during my adjustments: it all added up to a big change in my life. It's been an extreme makeover—God's way. Who wouldn't

A Chiropractor's Personal Miracle

I have seen many miracles in my years in practice, but none as closely as the miracle with my second son, Michael, when he was only sixty days old. I remember coming home late from giving a lecture at a local church that particular night, around 11 PM.

My wife, Melinda, told me she was worried about Michael, because he started to have a hacking cough with congestion. We decided to let him rest and sleep, but we planned to monitor him closely throughout the night. After showering and getting myself ready for bed, I could hear Michael's hacking cough getting progressively worse. Melinda and I were on high alert. A little after midnight when I jumped out of bed to comfort Michael, Melinda turned on the hot water in the shower to create a steam to ease his congestion.

After thirty minutes in our homemade steam room, his condition did not improve. We decided it was time to head to Emergency. While Melinda was trying to find a middle-of-the-night sitter for our other son, Christian, Michael's breathing worsened. During those tense moments, I decided to adjust Michael's spine. I started with his neck and worked my way down his tiny spine. I then picked him up and put him over my right shoulder, and that is when the miracle started to happen.

Michael rested his head on my shoulder, arched his back, and tucked his arms and legs under his chest. I could tell his body was preparing for something, but I didn't know what. All of a sudden, his arching back straightened skyward, his body started to fall back onto my chest, and he vomited over my shoulder.

Something special happened at that moment, because Michael immediately stopped coughing and hacking. He no longer had any trouble breathing. He was resting over my shoulder as if nothing happened. He was sound asleep. When I took off my shirt, I realized Michael had vomited mucus from his lungs, not the contents of his stomach. He slept soundly through the night and woke up fine the next morning.

His little body didn't need any drugs or poisons to get him back to health; he just needed his little body to work the way God had intended it to work. Once I removed his spinal subluxations, his body was able to function at a higher level of efficiency and heal itself.

The best defense a person can have against sickness, illness, and disease is to make sure that his spine is free from subluxations, allowing the Power that made the body to be the Power that heals the body.

> — DR. PATRICK ST. GERMAIN,
> director of St. Germain Chiropractic
> Clinics in Central Florida

love someone who did all that for her? I just think that for a while there I was getting gratitude and romance tangled up. I'm grateful to him. That's all."

"Right. And I'm the Easter Bunny."

"If you say so." Hope rolled her eyes.

"And Adam?"

"And Adam what?"

"Adam loves Eli too. I haven't seen him even speak to a male in the entire time I've known him, yet when he sees the doc he jumps into his arms like he's Santa Claus. You know that boy of yours loves Eli to pieces. And so do you. He's not Jacob and he's not your father. If you're going to take chances, take a chance on Eli."

"Easter Bunny, Santa Claus—I guess that makes me the Wicked Stepmother. Would you just look at the time?" Hope asked in her most exaggerated voice. "I simply must be running off now. See ya later, Easter Bunny!"

"Only if you stay in Ohio."

———

"The loss of one patient should be of no major concern to you," Benjamin said to his friend during their morning preshift prayer time. "You have many patients. One moves away; another moves in. It is what you would call 'No big deal.' Or is it?"

"Good try. But that won't work with me. It's common for patients to fall for doctors and doctors for patients. I'll forget about her in a few weeks and fall for someone else that I can't have."

"Elijah, you cannot run from this any longer. This is your

Three Simple Facts Changed Our Lives

As a pastor's wife, I thought God would protect me from having certain kinds of problems. So I didn't know what to think when our second child, Joshua, was not as responsive as I thought he should be.

At first, it was his hearing; several tests confirmed a loss of hearing in both ears. But the doctors weren't sure what was causing it.

Then I began to realize that Joshua was suffering from headaches. A medical doctor recommended drugs. But every time I gave him a dropper filled with medicine, I knew I wasn't fixing the problem.

By the time Joshua reached his preschool years, he was plagued with allergies. Again we tried medication, but I wondered if there was a connection between his allergy problems and his headaches. The doctors said only that there could be a connection. I was frustrated to no end. I wanted answers, but I wasn't getting any.

Soon his health problems grew in complexity. He required special hearing aid devices in both ears to pick up basic sounds we take for granted. Other children began to tease him.

Our daughter told us what she had learned from her chiropractor—three simple facts that helped her understand health and healing:

1. The most important part of the human body is fully enclosed in bone: the brain, surrounded by the skull; and the spinal cord, surrounded by the spinal column.

2. Misalignments in the spine cause stress to the nerves branching off the spinal cord, in turn causing miscommunication between the brain and the targeted organs and tissues controlled by those nerves.

3. Specific spinal adjustments remove nerve interference and allow the body to heal.

I decided to take Joshua in for a chiropractic examination. That day was the beginning of a miraculous healing. In a follow-up visit, our chiropractor reviewed Joshua's X-rays in detail and explained how specific areas of spinal misalignment could be linked to sinus and allergy problems, headaches, even hearing problems!

After the first week of spinal adjustments, Joshua's allergies didn't seem as bad. A few weeks later, Joshua mentioned that his headaches were decreasing and were almost gone completely. Joshua's teachers said he seemed more eager and more able to learn.

In only a few short weeks, my son's life has been changed, due to God's grace by way of chiropractic care. Fewer allergies, almost no more drugs or medications, fewer headaches, and improved hearing!

moment. You are in love. And not just with a woman—you love that boy as well. They are your family, the family you have wanted deep down inside you for all of your life," Benjamin said. "Now you must make it official. It is as simple as that."

"First of all, she's my patient."

"She is not going to be your patient anymore," Benjamin said.

"Second, you've heard me describe the perfect woman that God has for me. I'm still trying to find her."

"And how has that worked out for you?"

"Not well."

"Are you perfect?"

"I see where you're going, but it doesn't apply here."

"It doesn't? Listen, Doctor, materially, nothing is perfect. Spiritually, everything's perfect."

"I think the old days in the mine have finally caused your brain to deteriorate. What on earth does that mean?"

"Oh, I'm plenty sane. It's a simple concept. Nothing is just right, but everything is exactly as it is supposed to be. I am not perfect, you are not perfect, but we are exactly as God needs us to be. You will never find perfect either. The reason you love Hope—"

"I told you, I love her as a patient."

"The reason you love Hope," Benjamin repeated, "is because what you call 'imperfections' are the uniquenesses of her character. The very things you find imperfect are really what you love. God loves you, and you're a mess. When He's talking to His buddies, He probably doesn't admit He loves you either!" He laughed.

"Ms. Right is coming. I just need patience."

"You have known Hope for nearly a year. And you have been—

I can't wait to see what more God has planned for Joshua as we continue his chiropractic corrective care. Maybe God does intend for him to be a special leader like Joshua in the Bible— I've already seen him win a couple of very special battles!

—DORA DONNA,
patient of Keith Helmendach

Running the Race

When I started my practice in the hills of central Kentucky, my first patients were the Gibsons. Arvil Gibson was the maintenance man for the building I was renting, and getting him to come in for an adjustment was a battle, despite the back pain he suffered. Years before, another chiropractor had hurt him, and he was understandably reluctant—until he got to know me better. One by one the other family members started coming to the office for different health problems: shoulders, ankles, knees, headaches, neck pain, and so on.

One day, I had been invited to share a meal with the whole family. Grandchildren were running all over the yard—all but one, Justin. Quiet by nature, Justin was unable to join in since he walked with a limp and could not run. A doctor had told the Gibsons that Justin would grow out of it, and being protective of the child, they had not brought him in to see me. But that day, I asked Justin if he would let me take a picture of his hips and see if there was anything that I could do to help his body heal itself faster so he could play like the other kids.

I left it up to Justin to decide that there might be a chance for a change in his condition. To my surprise, Justin was in my office the next morning, ready to get started. By the end of the first week, he noticed an improvement in his stance and ability to walk. By the end of the first phase of chiropractic play, Justin was running and playing with the rest of the kids as if he never had a problem.

What made this especially meaningful to me was what happened next. Justin decided he wanted to try out for his elementary school's cross-country running team. Once again, his mother was understandably concerned and asked me to evaluate him to see if he could handle something so strenuous. I gave Justin the green light. And the more the boy ran, the faster he got. By the end of the season, Justin finished third in the state in his division.

To watch this young boy go from spectator to participant was a humbling experience, a genuine act of God. But nothing has been more gratifying than seeing him inspire his little brother and sister to do the same by chasing him on the cross-country team.

—DR. LEWIS MARTIN MISINAY,
a chiropractor in Kentucky

oh, what is that wonderful English word for it? Ah yes, you have been 'smitten' with her for most of that time. *Moyo wa kupenda hauna subira*—a heart deep in love has no patience. Therefore, you are not being true to your own heart. Why do you ignore this? You are deep in love, and yet you do not act. You do not tell her. You do not fight for her to stay. Be impatient, my friend! Impatient for the love to be fulfilled, to be realized. Be impatient, this one time."

On the way to Dr. Eli's office for her last visit, Hope's cell phone vibrated. She glanced at the caller ID; it was Dr. Jackson.

"Yes, Dr. Jackson, I had called you to make sure you had received my records," she said. "Yes, that's right—from Dr. Elijah Knight—or it might say Knight Chiropractic Wellness Center on the envelope. Good. You did get them. That's great. Well, we'll be in Detroit tomorrow. We're getting adjusted today, and Adam and I normally need only a weekly adjustment right now. So, we'd like to see you in a week. I don't want to miss any adjustments. Great. Thanks!"

Adam overheard the conversation from the backseat of the Honda where he was buried under the piles of pillows, towels, and blankets they were taking with them to Detroit. "Was that the new chiropractor, Mommy? Does he have a toy area like Dr. Eli?"

"He comes highly recommended by Dr. Eli. I'm sure he'll be great. With Mommy's new job, if he doesn't have any toys, we can buy him some." Hope loved the way that sounded.

No one will be like Dr. Knight. Oh well, this too shall pass. I'll get

Good-bye, Fibromyalgia!

I am fifty-three years old, and until five years ago I looked and felt much younger than my age at the time. I was lean, active (pursuing an orange belt in karate), and busy with family, church, and a job. I loved to shop, cook, teach, visit with friends, and take good care of myself.

I began experiencing all-over soreness and found myself unable to do a karate kick, sit Indian-style on the floor, even hold on to my purse. Stooping, bending, and walking without a limp or without support of some kind were difficult. Within a year, I was diagnosed with fibromyalgia. I soon got used to living with constant low-grade pain that escalated each night to a severe stabbing and tearing pain in my legs. I had asthma, headaches, and no sense of smell.

Within the first two weeks of chiropractic care, I realized I was sleeping better. My right leg was gaining strength; I could use it to pull my weight up the stairs without its buckling under or using my arms on the handrail to pull myself up. My headaches began diminishing, I could breathe more easily, and I started smelling and tasting things again. I had much more energy. Even in the first six weeks, I achieved more than I had anticipated so early on. Praise God!

—MICHELLE,
patient of Dr. Gavin Grant,
Orange County, CA

No More Medication

I'm thirty-six years old, and for years I've battled high cholesterol. When my cholesterol count hit 300, my doctor put me on Zocor, which reduced my cholesterol but caused liver damage. My doctor switched me to Lipitor, which caused my cholesterol level to actually increase. When my doctor next suggested switching to Crestor, I'd had enough. I was probably the most skeptical person on the planet when it came to alternatives, but I decided I needed to at least give them a try. So I decided to be guided by a local Body by God chiropractor. He got me to change my eating habits and started me on a regular adjustment program. In three months, my cholesterol was down to 235; in six months, it was down to 140, all without drugs. I also lost over twenty pounds.

—JOHN VANDERVOORT,
patient of Dr. Mark McCullough,
Battle Creek, Michigan

Even the Pediatrician Is Impressed

My three children and I have been seeing Dr. Debra for just over two and a half years. I am free of the migraines that troubled me for ten years! My children are free of ear infections and other childhood aches and pains. One of my children has

over all this silliness once I settle in and maybe even like Dr. Jackson more—as a chiropractor, Hope tried to convince herself.

———

Caroline was well prepared for their departure, with a good-bye balloon for Adam and a going-away card signed by all of the staff—and Benjamin—for Hope.

In the adjustment room, Hope tried to keep herself composed, but tears kept running down her face and ruining her makeup. She managed to cough out, "Dr. Eli, you'll be glad to know that Dr. Jackson got my records and has already scheduled my first appointment for me. We're actually going to see him next week. We'll really need it after the long ride and all of the unpacking."

Eli checked Adam's spine and said, "Well, I guess last week was his last adjustment from me. His spine is beginning to hold its healthy position for a couple of weeks at a time. I wish all kids could start life out this way." Always the doctor, Eli told Hope how sad they all were to be losing her as a patient.

"Hey, you're the one who convinced me I should do this," Hope said.

"What? Me? You never mentioned this plan to me until you had made the decision. I didn't have anything to do with it," Eli said, doing a lousy job of covering his distress.

Hope was shocked at his response. "You most certainly did! You asked me a really important question: 'What would you do if you knew you couldn't fail at it? Do not be afraid of making mistakes,

vision challenges; chiropractic relieves the pain in his neck and head due to eye strain. We are all free from antibiotics now. Chiropractic has changed our lives—just ask our pediatrician and my internal-medicine doctor.

I recently took my daughter in for her yearly wellness check. My pediatrician said, "Where have you guys been? This has been the worst cold and flu season. I've seen other patients two to three times more than usual, and I haven't seen you at all. What have you been doing to stay so healthy?" When I told her "chiropractic," she said, "Well, keep it up. It's certainly working!"

Truly, I can't believe we were once without the knowledge of all chiropractic can do. It's such a part of our lives now and contributes to our health and overall well-being in an amazing way!

—SHANA ALBRIGHT,
a patient of Dr. Debra Adams,
Kirkland Life Chiropractic,
Kirkland, Washington

The Miracles Have Begun

My daughter, Gabrielle (Gabbie), was a normal, healthy fifteen-month-old until July 10, 2003, when she fell into a small fishing pond and nearly drowned. She was pulled from the pond, given CPR, and rushed to Baptist East Hospital in Louisville, Kentucky, and later to Kosair.

Her prognosis was bad. Doctors found she had significant brain damage and doubted that she would live through the night. Our family, friends, and church family began a prayer vigil. We stood on such Scriptures as Isaiah 53:5, "By His stripes we are healed," and others.

After nearly two weeks at Kosair, having received the best that modern medicine had to offer, Gabbie was released and assigned to hospice care so she could die at home.

Her body had greatly deteriorated by this time. She was stiff and rigid, her eyes were rolled back in her head, and her tongue was protruding from her mouth as she gasped for every breath as if it was her last. We needed a miracle. On August 27, 2003, we got one!

We had gone to church that day, and the pastor asked us to bring Gabbie up front for prayer. While praying, Dr. Rick Hellmann, a chiropractor who is a member there, had a vision in which he saw Gabbie's skull hit a rock under water where she had fallen. The top two vertebrae in her neck had compressed the brain stem. This, he said, was causing her body to shut down, and he asked if he could adjust the compression right there in church. We agreed, and after Dr. Hellmann adjusted Gabbie's neck in one of the prayer rooms, wonderful things began to happen immediately.

just of not learning from your mistakes. Find a purpose'—all of that was you!

"And then that newsletter—well, that helped give me the courage to forgive my father and ask for his forgiveness. You had a whole lot to do with this decision."

"Don't go, Hope."

"What?"

"I—I mean, don't go unless you're sure it's the right thing."

"It feels like my purpose. Plus, we're leaving from here. Right now!"

Eli gathered himself, choked down his emotions, and focused on being her doctor one last time. "Hope, I didn't do anything other than help you discover the treasure buried deep inside you all that time. You've just now happened to trip over it and give yourself permission to follow your dreams and fulfill your purpose. You already have faced what some people never truly face in their lives. Everyone talks about surviving, but really they're just breathing. You are more than a survivor. You faced the dark place and the emptiness that was there crying out inside. You have kept on going in spite of it all. It's your conviction to hold fast to your dreams, not me, that is responsible for the fact that those dreams are now materializing.

"Hope, I want to share one more thing with you, because your name is so beautiful and symbolic. Remember, 'Faith is the substance of things *hoped* for.' Faith is something you have always had; you cannot get it and you cannot lose it; it was given to you by God. And since it is built on hope—which is not wishful thinking but rather confident expectation based on honoring true

That night, Gabbie slept for eight hours for the first time in her life! A miracle all in itself!

Since then, Dr. Hellmann has continued to adjust Gabbie on a daily basis (weekends included). He charges us nothing for his services, and Gabbie's health has slowly but surely improved. Now Gabbie can turn her head from side to side, sit up, and look around. She blinks her eyes, swallows, coughs, makes smacking noises with her mouth, eats without a feeding tube, moves her arms and legs, and opens her hands, which were once clenched tightly into fists. Her awareness and speech are coming back in the form of a cry.

Of course, we're believing that God has many more miracles in store for Gabbie. She needs a total healing and restoration in her brain, plus much more. But for right now, we're grateful. Grateful that Gabbie is still with us and grateful for people like Dr. Rick Hellmann.

—JENNY HOLLY,
whose daughter, Gabbie, is a patient
of Dr. Rick Hellmann, Trinity
Chiropractic, Louisville, Kentucky

Walking Without Pain

When I came to Dr. Harmon, I couldn't stand to lift up my right leg and walk because of the pain, soreness, and weakness in my heel and tendon area. I had suffered two years or longer with this pain.

Medical doctors treated me with Prednisone pills and injections and muscle relaxants, which helped until the medicine wore off, which made me think it was covering up the problem, not getting to the root of it. The doctor recommended surgery and the surgeons said they would have to shorten the tendon, resulting in my walking on my toes the rest of my life. I refused, believing God had a better way.

Then I met Dr. Harmon in 2004. After several adjustments, traction at home and at the office, and teachings by Dr. Harmon, I can walk without pain.

—ROSALEE DAVIS,
a patient of Dr. Terry Harmon

How Chiropractic Changed My Eyes, My Ears, My Life

Several years ago, chiropractic literally changed my life. For years I suffered from horrible pain and discomfort. As I aged I developed a terrible condition that affected not only my spine but my eyes and ears as well. My life became a nightmare. My visual condition was severe enough that normal daylight would put me in terrible pain and I needed to stay indoors or wear light-blocking sunglasses. My hearing problem was equally painful. Subtle noise or even normal everyday noises were amplified by the condition to a point of unbearable pain. Performing normal func-

desire—you can choose to live in faith. Faith is a decision when you boil it all down. It is something that you actually are learning to practice because you know your life depends on it. If you believe this is your purpose, then have faith and hope. Every decision you make by faith will show you just how much hope you have for the future."

Hope was shocked and speechless.

As Eli looked at the stunned Hope, he was stunned himself. He wished he hadn't said anything. If he wanted her to stay, it was too late now. He had just bought her a ticket. Realizing his little speech had now put him way behind with his work, and wanting to get away from what was becoming an obviously painful situation, Eli finally spoke, stumbling over his words: "Well . . . you'll be great— I'm sure I'll . . . we'll see you—"

"Mommy! Doc!" Adam ran into the room with his balloon waving behind him and gave Eli one last hug.

"Take care of your mom, Dr. Adam," Eli called as he sprinted to the next room.

When he got to the next room he couldn't believe it. "Benjamin, I hope they charged you extra to come in today."

"Thank God you're here, Dr. Eli. I thought you'd never leave that room with that woman you don't care about."

"How can I help you, Pastor?" Eli quickly changed the subject.

"I aggravated my disk again. I need your healing hands."

Eli put Benjamin in a position to take the pressure off his spine and left him in the room while he caught up on the mass of patients that had filled his office—and parking lot.

He came back and did his adjustment on Benjamin's spine.

tions such as driving caused me so much discomfort that I had to wear earmuffs to drown out the sound. Although I was an adult, I needed to live at home. My family and I spent a fortune at some of the top specialists in New York City. They performed test after test with no answers, no explanation, and no results at all.

At the time, my mom was a patient of Dr. Brad Butler's in Oakland, New Jersey. She kept asking me to see him. She knew he could help. I never listened. As I continued to suffer over more time, I knew I had to change something. Finally, I called his office. What I learned that day has changed my life. I learned that God made the body in such a way that health is our natural state and that all sicknesses, no matter what names used, are just signs that the body isn't functioning the right way.

After a few months of adjustments, my body began to regain normal functions for the first time in years. I was impatient at first. In fact, I tried to quit several times, but Dr. Butler kept after me. Thank goodness for that. As I write this, all of my visual and auditory problems have healed. I have a great job. I'm married and have a beautiful son. All of us get adjusted by Dr. Butler and plan that we always will.

—By Joel DePeri,
a patient of Dr. Bradford T. Butler,
DC Oakland, New Jersey

Depression and Anxiety Are Gone

For more than thirty years I suffered with severe depression and anxiety. It had consumed every waking minute of my life since I was five years old. It had affected every relationship I had; I hated my husband and he hated me. I considered divorce and honestly would not have blamed him if he had left me; *I* would have left me.

Throughout my life I was seen by the best doctors around for my depression. I was told that I had "mind problems" and was prescribed various medications that actually made the panic attacks come more frequently with increased severity. In April 2001, my husband dragged me into the office of Dr. Holly Ruocco. She took a few minutes away from her adjusting tables to explain how chiropractic care can benefit everyone; then she checked my spine and took X-rays. She had me return the following day for a report on her findings, and I reluctantly did so.

This was the moment that changed my life. When Dr. Holly stepped into the room, I knew there was a problem just by the look on her face. All of my worst fears were about to come true. She showed me my results and told me that I had a subluxation in my neck and this was impeding vital nerve flow from bringing life to every organ system in my body. I knew I was in trouble. The curve in my neck was going the opposite of normal. She explained that all health—physical, mental, and emotional—was given to us by God. That hit a nerve with me.

"That should get you fixing churches again, although I want you out of commission for tonight—flat on your back with an ice bag. No heat on a hot disk."

"Yes, Doctor, you are a blessing to me. I'll see you for prayer and another adjustment in the morning," Benjamin said as he stood up to leave.

"Benjamin," Eli called after him, "was it worth it?"

"Was what worth it, Eli?"

"Giving up the fortune you would have received, leaving the place you knew, the girl—you know."

"Eli, I'm not going to say I never wonder, *What if I had stayed?* But a man's heart is like an empty cup waiting to be filled by the love of a woman. We can deny this and try to fill the cup with other things, but then we find the emptiness remains. My Doris filled my cup in a way that work, achievements, and possessions never could have. Even with her death, her love is still there. Although I miss her now, I know I'll have her for all eternity. Was it worth it? Yes, it was worth it."

"See you tomorrow, Benjamin."

————

"That sure was a good meal. Thanks again," Miriam said to Eli. "You know I like it when we go out." She settled into the easy chair in her living room.

"No problem, Mom."

"Sit. Stay a while," she said. "You sound out of it."

For once, Eli was in the mood to stay. He dropped onto the couch.

"I heard that girl left with her son for Detroit today."

When Dr. Holly made her recommendations, my first thought was, *No way; I am committed to my work,* and time would not permit me to get to her office before 6 PM. Then I realized just how backward my priorities were, and I decided to get adjusted. It scared me, but everything in her report made sense, so I decided to fight through that fear.

When I received my first chiropractic adjustment, I had immediate energy that I had not felt in years. That night I found myself dancing around the house. Ken noticed a difference too. He said I had a sparkle in my eyes that he had not seen in years. It was like life had entered my body. It was the first night in years Ken didn't go outside to clean his car or find something to do to avoid me.

All my bad thoughts have gone away, and I no longer suffer from anxiety attacks. It has been three years, and I love my life.

Through the years of being with Dr. Holly, I have met countless others who have had their "moment" in her office. From depression and anxiety to migraines and pain to ulcers and infections. We are all in agreement: remove the interference from your nervous system and let the power that made your body, heal your body. I know that my body is a self-healing gift.

— TRISH DIGRAZIA,
a patient of Dr. Holly Ruocco

There's a Difference Between Chiropractors

My name is David Parkhurst, and I am forty-nine years old. For three months I have been receiving chiropractic adjustments and traction three times a week from Dr. Pamer.

About three years ago I pinched a nerve in my neck from driving a semitruck. At the time, I was told by a chiropractor that it probably caused permanent damage to my spine. I had to quit my job, take a nine-month leave, and change occupations. When I saw Dr. Pamer several years later, I still had numbness in my left thumb, occasional pain in my left shoulder, and an uneasiness about how fragile my body actually was. Dr. Pamer took some X-rays and showed me how my spinal geometry was still misaligned and explained that this misalignment was causing interference of the central nervous system.

My first chiropractor did mention that my problem could possibly be reversed, but that it would probably be too expensive because he was not set up to give the kind of long-term, intensive, and affordable treatment that was necessary for me to recover. My first chiropractor was used to seeing patients only during times of discomfort and saw them only until their pain was relieved. My condition was irreversible only because of a lack of knowledge on my part; I didn't know there were different kinds of chiropractors.

Dr. Pamer made it possible for me to have much more mobility and energy, and

"What is with everyone? How did you find out about that?"

"I'm your mother. I get paid good money to know these things."

This should be interesting, Eli thought. They had pretty much talked everything out over Miriam's birthday dinner: the typical "You work too much, you should take a vacation," but she never brought up Hope. This felt like a setup.

Eli got up and walked into the kitchen. "Do you have any bottled water, Mom? That meal was salty." Eli grabbed a bottle and sat back on the sofa ready to resist.

"So, what's the story?"

"Are you talking about Hope and Adam? They're gone, Mom. I was just a vessel, someone God used to help Hope get whole again and find her purpose. I was an agent of healing. Nothing more and nothing less. It was just not meant to be."

"Maybe something did happen, and you're just afraid to take a chance. All relationships aren't like ours, and all fathers aren't like your dad."

"Sounds like it's time for me to go. Happy birthday again, Mom." He kissed her on the cheek and rushed out the door before she had any more time for *Amateur Psychologist Hour.*

Somehow, though, what she said had pierced him. He unlocked his car door, got in, but before he could turn on the ignition he felt a strange yet familiar feeling. He felt as if he were seven years old again, sitting in a hospital room, confused, scared, and struggling for every breath—wondering if one of them would be his last. He could see everything; the monitors, the white sterile walls, the chrome at the end of the bed, the old TV, the tubes sticking in his arms, and the frustrated look on the nurse's face. He felt cold, but

I can now exercise pain-free. I really believe that I am now free to live life at 100 percent and not be distracted by memories of pain and sorrow.

— DAVID PARKHURST,
a patient of Dr. Matt Pamer

Help in My Pain and My Pregnancy

Before I came to see Dr. Terri, I didn't think anything could be done for my headaches, my difficulty with balance, and poor circulation in my feet. I just took pills for my pain and put up with the rest. I had no idea the problems were related to my spine.

My sister, Michelle, who was Dr. Terri's chiropractic assistant, had been telling me about the benefits of chiropractic, so I thought I'd give it a try. After starting the care I became pregnant. I had had horrible back labor with my first child, and I didn't want to go through that again.

From the X-rays and computerized scans Dr. Terri took on my first visit, I could see that there was a subluxation in the first vertebra in my neck as well as in my pelvis. I have been under chiropractic care for ten months and have had fantastic results. My headaches are gone, my circulation has returned to normal, and my balance is great. Most exciting of all is that my pregnancy and delivery were very smooth.

— PATTI MERKEL,
patient of Dr. Terri Well

Police Officer Sheds Asthma, Lupus, and Fibromyalgia

Stephanie is a local police officer and has suffered from fibromyalgia, lupus, allergies, and asthma all of her life. She had chronic pain throughout her entire body. She had suffered for fourteen years, especially in the six months leading to her experience with chiropractic. She had tried all kinds of medication and was getting worse—and she was losing hope.

When Stephanie visited Dr. Laszlo's office, he found several areas of her spine that were out of normal position. Through adjustments, he and Stephanie began to restore the proper position of her spinal bones, releasing pressure and tension on her spinal cord. Her body began to heal.

Since Stephanie started receiving chiropractic care, her asthma has disappeared. She no longer takes any medication. Her chronic pain from the lupus and fibromyalgia has also disappeared. She can now work out, run, and enjoy life without the constant pain.

— DR. KEPPEN LASZLO

he began to sweat. His stomach began to churn and his legs started to feel weak, as if he couldn't even move the car pedals if he tried.

When he was a kid and he felt like this, there would be no relief in sight, he'd have nowhere to turn and no one to turn to. Even at an early age, Eli knew on some level that if he didn't fight, he wouldn't make it. He'd always known that if you run, you die. Several times, alone in a cold, dark hospital room, he was forced to make that decision. Some way, somehow he always found the will to stand and fight.

In a cold, dark car, for the first time since he was a kid, he felt he had to make that life-and-death decision again.

Benjamin woke with a start. Two in the morning—even for an early riser like Benjamin, this was early. But Benjamin knew the drill well. Whenever he awoke that suddenly, at such an unusual hour, that meant it was time to pray. He seldom knew what it was that he should be praying for. He simply considered unusual interruptions in his sleep to be a wake-up call from God, and so he prayed about whatever came to mind.

Kneeling by his bed—during his nighttime prayers, he always knelt by the bed, a holdover from those rare prayer times with his grandparents in Africa—he began praising God, first in English, then in Swahili, and then from the silence of his heart. Somewhere, something was happening—something monumental, something life-changing. And Benjamin was a part of it, though he had no idea what that something was.

Whatever it was, an hour later Benjamin sensed that God's will

A Major Breakthrough—Without Medicine

My youngest son, Mark Aaron, was born on December 17, 2001. For the first two years of his life, Mark was on antibiotics and other medicine for ear infections and asthma. My pediatrician convinced me to pump him full of various medicines, and I was doing it.

Then I met Dr. Stender, who offered me a job in his office. Little did I know that God was up to something much bigger. Mark Aaron has been receiving care from Dr. Stender for six months, three times a week, and in that six-month period I have put him on his breathing treatment only one time, and that was because I was not sure what to expect from the treatments.

Mark Aaron has been drug-free for the past six months, and he has not even had one cold, or allergy attack, or flu, ear infection, or asthma. I can't wait to tell his pediatrician how remarkable his health has been because of chiropractic care.

— ROBIN MARLOWE,
patient of Dr. David Stender

Feeding Tube Gone, Five-Year-Old Boy Begins to Thrive

In September 2003, my family began coming to Dr. Dan for chiropractic care. My husband had severe headaches, and I suffered with back pain. At the time, we didn't realize that Jack, our five-year-old youngest son, would be the one to benefit the most from Dr. Dan. He would soon have his life back.

Jack was born with several medical problems, including Sabglottic [**subaortic?**] stenosis, severe reflux, dysphagia, and failure to thrive. Jack couldn't breathe well or swallow. Whatever he swallowed came back up through his nose. At one time Jack was under the care of a gastroenterologist, otolaryngologist, pulmonologist, neurologist, physical therapist, occupational therapist, primary pediatrician, and in-home nurse.

Jack did not crawl until he was a year old and didn't walk until age two. At five months he was on twenty-four-hour feedings via feeding pump and twenty-four-hour oxygen. He didn't even eat anything significant by mouth until age two and a half, when he started with a half cup of chocolate pudding.

In the initial consult, Dr. Dan was clear that he would not promise to "heal" anyone. He did promise to remove interference and thus allow the central nervous system to flow freely through the spine. Dr. Dan said that only God could heal, and I firmly believed that He could use Dr. Dan to help Jack in his fight to eat by mouth.

Since starting with Dr. Dan, Jack has been able to discontinue all his breathing treatment medicines, and his swallowing ability has improved greatly. He is eating exclusively by mouth, and his feeding tube has now been removed permanently.

— UNSIGNED,
patient of Dr. Dan Yachter

had been accomplished and climbed back into bed, gratified to be a part of the invisible community of God summoned to prayer in the middle of the night.

At 6 AM, Benjamin awoke without the benefit of an alarm clock. No need; his internal alarm was faithful to awaken him at just the right time. Thursday morning—prayer time with Eli.

———

The morning air was thick with fog. But even from a distance, Benjamin could see that the parking lot at Knight Chiropractic Wellness Center was empty. He was the first one there, as usual.

As he neared the back door—the one Eli always kept open for him on Thursday mornings—he found it locked. He went around to the front and saw what appeared to be a note on the door. Maybe Eli had an emergency and left him a message. Pulling his glasses from his breast pocket, Benjamin read the note—it was to all of the patients, but he knew it was specifically designed for him.

> *Dear Patients:*
> *For the first time ever, we are closed.*
> *We'll be back in a week.*
>
> *Moyo wa kupenda hauna subira.*
> *(A heart deep in love has no patience.)*
>
> *I'm off to fill my cup with Hope.*
>
> *—Dr. Eli*

Drug-Free and on the Way to Total Health

After three severe car accidents when I was eighteen, my life has never been the same. I am now thirty-six, and having undergone a spinal fusion, chronic back and neck pain had become a fact of life for me. My ability to function as a normal person was a real struggle.

In one year's time I had seen seven neurologists. After being diagnosed with MS, Parkinson's disease, and numerous other diseases, I began to believe that my life counted on a prescription pad. At one point, I was on fourteen different medications, including steroids, pain medicines, blood pressure medicine, and antidepressants. Each medicine just gave me new problems.

My pain caused my blood pressure to soar to stroke levels almost every day. I tried to tell the doctors that it felt as if I had a pinched nerve at the base of my skull, but I couldn't find a doctor who would listen.

When a friend gave me the Gift of Health gift certificate from the Pamer Family Chiropractic Center, I was skeptical because I had already been treated by a chiropractor for many years. But my friend begged me to give this chiropractor just one chance, so I did. With my family in mind, I took my six-inch stack of MRIs, CT scans, spinal tap results, and myelograms to Dr. Pamer for her review. She spent many hours reviewing my files and took X-rays of her own.

When I followed up with Dr. Pamer to see if there was any hope left for my condition, she said that my spine was in pretty bad shape. But after only a few visits I knew that I was in the right place.

It has been two and a half months since I first began going to Dr. Pamer, and I have been drug-free since.

—JENI REIDA,
patient of Dr. Mackenzie Pamer,
Pamer Family Chiropractic,
Powell, OH

Notes

1. Reuters London, March 25, 2002.

2. Norman D. Ford, Health Report.

3. B. Starfield, "Is US Health Really the Best in the World?" *JAMA* 284(4) (July 26, 2000): 483–85.

4. Ibid.

5. Ibid.

6. Reported and available at www.lef.org through the investigation of Gary Null, PhD; Carolyn Dean, MD, ND; Martin Feldman, MD; Debora Rasio, MD; and Dorothy Smith, PhD.

7. U.S. National Center for Health Statistics, *National Vital Statistics Report,* vol. 51, no. 5, March 14, 2003.

8. Nationwide poll on patient safety: National Patient Safety Foundation, "100 million Americans See Medical Mistakes Directly Touching Them" [press release], McLean, VA: October 9, 1997. See also: "Drug giant accused of false claims," *MSNBC News,* July 11, 2003. Available at: http://msnbc.com/news/937302.asp?0sl=-42&cp1=1.

9. E. J. Thomas et al., "Incidence and Types of Adverse Events and Negligent Care in Utah and Colorado," *Medical Care* 38(3) (March 2000): 261–71.

   E. J. Thomas et al., "Costs of Medical Injuries in Utah and Colorado," *Inquiry* 36(3) (Fall 1999): 255–64.

10. Nationwide poll on patient safety: "100 Million Americans See Medical mistakes." See also the following:

    G. C. Xakellis, R. Frantz, and A. Lewis, "Cost of Pressure Ulcer Prevention in Long-Term Care," *Journal of the American Geriatrics Society,* 43(5) (May 1995): 496–501.

    C. A. Barczak et al., "Fourth National Pressure Ulcer Prevalence Survey, *Advances in Wound Care,*" 10(4) (July–August 1997): 18–26.

11. R. A. Weinstein, "Nosocomial Infection Update," *Emerging Infectious Diseases* 4(3) (July–September 1998): 416–20 (also found at www.cdc.gov/ncidod/eid/vol4no3/weinstein.htm). See also:

    Fourth Decennial International Conference on Nosocomial and Healthcare-Associated Infections, *Morbidity and Mortality Weekly Report* 49, no. 7 (February 25, 2000): 138.

12. S. G. Burger, J. Kayser-Jones, and J. P. Bell, "Malnutrition and Dehydration in Nursing Homes: Key Issues in Prevention and Treatment," National Citizens' Coalition for Nursing Home Reform (June 2000). Available at: http://www.cmwf.org/programs/elders/burger _mal_386.asp.

13. B. Starfield, "Is US Health Really the Best in the World?" *JAMA* 284(4) (July 26, 2000): 483–85. Also see the following:

    Starfield, "Deficiencies in US Medical Care," *JAMA* 284(17) (November 1, 2000): 2184–85.

    Injuryboard.com, "General Accounting Office Study Sheds Light on Nursing Home Abuse," July 17, 2003, www.injuryboard.com/view.cfm/Article=3005 (accessed December 17, 2003).

14. HCUPnet (Healthcare Cost and Utilization Project), an agency for healthcare research and quality, http://hcup.ahrq.gov/HCUPnet.asp.

NOTES

For calculation detail, see "Unnecessary Surgery." Sources: HCUPnet, http://hcup.ahrq.gov/HCUPnet.asp; and US Congressional House Subcommittee Oversight Investigation, *Cost and Quality of Health Care: Unnecessary Surgery* (Washington, DC: Government Printing Office, 1976). Cited in: G. B. McClelland, Foundation for Chiropractic Education and Research, testimony to the Department of Veterans Affairs' Chiropractic Advisory Committee, March 25, 2003.

15. S. R. Tunis and H. Gelband, "Health Care Technology in the United States," *Health Policy* 30(1–3) (October–December 1994): 335–96.

16. L. L. Leape, "Error in Medicine," *JAMA* 272(23) (December 21, 1994): 1851–57. See also:

    D. W. Bates et al., "Incidence of Adverse Drug Events and Potential Adverse Drug Events— Implications for Prevention," *JAMA* 274 (July 5, 1995): 29–34.

    C. Vincent, N. Stanhope, and M. Crowley-Murphy, "Reasons for Not Reporting Adverse Incidents: an Empirical Study," *Journal of Evaluation in Clinical Practice* 5(1) (February 1999): 13–21.

    D. W. Bates, "Drugs and Adverse Drug Reactions: How Worried Should We Be?" *JAMA* 279(15) (April 15, 1998): 1216–17.

    J. G. Dickinson, "FDA Seeks to Double Effort on Confusing Drug Names," *Dickinson's FDA Review* 7(3) (March 2000): 13–14.

    H. Wald and K. G. Shojania, "Incident Reporting," in K. G. Shojania et al., eds., *Making Health Care Safer: A Critical Analysis of Patient Safety Practices* (Rockville, MD: Agency for Healthcare Research and Quality, 2001): chapter 4; and Evidence Report/Technology Assessment No. 43, AHRQ publication 01-E058.

    M. J. Grinfeld, "The Debate over Medical Error Reporting," *Psychiatric Times* (April 2000).

17. *New England Journal of Medicine* 345 (December 20, 2001): 1801–8.

18. Ibid. See also:

    American Association for the Study of Liver Diseases, *Hepatology* 40, no. 1, 6–9 (published online June 30, 2004).

19. Centers for Disease Control and Prevention, CDC antimicrobial resistance and antibiotic resistance—general information, http://www.cdc.gov/drugresistance/community/ (accessed December 13, 2003).

20. R. Rabin, "Caution About Overuse of Antibiotics," *Newsday* (September 18, 2003).

21. Ron Law, member of the New Zealand Ministry of Health Working Group.

22. Centers for Disease Control, January 16, 2004.

23. Barbara Loe Fisher, www.909shot.com; www.mercola.com.

24. Quoted by Robert Hoffman; source: *Time* magazine, April 9, 2001, and the *New England Journal of Medicine.*

25. Quoted by Robert Hoffman; source: *USA Today* (no date given).

26. Quoted by Robert Hoffman; source: *USA Today*, February 7, 2002.

27. Fred A. Baughman Jr., MD (2/4/98); Peter R.Breggin, *Talking Back To Ritalin: What Doctors Aren't Telling You About Stimulants and ADHD* (Monroe, ME: Common Courage Press, 1998).

28. Gardiner Harris, "Study Links a Fourth Painkiller to an Increase in Heart Problems," *New York Times*, December 21, 2004.

29. Ibid.

30. Ray Moynihan, Iona Heath, and David Henry, "Selling Sickness; the Pharmaceutical Industry and Disease Mongering," *British Medical Journal* 324, April 13, 2002: 886–91.

31. S. Haldeman, "Neurologic Effects of the Adjustment," *Journal of Manipulative & Physiological Therapeutics (JMPT)* (2000): 23. See also:

C. A. Lantz, "The Vertebral Subluxation Complex, Part 2: The Neurophysiological and Myopathological Components," *Chiropractic Research Journal* 1 (4) (1990).

P. Bolton, "Reflex Effects of Vertebral Subluxations: The Peripheral Nervous System," *JMPT* 23 (2) (2000).

The Association of Chiropractic Colleges Guidelines for Subluxation: "A subluxation is a complex of functional and/or structural and/or pathological articular changes that compromise neural integrity and may influence organ system function and general health."

32. J. D. Grostic, "Dentate Ligament-Cord Distortion Hypothesis," *Chiropractic Research Journal* 1(1) (1988): 47–55. See also:

H. S. Crow and T. Kleinman, "Upper Cervical Influence on the Reticular System," *Upper Cervical Monograph* 5(1) (1991): 12–14.

K. Abbot, "Foramen Magnum and High Cervical Cord Lesions Simulating Degenerative Disease of The Nervous System," *Ohio State Medical Journal* 46 (1950): 645–47.

R. Sweat and T. Sievert, "Chiropractic and Vertebral Arteries," Parts 1 & 2, *Today's Chiropractic* (September/October1984): 45–48 and (November/December 1984): 23–24.

33. Wolf's Law of Physics. See:

C. A. Lantz, Part 2: The Subluxation Complex, in Meridel Gatterman, ed., *Foundations of Chiropractic: Subluxation* (St. Louis: Mosby Year Book, January 1995).

Lantz, "Immobilization Degeneration and the Fixation Hypothesis of the Chiropractic Subluxation," *Chiropractic Research Journal* 1, no. 1 (1988).

34. J. C. Keating Jr., and D. T. Hanson, "Quackery vs Accountability in the Marketing of Chiropractic," *Journal of Manipulative & Physiology Therapy* 15 (1992): 459–79 [Medline]. See also:

J. H. Donahue and Morris Fishbein, MD, "The 'Medical Mussolini' and Chiropractic," *Chiropractic History* 16 (1996): 39–49.

D. Chapman-Smith, "The Wilk Case," *Journal of Manipulative & Physiology Therapy* 12 (1989): 142–46 [Medline].

D. Coburn and C. L. Biggs, "Limits to Medical Dominance: The Case of Chiropractic," *Soc Sci Med* 22 (1986): 1035–46 [CrossRef][Medline].

M. Kimbrough, "Jailed Chiropractors: Those Who Blazed the Trail," *Chiropractic History* 18 (1998): 79–100.

J. K. Simpson, "The Iowa Plan and the Activities of the Committee on Quackery," *Chiropractic Journal* 27 (August 1997): 5–12.

35. Donahue and Fishbein, "The 'Medical Mussolini.'"

36. Simpson, "The Iowa Plan," 5–12.

37. Chapman-Smith, "The Wilk Case,"142–46 [Medline]. See also Simpson, "The Iowa Plan."

38. I. A. Kapandji.

39. To see specific spinal hygiene programs, go to "Straighten Up, America." Copyright© 2003, http://www.life.edu/spinalhygiene/index.html (Life University, College of Chiropractic, College of Arts and Sciences, Dr. Ron Kirk, 1269 Barclay Circle, Marietta, GA 30060, 770-426-2925 / 800-543-3203).

40. C. Shepeher, BS, DC, and Ron Kirk, BS Ed., MA, DC, "Spinal Hygiene and Its Impact on Health and General Well-Being," *Journal of Vertebral Subluxation Research (JVSR)* (August 16, 2004).

41. I. D. Coulter et al., "Chiropractic Patients in a Comprehensive Home Based Geriatric Assessment, Follow Up and Health Promotion Program," *Topics in Clinical Chiropractic* (1996).

42. *Psychosomatic Medicine* 62 (September/October 2000): 633–38.

43. M. Fleshner, *Journal of Applied Physiology* 97 (August 2004): 491–98; news release, American Physiological Society. See also the following:

    Neurology 64(4) (February 22, 2005): 664–69.

    Medical News Today (February 22, 2005).

    Cancer 92 (September 15, 2001): 1638–49.

    Obstetrics and Gynecology 96 (October 2000): 609–14.

    Journal of the National Cancer Institute 89 (1997): 948–55.

44. Gary Greenberg, "The Serotonin Surprise," *Discover* 22, no. 7 (July 2001).

45. Ibid.

46. "Sugar Pills as Good as Antidepressants," *Washington Post,* May 7, 2002, A1.

47. Ibid. See also:

    Jay Dixit, "Fake," *Washington Post,* May 18, 2002.

    Richard A. Friedman, MD, "SSRIS vs. Therapy," *New York Times,* August 27, 2002.

    Elizabeth Querna, "Medication vs. Therapy for Social Phobics," *U.S. News & World Report,* January 14, 2005.

48. World Health Organization, *Progress in Reproductive Health Newsletter,* no. 63.

49. American Medical Association records released in 1987 during trial in U.S. District Court, Northern Illinois Eastern Division, No. 76 C 3777. See also:

    Per Freitag; expert testimony of Pertag, MD, PhD, comparing the results of two neighboring hospitals, U.S. District Court Northern Illinois Eastern Division, No. 76 C 3777, May 1987.

50. M. McMullen. "Physical Stresses of Childhood That Could Lead to the Need for Chiropractic Care," Proceedings of the National Conference on Chiropractic and Pediatrics, San Diego, California., International Chiropractors Association, 1991.

51. A. Towbin, "Latent Spinal Cord and Brain Stem Injury in Newborn Infants," *Developmental Medicine and Child Neurology* 11 (1) (February 1969): 54–68. See also:

    H. J. Biedermann, "Kinematic Imbalances Due to Suboccipital Strain in Newborns," *Manual Medicine* (Springer-Verlag, 1992), 151–56.

    L. E. Koch, H. J. Biedermann, and K. K. Saternus, "High Cervical Stress and Apneoea" *Forensic Science Int* 97 (1) (October 12, 1998): 1–9.

52. G. Gutmann, "Blocked Atlantal Nerve Syndrome in Infants and Small Children," originally published in *Manuelle Medizine* (Springer-Verlag, 1987). English translation published in *International Review of Chiropractic,* July–August 1990. See also:

    L. A. Hospers, J. A. Daso, and L. V. Steinle, "Electromyographic Patterns of Mentally Retarded Cerebral Palsy Patient After Life Upper Cervical Adjustment," *Today's Chiropractic* 15(5) (1986): 13–14.

    L. A. Hospers et al., "Response of a Three Year Old Epileptic Child to Upper Cervical Adjustment," *Today's Chiropractic* 15 (15) (December–January 1987): 69–76.

    G. Young, "Chiropractic Success in Epileptic Conditions," *ACA Journal of Chiropractic* 19 (4) (1982): 62–63.

    "Ear Infection: A Retrospective Study Examining Improvement from Chiropractic Care and Analyzing For Influencing Factors," *Journal of Manipulative & Physiology Therapy* 19 (3) (March 1996): 169–77.

NOTES

J. M. Fallon, "The Role of Chiropractic Adjustments in the Care and Treatment of 332 Children with Otitis Media," *Journal of Consulting and Clinical Psychology* 2 (1997): 167–83.

T. R. Bachman and C. A. Lantz, "Management of Pediatric Asthma and Enuresis with Probably Traumatic Etiology," 1992, International Chiropractic Association conference on Pediatrics.

53. Gutmann, "Blocked Atlantal Nerve Syndrome."

54. McMullen, "Physical Stresses of Childhood."

55. Gutmann, "Blocked Atlantal Nerve Syndrome."

56. Towbin, "Latent Spinal Cord and Brain Stem Injury in Newborn Infants." See also:

Gutmann, "Blocked Atlantal Nerve Syndrome."

Hospers, Daso, and Steinle, "Electromyographic Patterns of Mentally Retarded Cerebral Palsy Patient," 13–14.

Hospers et al., "Response of a Three Year Old Epileptic Child," 69–76.

Young, "Chiropractic Success in Epileptic Conditions," 62–63.

"Ear Infection: A Retrospective Study Examining Improvement from Chiropractic Care and Analyzing for Influencing Factors," *Journal of Manipulative & Physiology Therapy* 19 (3) (March 1996): 169–77.

Fallon, "The Role of Chiropractic Adjustments," 167–83.

Bachman and Lantz, "Management of Pediatric Asthma and Enuresis."

57. E. Dretakis et al., "Electroencephalographic Study of Schoolchildren with Adolescent Idiopathic Scoliosis," *Spine* 13 (1988): 143–45. See also:

"Equilibrium Dysfunction," *Spine,* 2, no. 3: 65146.

R. Herman et al., "Idiopathic Scoliosis and the Central Nervous System: A Motor Control Problem," *Spine* 10 (1985): 1–14.

58. W. M. Vanbreda and J. Vanbreda, "A Comparative Study of Health Status of Children Raised Under the Health Care Models of Chiropractic & Allopathic Medicine," *American Chiropractor,* September 1993.

59. Anne C. C. Lee, BSE; H. Dawn, LI, MD; Kathi J. Kemper, MD, MPH, "Chiropractic Care for Children," published in the *Archives of Pediatric and Adolescent Medicine* 154, no. 4 (April 2000): 401–7.

60. Clayton J. Campbell, Christopher Kent, Arthur Banne, Amir Amiri, and Ronald W. Pero, "Surrogate Indication of DNA Repair in Serum After Long-Term Chiropractic Intervention," *Journal of Vertebral Subluxation Research* (JVSR.com).

61. Ogi Ressel, BSc, DC, DACBR(C), FICPA, and Robert Rudy BSc, DC, FICPA, "Vertebral Subluxation Correlation with Somatic, Visceral and Immune Complaints: An Analysis of 650 Children Under Chiropractic Care," *Journal of Vertebral Subluxation Research,* October 18, 2004.

Seleno, Pfleger, Grostic et al., "The Effects of Specific Upper Cervical Adjustments on the CD 4 Counts of HIV Positive Patients," *Chiropractic Research Journal* 3 (1).

62. R. W. Dishman, "Static and Dynamic Components of the Chiropractic Subluxation Complex: A Literature Review," *JMPT* 11(2)(1988).

Charles A. Lantz, "Immobilization Degeneration and the Fixation Hypothesis of Chiropractic Subluxation," *Chiropractic Research Journal* 1 (1) (1988).

D. D. Harrison et al., "The Efficacy of Cervical Extension-Compression Traction Combined with Diversified Manipulation and Drop Table Adjustments in the Rehabilitation of Cervical Lordosis," *JMPT* 17(7) (1994): 454–64.

NOTES

D. E. Harrison et al., "New 3-Point Bending Traction Method of Restoring Cervical Lordosis Combined with Cervical Manipulation: Non-Randomized Clinical Control Trial," *Archives of Physical Medicine and Rehabilitation* 83, no. 4: 447–53.

63. Shepeher, "Spinal Hygiene and Its Impact on Health." See also:

Sean M. Hannon, BA, DC, "Objective Physiologic Changes and Associated Health Benefits of Chiropractic Adjustments in Asymptomatic Subjects: A Review of Literature," *Journal of Vertebral Subluxation Research*, April 26, 2004.

Special thanks to these doctors,
who have been and continue to be strong supporters
of my first book, *Body by God.*

Arizona

Dr. Mitchell Borst
Scottsdale

Dr. Dave Stender
Tucson

Colorado

Dr. Keppen Laszlo
Arvada

Florida

Dr. Mickey Cohen
Plantation

Dr. Patrick St. Germain
Apopka

Idaho

Dr. Keith McKim
Nampa

Dr. Zane Sterling
Boise

Kentucky

Dr. Terry Harmon
Morgansfield

North Carolina

Dr. Keith Helmendach
Charlotte

Dr. Terri Wells
Shallotte

Dr. Megan Powell
Shallotte

Dr. Sonya Young
Wrightsville Beach

New Hampshire

Dr. Holly Ruocco
Salem

New Jersey

Dr. Brad Butler
Hewitt

Dr. Mackenzie Pamer
Powell

Dr. Matt Pamer
Mansfield

Pennsylvania

Dr. Tom Horn
Towanda

Washington

Dr. Deborah Adams
Kirkland